CLINGING TO MAMMY

Clinging to Mammy

THE FAITHFUL SLAVE IN
TWENTIETH-CENTURY AMERICA

Micki McElya

HARVARD UNIVERSITY PRESS

Cambridge, Massachusetts, and London, England · 2007

Parts of Chapter 4 originally appeared in a different form in *Monuments to the Lost Cause: Women, Art, and the Landscape of Southern Memory*, edited by Cynthia Mills and Pamela H. Simpson. Copyright © 2003 by the University of Tennessee Press. Used with permission.

Library of Congress Cataloging-in-Publication Data
  McElya, Micki, 1972–
  Clinging to mammy : the faithful slave in twentieth-century America / Micki McElya.
    p. cm.
  Includes bibliographical references and index.
  ISBN-13: 978-0-674-02433-5 (alk. paper)
  ISBN-10: 0-674-02433-8 (alk. paper)
  1. African American women in popular culture—History—20th century. 2. African Americans in popular culture—History—20th century. 3. Women slaves—United States—History. 4. Slavery—United States—History. 5. African American women—History. 6. Racism in popular culture—United States—History—20th century. 7. Stereotypes (Social psychology)—United States. 8. Stereotypes (Social psychology) in advertising—United States. 9. Jemima, Aunt. 10. United States—Race relations—History—20th century. I. Title.
  E185.86.M397 2007
  306.3′620820973—dc22   2007001231

For my family

CONTENTS

ILLUSTRATIONS

CLINGING TO MAMMY

INTRODUCTION:
THE FAITHFUL SLAVE

WHEN NEWSPAPERS reported her death in 1923, many obituaries sounded a common refrain summed up by a headline in the *Missouri Farmer:* "Aunt Jemima Is Gone." Americans had first fallen in love with the ex-slave cook and her secret recipe for pancakes at the World's Columbian Exposition in Chicago in the summer and fall of 1893. By all accounts her debut there had been glorious. Fairgoers were drawn to the giant barrel-shaped concession of the R. T. Davis Milling Company by the smell of buttery hotcakes and the sounds of laughter and applause. Rising above the general roar of thousands of people moving through the Agriculture Building, a singular voice called to them with a southern cadence reminiscent of the old days. It was the voice of an old black woman they would soon come to know as Aunt Jemima. As she slid steaming pancakes onto platters, the woman described her days as a slave. Winking and grinning at the audience she held enthralled, Aunt Jemima told of happy times passed on a beautiful plantation, of endless parties and parades of houseguests for whom she cooked bountiful stacks of her delicious pancakes, which were famous throughout the South. Oh, how they loved those hotcakes! And now, thanks to the Davis Milling Company, people all over the country could have pancakes made from Aunt Jemima's secret recipe. All you had to do was add water to the mix, she explained; no need to measure or have eggs and milk on hand, just a little water and a hot griddle for perfect pancakes every time. They were so easy to make, and so delicious. It was as if Aunt Jemima herself was in your kitchen making them for you. People in the dense crowd at the exhibition stand crushed forward to get a better glimpse of the woman who had been a slave and to sample her pancakes. Aunt Jemima kept the spirituals, work songs, and stories coming while she flipped hotcakes, poured fresh discs of batter, and filled plates for her hungry audience. They were hungry for the food, hungry for grand plantation abundance and refined southern hospitality, but most of all, they were hungry for her.[1]

The elderly woman whose death was reported in 1923 was not Aunt Jemima. No such person had actually existed. The woman who was struck by a car and killed, who for thirty years had held the job of *acting* the role of "Aunt Jemima," was Nancy Green. While Aunt Jemima was dubbed "The Most Famous Colored Woman in the World" after the Columbian Exposition, Nancy Green's life was obscured by the trademark figure she portrayed and by the faithful slave image she embodied. Green, born into slavery in Kentucky, had made her way north to Chicago, where she worked as a domestic servant like so many other African American women before and after her. Someone visiting her employer's home believed that she might satisfy R. T. Davis's search for a black woman to demonstrate his new product. Perhaps it was her skill, her convenient location in Chicago, her force of personality, or all of these attributes that suggested her suitability to portray "Aunt Jemima." What is clear is that Green did not come to Chicago at the behest of a milling concern, nor had she arrived with a secret recipe for terrific pancakes, and no one had ever called her "Aunt Jemima" before. Vivid accounts of her debut at the fair have been told over and over, yet they all ultimately trace back to advertisements and promotional materials produced after the event, not to eyewitnesses, and not to Green herself. Nancy Green's experience of working at the exposition was transformed, through ads and a pseudo-slave narrative produced by the R. T. Davis Company, into an event in the commercially constructed life of Aunt Jemima. And when the real Nancy Green was accidentally killed, her popular eulogy became "Aunt Jemima Is Gone."[2]

But in 1923 Aunt Jemima was not gone. Both the trademark and the popular figure of the slave mammy outlived Nancy Green. Stories and images of the slave as a faithful and loving dependent, of which the mammy has been the most popular representation, drenched American culture and politics throughout the twentieth century and persist to this day. Another popular variation is Scarlett O'Hara's feisty but adoring and loyal mammy in the film *Gone With the Wind* (1939) as she was played by Hattie McDaniel.[3] The fictional character whose only name was her descriptor, "Mammy," remains dear to the hearts—and plantation fantasies—of many. Yet Aunt Jemima, her smile beaming still from store shelves, freezer sections, and kitchen cupboards, is the most enduring image of the faithful slave. The drama of Nancy Green's life eclipsed by the mammy figure has been played again and again in the experiences of black women in the United States. The myth of the faithful slave lingers because so many white Americans have wished to live in a world in which African Americans are not angry over past and present injustices, a world in which white people were and are not complicit, in which the injustices themselves—of slavery, Jim Crow, and ongoing structural racism—seem not to exist at all. The mammy figure affirmed their wishes. The narrative of the faithful slave is deeply rooted in the American racial imagination. It is a story of our national past and political future that blurs the lines between myth and memory, guilt and justice, stereotype and individuality, commodity and humanity.

"Mammies," as they have been described and remembered by whites, like all faithful slaves, bear little resemblance to actual enslaved women of the antebellum period. Black women did work in white homes, cooked innumerable meals, cared for white children, and surely formed emotional ties to white family members at times, but the mammy was—and is—a fiction. She is the most visible character in the myth of the faithful slave, a set of stories, images, and ideas that have been passed down from generation to generation in the United States, through every possible popular medium, from fine art and literature to the vaudeville stage and cinema, and in countless novelty items from ashtrays to salt and pepper shakers.[4] These narratives are locked emotionally and politically to the slave narrative genre. Early versions produced in the antebellum period by proslavery white southerners were explicitly reactionary. The stories were designed to provide reassurance that their authors' patriarchal benevolence was real, and was recognized and appreciated by those they enslaved. They were hurled northward in response to the publication of slave narratives detailing the horror and inhumanity of the institution, the speaking tours by activist runaways, and the impact of abolitionist works such as *Uncle Tom's Cabin*. As personally satisfying as they were politically and economically potent, tales of faithful slavery appeared with ever greater frequency.

The mammy narrative embodied in the Aunt Jemima trademark dates back at least to the 1830s, when members of the planter class began using these stories to animate their assertions of slavery as benevolent and slave owning as honorable. "When my mother arrived in Charleston, she sought out a faithful servant as a nurse for her young family. Margaret was her name, which we soon contracted into the endearing appellative of 'Mammy Marget,'" a South Carolina gentleman explains to his visitor from New York City in a serial installment titled "Diary of an Invalid" in the *Southern Literary Messenger* in 1836. "She was the most devoted and faithful servant I ever knew. I loved and venerated her next to my mother."[5] The account, framed as the diary of a consumptive New Yorker who travels the globe seeking cures for his ailments, more amenable climates, and stories from the locals, shows that the popular mammy narrative was already well established by this time. Upon his arrival at the grand Charleston home of Colonel H. B. Ashton, the wan narrator is bewitched by the portrait of a young woman that hangs in the parlor. He learns that she is the colonel's cousin who was driven mad and died young and "unspoiled" in the midst of the Revolutionary War when she learned in a single afternoon of the deaths of both her naval officer father and her soldier fiancé. While it is her story that drives the narrative, it is the affection and attention of "Mammy Marget" that makes the young woman's character apparent and illuminates her love for these two men. With her last dying breath, fevered and hallucinating, she calls to her enslaved caretaker: "Mammy Marget . . . bring my bridal dress—the procession is waiting for me; to the church you know we must go to be united: there is Alfred and father too. Haste! Haste!"[6]

Several key themes of the faithful slave narrative generally, and the depiction of the mammy explicitly, are revealed in this story. Accounts of enslaved people's fidelity constituted the ultimate expression of southern paternalism, which held that the relationship of the master to the slave was removed from market forces and economic exigency and functioned more like a familial relationship between father and child based on a set of mutual obligations and responsibilities as well as affection. Proslavery theorists argued that this was very different from the cold contract of "free labor," under which bosses owed nothing but wages to the laborers they employed and could fire them at will. Slave owners claimed, by contrast, to be responsible for providing every aspect of enslaved people's well-being, including clothing, food, housing, and medicine, and they bore this burden for the lifetime of their slaves as their obligation. The only thing required of the carefree slave in this scenario was work and loyalty. The faithful slave narrative, however, went one step further to argue that enslaved people appeared faithful and caring not because they *had* to be or were violently compelled to be, but because their fidelity was heartfelt and indicative of their love for and dependence on their owners. At their core, stories of faithful slavery were expressions of the value, honor, and identity of whites. They had little if anything to do with the actual perceptions and attitudes of the enslaved. The conceit of a slave owner and Revolutionary War veteran recounting the story of his cousin and her mammy to his visitor from New York promotes this paternalist conception of slavery and underscores its significance for the periodical's predominantly southern readership.

Such justifications were necessitated by the increasing radicalization of abolitionism in the United States in the 1830s and the appearance of exposés of the domestic slave trade and the brutalities of southern slavery. Accounts of sexual terror, violent punishment, and the torture of enslaved people were becoming more commonplace. The rapid expansion and movement of slavery to the South and West between 1820 and 1860 was made possible through a thriving intraregional market in slaves. In that forty-year period, at least 875,000 enslaved people were forcibly moved from the upper to the lower South, and several thousand more were regularly hired out for year-long contracts. Each one of their number represented the severing of family, friendship, and community ties. Contrary to the claims of owners, the trade was not distant from the everyday experiences of enslavement or slave owning. The relationship between owner and enslaved was defined by the market. Responding to the persistent abolitionist focus on the evils of the trade and its massive dislocations of black people and families, slave owners and their allies told tender tales of grand plantations populated by elderly "aunties" and "uncles" and old mammies who could no longer work but were well cared for and held dear. The story of the faithful slave became a cornerstone of paternalist defenses of slavery and rationales for elite southern patterns of domesticity.[7]

"Diary of an Invalid" elaborates several aspects of the mammy figure's character and relationships to whites that would come to dominate tales of faithful slavery, particularly its gendered elements. Recounted by a southern gentleman who insists that he loved his mammy like his mother, the colonel's story dwells on the enslaved woman's connections to white women in the household, first to his mother and then to his young cousin. This juxtaposition of black and white womanhood remained a key facet of the mammy narrative. Black and white women had been called "mammy" before the 1830s, whether as a maternal endearment or an indication of enslavement, but in the context of spreading abolitionist sentiment, countered by increasingly detailed visions of planter paternalism and refinement, the name and descriptor took on a very specific meaning. The figure of the faithful slave came to bear much of the burden of slavery's defense. This is made clear in another story from the *Southern Literary Messenger* published two years later. Similarly framed as a story told among whites, "A Couple of Loveletters" is intended to be a humorous tale of a young man's meddling in the affairs of "old Aunt Dinah," with the unwitting help of his enslaved playmate, Charles. The now grown narrator relates that Charles's mother died when the boy was an infant. Pointing to his own mother's benevolence, the man explains: "There happened to be no nurse on the plantation at the time, and so my mother took him into the house and raised him along with myself. The poor little fellow used to amuse us very much, by calling her 'mammy,' until he was taught differently, but his devotion to herself and to the family has never subsided, and, to this day, her grave is to him the holiest spot of all the earth."[8] By 1838 the thought of a black child calling a white woman "mammy" was a great joke, suggesting the depth of the association of the name with a black enslaved woman.

With each passing year planter-class accounts of faithful slavery grew more nuanced and richer with detail and reiterated themes. They also became more common as resistance to slavery and its spread deepened and sectional politics became more heated. The image of the grandmotherly mammy, described as a beloved cook and a loving caretaker, was offered in response to abolitionists' charges that the institution of slavery was wracked with sexual depravity and the rape and concubinage of black women by white men. In this way, southern proslavery writers sought to legitimize relations between black women and white men as maternal and nurturing, not sexual. Their elaborate construction of the mammy included not only her physical attributes, which stressed her advanced age or wide girth, but also her spirited character. She loved her white "family" and would defend and protect them fiercely, but she could be cantankerous with them and was a disciplinarian of white children. Mammy was endearing in her gruff demeanor and unrefined features, but she was the antithesis of desirable white femininity, an answer to charges of rampant, violent sexuality and white men's fathering of black women's children that were promoted by abolitionists and the accounts of runaway slaves.[9]

The idealized mammy figure set the contours of the faithful slave narrative. The scene of black loyalty was almost always the white home, whether in terms of domestic work or, particularly in the case of male slaves, the protection of the home in the wartime absence of male patriarchs. These black figures and their relationships to white people were usually expressed by the assertion that they were "like one of the family." This expression of paternalism, which included both the giving and the taking of care, affection, and responsibility, worked to obscure the brutal coercion of slavery. Drawing the mammy or manservant into the folds of white domesticity occluded his or her essential role in black family life and community as well as slavery's devastation of so many black families. Furthermore, identifying some slaves as being *like* family members denied the fact that many indeed *were* the biological children of owners and overseers.

By the 1850s, the southern figure of the faithful mammy was well on its way to becoming a national icon. This was ironically due in large measure to the reach of Harriet Beecher Stowe's abolitionist novel *Uncle Tom's Cabin* (1852). Stowe also employed the image of faithful slaves—faithful to a Christian God, to their families and friends, and even to their owners—but she used it to emphasize the horror of their abuse and the systematic terror of slavery. The figure of the enslaved black mother ensconced within the setting of southern white domesticity became a familiar one nationally and internationally owing to the widespread sentimental appeal of the book, which was one of the most widely read works of the nineteenth century. Stowe's description of Uncle Tom's wife, Aunt Chloe, may even have been the model for ensuing representations of the mammy figure.[10] In a passage that portrays Aunt Chloe in terms of the food she is so good at preparing, Stowe writes: "A round, black, shiny face is hers, so glossy as to suggest the idea that she might have been washed over with the whites of eggs . . . Her whole plump countenance beams with satisfaction and contentment from under a well-starched checked turban, bearing on it, however, if we must confess it, a little of that tinge of self-consciousness which becomes the first cook of the neighborhood, as Aunt Chloe was universally held and acknowledged to be."[11] Aunt Chloe bears an uncanny resemblance to the trademark Aunt Jemima, a figure that can in turn be traced to the minstrel stage of the nineteenth century, which generated endless adaptations of *Uncle Tom's Cabin* for blackface performance. Despite the apparent contradiction, the role of the powerful abolitionist novel in promoting the faithful slave narrative is actually not surprising. The middle-class northern reading public that fueled the popularity of *Uncle Tom's Cabin* prefigured the public that would romanticize the plantation South after Reconstruction. And the same sentimental characteristics that humanized enslaved people in Stowe's eyes were present in the paternalistic myths espoused by the proslavery writers who challenged her critique.[12]

Far from ending this romance with the faithful slave mammy, the Civil War made it all the more insistent. The narrative surged in popularity and proliferated nationally as well as regionally. Celebrated in antebellum southern letters and proslavery ideology, the concept was imbued with fresh energy and new urgency after emancipation. The racial and gender hierarchies of the antebellum South were grounded in domesticity—in patriarchy and paternalism. This was certainly not unique to the region, yet the specific forms they took and the ideas that sustained them were distinctly shaped by slavery.[13] This was true for slave-owning and non-slave-owning whites alike.[14] The domestic underpinnings of southern society and political culture persisted after the Civil War, bolstered by attempts to reconstruct these hierarchies in the aftermath of emancipation and black mobility, massive human loss and injury, and the devastation of natural and built environments. Amidst the general upheaval, white southerners would come to rely more and more on appeals to popular nostalgia for the days of slavery and seek refuge in recollections of the faithful slave.

Sentimental evocations of plantation abundance and benign slavery held increasing allure for non-southern whites as well, as it appealed to their own racism, fears, and postwar concerns. The image of the faithful slave spread through regional literature and contributed to the dismantling of Reconstruction. Like black codes and racist violence, these myths aided white southerners' attempts to shape and limit black freedom, both literally and imaginatively. Unlike other forms of coercion, however, stories of faithful slaves were always constructed with at least one eye glancing northward. Echoing antebellum arguments citing the contented and well-cared-for slave as proof of benevolent paternalism, they asserted the existence of idyllic race and labor relations in the past. For their part, many beyond the geographic confines of the South read hungrily and with pleasure these tales of plantation grandeur, contented black workers who "knew their place," and the hospitality of rural plenty. Alongside growing critiques of Radical Republican programs for social change and racial equality, faithful slave narratives provided a nostalgic alternative to the economic depression and labor turmoil of the post–Civil War period. They acted as a kind of emotional and political salve, a potion to speed the conclusion of federal Reconstruction and the subsequent reversion to "home rule" in the southern states.

The collapse of radical Reconstruction and the final withdrawal of a federal presence from the old Confederacy in 1877 sparked a mass migration of black working people out of the South. The source of intense local concern and national curiosity, the flight of these "Exodusters" to Kansas suggested the vicious realities behind those declarations of love for the "old-time darkies."[15] Unwilling to accept the place designated for them within the class and racial hierarchies of the emerging New South, nineteenth-century black migrants, like those who would follow them farther north and west in the twentieth century, exposed how incomplete that reconstruction had been.

The 1880s witnessed daily struggles to define both locally and nationally the meaning of the Civil War and the recently dismantled system of Reconstruction. Various interests north and south attempted to shape the popular memory of these events and to mobilize their versions of the past as a means of determining the process of reunification and the direction of contemporary political and social life.[16] As white southerners promoted the rise of the New South and dwelled on its nostalgic corollary, the Lost Cause, a group of regional authors generated an enormously popular national literature devoted to antebellum moonlight and magnolias, cavaliers and fine ladies, and of course faithful slaves. These writers were commonly referred to as the Plantation School. Although their work was often derided by twentieth-century scholars of modernism and the Southern Renascence as overly sentimental and even hackneyed, Plantation School authors such as Thomas Nelson Page and Joel Chandler Harris were literary stars in the late nineteenth century, publishing books or serialized works, traveling to speaking engagements around the country, and topping the A-list at social, literary, and political functions. As the most famous of the group, Page and Harris continue to enjoy significant readerships to this day.[17]

No one understood the threat posed by this literature better than Frederick Douglass. He watched the rise of the Plantation School's faithful slave narrative and the diminishing popularity and understanding of genuine slave narratives like his own with astonishment and horror. As early as 1870 he cautioned: "The South has a past not to be contemplated with pleasure, but with a shudder. She has been selling agony, trading in blood and in the souls of men. If her past has any lesson, it is one of repentance and reformation."[18] Douglass campaigned tirelessly against the tightening grip of Lost Cause mythology on the imaginations and political visions of nineteenth-century white Americans, but he could not loosen their hold on mammy.

The role of "Aunt Jemima" that Nancy Green assumed in 1893 carried on this baleful history and capitalized upon it to sell pancake mix. With the rise of consumer capitalism, commodity culture, and technological innovation, far from dwindling in power or quantity, stories and images of the enslaved mammy became more prevalent nationally than ever.[19] One would be hard-pressed to find any area of modern American culture that was not suffused with images, sounds, and stories of the faithful slave. Romanticized narratives of slavery and black fidelity to white masters proliferated long after emancipation because they served a wide range of emotional, economic, and political needs for white and black Americans. The mammy figure in particular was an essential site for grappling with the meaning and burden of slavery for American capitalist democracy. Loving, hating, pitying, or pining for mammy in the twentieth century became a way for Americans to define the character of the nation, the meaning of freedom, and the racial and gender boundaries of the citizenry.

W. E. B. Du Bois famously predicted in 1903 that the twentieth century would be defined by "the problem of the color line."[20] This book examines how that line was drawn and violently maintained through stories of interracial affection and faithful slavery, and how it was given shape in fantasies about black women who crossed it. It also explores the diversity of black activisms that have challenged, and at times strategically affirmed, this version of black womanhood and history, and to what ends. The problem of the color line, with its animating faithful slave narratives, has persisted into the twenty-first century. If we are to reckon honestly with the history and continued legacies of slavery in the United States, we must confront the terrible depths of desire for the black mammy and the way it still drags at struggles for real democracy and social justice.

1 THE LIFE OF "AUNT JEMIMA"

Dream about der possum and hoecake,
Yer Aunt Jemima's gwine to make yer pancakes when
yer wake.

—"Aunt Jemima's Lullaby," 1896

FAIRGOERS TINGLED with a sense of being on the cusp of a new
and different age as they celebrated the advance of American
civilization at the Chicago World's Columbian Exposition of
1893. An early crystallization of what would become the
predominant cultural, economic, and imperial trends of the
twentieth century, the fair helped to usher in modernity in
the United States. Nancy Green's first performance as Aunt
Jemima at that fair placed the faithful slave narrative—and in
particular the mammy figure—at the very heart of this transition. The R. T. Davis Milling Company capitalized on a
mythic southern past to sell a thoroughly modern product
made possible by the technological advances displayed elsewhere at the fair. Aunt Jemima pancake mix would ride the
leading edge of innovation in production, packaging, advertising, and distribution for much of the twentieth century,
while its supposedly essential characteristics—convenience,
wholesomeness, and good taste—were deemed best represented by an enslaved woman and the Old South.

The trademark told a story of the post-Reconstruction reunification of North and South brought about through the loving labors of a black woman and made available to all through modern capitalism. As the dialect lyrics of the company's commissioned song, "Aunt Jemima's Lullaby," assured American consumers, to buy the pancake mix was to buy into a collective white dream that when they awoke, no matter where they were in the country, and despite the passage of nearly thirty years since emancipation, they would be greeted by a black mammy with a stack of warm pancakes and a ready smile. Reaching a much larger audience than the popular fiction of the Plantation School ever would, the Aunt Jemima trademark cemented an idea of what a mammy looked and acted like for generations of consumers. The millions who saw Nancy Green at the fair or later at one of her many personal appearances around the country would be encouraged to believe that they had seen the "real" Aunt Jemima, and that they had been close to, and perhaps eaten food prepared by, an actual former faithful slave. The distortion of Nancy Green's life through this trademark was doubled in these moments, for not only was her true identity concealed behind the mask of Aunt Jemima, but also her lived experience of slavery was erased in plantation fantasy.

Aunt Jemima and other popular images of faithful slavery in the twentieth century equated the African American's place in modern life with servility, obedience, and joviality. Any other attitude on the part of blacks, from anger to aspiration, was considered symptomatic of a growing contemporary "Negro problem" that beset not just the (white) South but the nation. In the last decade of the nineteenth century, southern states constructed the legal frameworks of disfranchisement and widespread segregation with a speed born of popular racism, white fears about this looming "problem," and national sanction. At the same time, escalating racial violence terrorized southern black communities. The year of the official dedication of the Columbian Exposition, 1892, witnessed the largest number of recorded lynchings in U.S. history, 230, of which an overwhelming majority of the victims were black and southern.[1] That year also saw the publication of Ida B. Wells's influential protest tract *Southern Horrors*, which she released while a fugitive from her home in Memphis, Tennessee, where her own life had been threatened because of her activism. Although Wells would be denied a role in the Chicago exposition and the version of American progress it promoted, the faithful slave mammy would be there in the figure of Aunt Jemima.[2]

Part of what made the image of the faithful slave so tenacious in modern American politics and culture in this period was its malleability. This was exemplified at the next world's fair held in the United States, at which several performances of faithful slavery were staged, including another on behalf of Aunt Jemima pancake mix. Intended to be a spectacular showcase of the New South, the Atlanta Cotton States and International Exposition of 1895 would become best known for bringing Booker T. Washington into the national spotlight and helping to establish him as the most powerful black political figure of the early twentieth century. Washington joined other prominent black southerners who sought to use the Atlanta fair as a platform for broadcasting African American progress in the thirty years since emancipation and asserting the essential roles black people would play in the progress toward regional prosperity in the coming century. His address on the opening day of the fair articulated a vision of black partnership in the economy of the New South as a gradual path to self-sufficiency and citizenship founded on a shared history of slave-owner paternalism and the loyalty of the enslaved. Black aspirations and a fully realized democracy, he suggested to the segregated black and white audience before him, were inextricably tied to this Plantation School vision of the history of slavery.

The origins of the Aunt Jemima trademark lay in the theatrical performances of post–Civil War minstrelsy and vaudeville. In popular accounts of the story, Chris Rutt, one of the co-developers of the self-rising pancake flour, came upon the name in the autumn of 1889 when he saw the minstrel team Baker and Farrell perform the song "Old Aunt Jemima" in his hometown of St. Joseph, Missouri. One of the pair would sing the number as part of a cakewalk finale while wearing a dress, apron, and red bandanna, as well as burnt cork blackface makeup. The song, which in this context was performed by a white man masquerading as a black woman, had itself been composed in 1875 and performed thousands of times by Billy Kersands, an African American comedian and vaudevillian who also performed in blackface.[3] The layers of racial and gender crossings, including the blacking up of an already black performer, were complex. They would only become more so when a formerly enslaved black woman was asked to take on the fictional role of a formerly enslaved black woman.

The story of the trademark is surrounded by a thick murk of fabrication, scanty documentation, and oft-repeated historical inaccuracies. It is likely that the show Rutt saw was a solo act by Pete F. Baker, who portrayed Aunt Jemima, among other characters, and who had appeared previously in St. Joseph with another vaudevillian named T. J. Farron.[4] Yet the popular version has been told so frequently and consistently that it has lent credibility to the tale.[5] After the success of Green's appearance at the fair as Aunt Jemima, Purd Wright, a St. Joseph librarian who had served as the first taste-tester for Rutt and his partner, Charles Underwood, made a signal contribution to national advertising for the product. He produced an illustrated pseudo–slave narrative titled *The Life of Aunt Jemima, the Most Famous Colored Woman in the World* (1895). It purportedly blended stories told by Green herself with a biography of Wright's invention claiming that Aunt Jemima's pancake recipe was her own, and that it had first been tasted by a northerner during the Civil War. It was this man, in Wright's story, who had searched out the maker of those delicious hotcakes during Reconstruction and persuaded her to come back north with him. Several of Wright's anecdotes, including Aunt Jemima's famed debut in Chicago, with its symbolic national reunion of northern industrial capital and Old Southern refinement and faithful slavery, reappeared as part of a popular national magazine ad campaign produced in the 1920s by the J. Walter Thompson advertising firm. Illustrated by the masterly N. C. Wyeth, the full-page narrative ads elaborated a picture of a lush world of antebellum plantation grandeur and loyal slaves, and promoted sectional reconciliation through capitalism. His rich illustrations embellished the story for a broad national audience.[6] In 1925 the Quaker Oats Company purchased the trademark and flour recipe. When a corporate history titled *Brands, Trademarks, and Good Will: The Story of the Quaker Oats Company* appeared in 1967, it repeated many of these fictions as facts about the trademark's past, giving them authority as the true history of the product and its spokesperson almost seventy-five years after Green's first Chicago performance. In this morass of commercially driven inaccuracies and lingering plantation fantasies, two key facts remain clear. First, the recipe for Aunt Jemima's pancake mix was conceived by Rutt and Underwood through trial and error in the late 1880s in Missouri, not by an enslaved black woman in the antebellum South. Second, the figure of Aunt Jemima was not drawn from history or indicative of the realities of American slavery but came out of the minstrel theater.

Within a year of naming the flour mixture and trying unsuccessfully to market it, Rutt and Underwood sold the recipe to the R. T. Davis Milling Company, which was the
largest miller in the county and a primary supplier for the
Missouri Valley. Davis Milling had the distribution networks,
capital, and industry knowledge needed to transform the
product and get it into more homes, which it did. Among
Davis Milling's changes to the recipe was the addition of
powdered milk, which meant that all one had to do to make
the batter was add water. Aunt Jemima pancake mix thus became one of the first ready-mix products on the market. It
made cooking pancakes quick, easy, and consistent. It was
like having a "slave in a box."[7] Davis Milling planned to introduce the product to a national audience at the Columbian
Exposition. In doing so, R. T. Davis would make another key
contribution to the trademark's development: he would bring
the slave to life by having the product demonstrated at the
fair by a black woman identified only as "Aunt Jemima."[8]

In the short span of four years, Aunt Jemima mix went
from being a locally available midwestern product to a national consumer phenomenon via the spectacle that was the
Columbian Exposition. Imperial in its design, the fair took as
its theme the commemoration of Columbus's discovery of
the New World. Its aim, however, was to showcase the global
power and great technological, industrial, and economic advance of the United States at the end of the nineteenth century. Because of this, the fair became a great testing ground
for establishing whose voices would be included in this surge
of power and progress and how they would be heard.

One celebrated example of inclusion at the fair was the
Woman's Building, overseen by a National Board of Lady
Managers and representatives from each state. Despite pressure from several black clubwomen, Ida B. Wells notable
among them, the national and state boards were almost en-

tirely white in constitution. J. Imogen Howard, a teacher from New York City who was appointed to the New York Board of Women Managers, was the only black woman to serve in an official capacity. Notably, she made it her goal to include in the New York State exhibit statistics on black women's paid labor and wider contributions.[9] While some sought this form of inclusion, other women, black and white, challenged the logic of having a separate building for celebrating women's contributions. They argued that their achievements should be interspersed across the fair's buildings and exhibits on equal footing with men's, that it was ultimately their ingenuity and strengths that were important, not their gender. White American sculptor Harriet Hosmer declared that her work and that of other female artists should be included in the Fine Arts Building's galleries and judged on its own merits rather than placed in the Woman's Building, where it would be gauged by different, gendered standards.[10]

These racial and gender critiques combined in the National Board's attempts to shut down black women's protests. In the early summer of 1892, the members of the National Board of Lady Managers published a response to their critics and provided their rationale for not explicitly seeking black representatives. They did not wish to specify race anywhere in their building, because they were "endeavoring to show the work of industrial women for all countries in the world without discrimination as to race or color."[11] Foreshadowing late-twentieth-century conservative critiques of affirmative action and multiculturalism in their claims to be fighting discrimination while aggressively attempting to craft an all-white board, the Lady Managers heralded separation as celebration and progress where white women's exhibits were concerned while championing white supremacy through the rhetoric of racial equality.

Debates over the meaning and political expediency of seeking inclusion in all exhibits as opposed to separate representation of some kind were intense within black activist circles but receded as it became clear that African Americans would find no meaningful representation at all at the fair. Responding tardily to criticism, fair managers designated August 25, 1893, as "Colored People's Day," with special trains and events, including a watermelon sale. Arguing not only that this was adding insult to injury but also that it was a cynical ploy to attract black fairgoers and their dollars, Ida B. Wells led a campaign to boycott the event. Some black visitors did attend on August 25, but figures were very low.[12] Several prominent black activists and community leaders found other ways to participate in the fair to generate positive images of African Americans and their abilities. Hallie Quinn Brown, Anna Julia Cooper, and Fannie Barrier Williams participated in the World Congress of Representative Women, while Booker T. Washington attended a session of the Labor Congress devoted to black workers. Frederick Douglass represented Haiti at the fair on the basis of his previous service as the U.S. minister to that country. Most famously, Douglass, Wells, and others publicized the struggle for a significant black American presence in the fair's organization and execution and detailed the contributions of African Americans historically and contemporaneously in a widely circulated pamphlet titled *The Reason Why the Colored American Is Not in the World's Columbian Exposition* (1893).[13] The absence indicated by the title was not so much that of actual black people, although inclusion of any kind was clearly limited, but of individuals or exhibits that could be considered positive representations of racial progress and national power.

The forward march of modernity was represented by at least one "colored American" at the fair, however, in the

The site of the R. T. Davis Milling Company display in the Agriculture Building at the World's Columbian Exposition in Chicago in 1893 (back row). (Photo courtesy of The Newberry Library, Chicago, Illinois.)

faithful enslaved mammy personified by Aunt Jemima. Nancy Green was presented as *the* Aunt Jemima, ex-slave cook and bearer of the always delicious and easy-to-make pancake recipe, courtesy of the Davis Milling Company. Green presided over a hot griddle and served pancakes while promoting the mix and spinning tales of glorious old days on the plantation for hordes of hungry visitors at a booth shaped like an enormous flour barrel. The booth and Green's demonstration were located on the Agriculture Building's second-floor gallery, all of which was devoted to food preparation, preservation, and distribution. The ground level of the hall, which covered fifteen acres, was filled with large exhibits of the agricultural products of each state in the United

States, several foreign countries, and a number of colonial territories. Visitors were guided upstairs by large signs detailing the foodstuffs, sweets, and beverages that were on exhibit and available in the galleries.[14] On display there were examples of the technological advances necessary for turning all of the raw commodities exhibited on the first floor into finished consumer goods, the technology often represented by the consumable product itself. Corporate entities rather than political boundaries defined the geography of the galleries. The building's design and layout equated progress and the modern with consumption. Through Aunt Jemima, the Davis Milling Company combined all of these elements with a version of history defined by agrarian abundance, hospitality, and white leisure, all made possible by faithful slaves. The trademark character suggested that slavery itself had been a necessary stage in the progress of capitalist civilization. With every sweet and buttery bite, fairgoers were transported to the Old South of popular imagination as they marveled at their own modern good fortune.

In *Brands, Trademarks, and Good Will*, Arthur Marquette reports that it was not only Green's gregarious nature and fine cooking skills that caught the attention of the Davis Milling Company but also the fact that she "loved to talk about her own slave days." Her stories, he qualifies, were "no doubt apocryphal but nonetheless entertaining." Green shared these wonderfully entertaining tales and old songs with fairgoers, Marquette continues, in a presentation that was largely of her own creation and that surpassed all other food demonstrations at the fair in popularity and impact. Aunt Jemima and her pancakes were in such demand, he claims, that extra police had to be hired for the gallery to keep the flow of traffic moving around the Davis Milling booth.[15] The popularity verging on hysteria that Marquette and others describe may well be a product of subsequent advertising.

Extant firsthand accounts of the demonstration say nothing about enormous or unmanageable crowds; crowds are mentioned mostly in the context of reports about the abundance of free food available in the Agriculture Building. "Exposition wits tell many amusing stories of the crowds which surge toward the galleries of Agricultural hall as the lunch hour approaches, as it is generally known that a number of exhibitors distribute their specialties in food and drink for advertising purposes," notes one contemporary report.[16] Some make reference to Aunt Jemima, "a genuine southern cook," by name, while others, such as one that referred to a "colored woman" demonstrating a "special mixture of flour," do not identify the product or its demonstrator. One report erroneously advised visitors to get "one of Aunt Dinah's pancakes, hot from the griddle."[17]

Within a few years of the Chicago fair, it would be rare for an American reporter to mistake the trademark's name. In part, this would be due to the range of advertising media that came to bear the image of the trademark mammy. Many visitors to the Davis booth received a lapel pin emblazoned with her picture, a bandannaed black woman with a toothy grin, above which was printed the slogan "I'se in town, honey!" Drawing on popular dialect forms and seeking to enfold the potential consumer in the affective "Honey," the button apparently said nothing about pancakes or flour, nor did the full product name appear. At a time in the product's history when Aunt Jemima's smile did not necessarily elicit brand recognition, the buttons promoted the idea of a beaming mammy more than they did pancakes.

These buttons were an early attempt to identify brand awareness with status, a central feature of modern consumer culture. Drawing on an established tradition of political ephemera such as lapel pins that promoted parties and politicians and denoted the wearer's membership or support,

"Aunt Jemima's Lullaby." Words by George Cooper, music by S. H. Speck, 1896. (Photo courtesy of Brown University Library, Providence, Rhode Island.)

the Aunt Jemima buttons were an early form of the advertising premiums that the Davis Milling Company used to generate brand loyalty. In 1897, four cents' worth of stamps sent to the company would bring its customers a copy of Purd Wright's *Life of Aunt Jemima*, a set of "pickaninny dolls" ready for stuffing, and piano sheet music for "Aunt Jemima's Lullaby," a song composed expressly for the product.[18] Consumers were encouraged to gather friends and family around the piano to sing songs about Aunt Jemima, read a "slave narrative" about her and her recipe, and tuck the kids into bed with dolls bearing the product name. Items such as these infiltrated the intimate spaces of people's daily lives and reinforced ideas of white supremacy and black servility as much as they sold products. They represented an early-twentieth-century commodity culture that promoted the faithful slave and other derogatory black images in print media and mass-produced material goods such as statuettes, coin banks, dishes, and ashtrays aimed at predominantly white consumers. Over the next sixty years, many additional items would become Aunt Jemima premiums, available for a specified number of box tops plus shipping charges, and designed to be displayed in collectors' homes.[19]

Nancy Green, the woman handing out Aunt Jemima buttons at the Columbian Exposition, who was said to have been born a slave in the Kentucky bluegrass, was working in Chicago as a domestic servant when a wholesale distributor met her in the home of her employer, his friend Charles Walker. He notified R. T. Davis that he had found just the black woman the company owner was looking for to demonstrate his new product at the fair. Davis met her and offered her the job. From that point on Green's life changed significantly, as her own history and experience were eclipsed by the figure of Aunt Jemima. The trademark's "history" relayed through *The Life of Aunt Jemima, the Most Famous Colored Woman in the World*, and subsequent ad campaigns embellishing the story absorbed aspects of Green's life into Aunt Jemima's. The power of the faithful slave narrative, mammy iconography, and the J. Walter Thompson Company's ads combined to blur her biography and transform her for posterity into not just the embodiment but the very being of the beloved trademark. In this, Green's story is emblematic of the experiences of the thousands of black women in the early twentieth century whose identities and labor were shaped and at times overwhelmed by the figure of the mammy.

When Nancy Green was hit by a car and killed in late August 1923, few people outside of her immediate circle of family, friends, and fellow parishioners at the Olivet Baptist Church knew that she had been appearing as Aunt Jemima since the fair. When the *Chicago Tribune* first ran Green's obituary and a short item reporting the fatal accident, there was no mention of her job portraying Aunt Jemima.[20] This all changed the following week, when the connection was drawn between Green and the trademark at a coroner's inquest. The day after, the *Tribune* reported the legal proceedings and a detailed obituary under the headline "'Aunt Jemima' of Pancake Fame Is Killed by Auto." The article declared, "'Aunt Jemima' is dead," much like the *Missouri Farmer*'s later proclamation, "Aunt Jemima Is Gone."[21] Although the article is framed as the saddening revelation of Green's supposed dual identity, it slips quickly into collapsing the two, recounting a tale of Green's life that is much more that of the fictional Aunt Jemima. The article adds elements to the narrative that further depict Green as a faithful enslaved mammy by implying that she had traveled to Chicago as a slave of the Walker family:

> "Aunt Jemima" was born in Montgomery County, Ky., in 1834 and came to Chicago as a nurse for the Walker family. She nursed and made pancakes for the late Circuit Judge Charles M. Walker, chief justice of the municipal court, and his brother, Dr. Samuel Walker, now a leading north side physician, when they were boys. They spread her fame among their boy chums, and before long "Aunt Jemima's pancakes" became a common phrase in Chicago when good things to eat were discussed.
>
> A milling concern heard of her, searched her out, obtained her recipe and induced her to make pancakes at the World's fair. After that she went from one exposition to another demonstrating her skill. There was one, however, that she re-

fused to attend—the Paris exposition. All inducements that could be made were put forward, but "Aunt Jemima" refused to budge.

To animate Green's refusal to go to Paris, the article shifts into dialect in a passage attributed as a quotation, much like the "I'se in Town, Honey" slogan long associated with the trademark: "I was bo'n in this country an' I'm gonna die heah, not somewheah 'twixt heah an' somewheah's else."[22]

The *Tribune*'s second obituary of Green characterizes her as a domestic laborer/faithful slave within the Walker home, and as Aunt Jemima. A reprint of this obituary under a different headline a month later reinforced this connection. The *Cook County Herald* of Arlington Heights, Illinois, titled the obituary "'Aunt Jemima' Victim of Auto—Colored Mammy of Pancake Fame Crushed to Death in Chicago; Born in Kentucky."[23] The only information about Green provided to readers that is unrelated to the trademark is a note that she was an organizing member of her church, described as "the largest colored church in the world," and a missionary worker. While this does locate Green within a black community and identifies her as an individual person of faith, in the wider context of the obituary this fact serves more to reinforce the generic construction of the enslaved mammy figure as supremely pious. It is probable that the story, incorrect both in much of its detail about Green's life and in its version of the pancake mix's history, came from the inquest, where elements of Green's history and of advertising copy were blended in testimony. All of this took place in the context of a legal proceeding, the aim of which was to decide whether to hold the two drivers involved in the death criminally culpable.[24] It is clear that the dialect speech came from the *Tribune* journalist's imagination.

Although some of these errors persisted in local black press coverage of Green's death, there are important and telling differences in the *Chicago Defender*'s obituary. A small photo of Green that ran under the *Tribune* headline was labeled only "Aunt Jemima." This same picture appeared four days later in the *Defender*'s front-page article identified as "Mrs. Nancy Green." The *Defender*'s label rejects the "Aunt" moniker of enslavement, which had been designed to avoid the need for formalities when whites addressed black people and denoted a kind of interchangeability among all black women. While it describes her work for the Walkers and does not provide any further information about when or why she traveled from Kentucky to Chicago, the black-owned paper locates Green more solidly within black communities, noting: "Mrs. Green was one of the first missionary workers of Olivet Baptist church, which she helped organize . . . Her funeral was held from there Saturday. She was a member of many fraternal organizations. She is survived by several relatives."[25] This last line places her within her own family, not the white Walker family for which she worked.

In a later *Defender* piece on Green, columnist A. L. Jackson suggested that budding black businessmen could take a lesson from the lucrative popularity of "her" pancakes. Referring to black criticisms of the trademark, Jackson countered:

> Many will say that this dear old lady was exploited by this rich concern, but they will fail to reckon upon the fact that there are perhaps hundreds of others who could make cakes just as delicious as Aunt Jemima who will never be known to the world . . . There are other things than pancakes which our mothers know how to make better than other women. There is no good reason why some wide-awake young business man from our own crowd should not seize upon that skill and capitalize it for himself and the Race as these white men did with Aunt Jemima.[26]

Jackson's suggestion that some black man should summon both the gumption and the race pride to exploit the skill and persona of black women leaves little room for imagining that one of those women might do this herself. It is the black male economic subject, independent, wealthy, and primed to demand his full rights as a citizen, with whom Jackson is most concerned.

Although limited, Jackson's attempt to resituate Aunt Jemima as a misappropriation of black ingenuity by white economic interests, and his caution that readers should not imagine her simply as an exploited woman, remind us that Nancy Green was making choices within a restricted range of options. Despite their silences and distortions, Green's obituaries reveal her to have been a prominent figure within one of black Chicago's most powerful churches and an active community member. Census records provide some picture of her southern past, family relationships, and work life. It is likely that she was in fact born into slavery in Kentucky, but the year was 1844, not 1834, as most obituaries reported. This made her forty-nine years old when she assumed the role of Aunt Jemima and seventy-nine when she died. In Chicago, Green lived with the Hayes family and a collection of unrelated boarders, first with Nelson and Mamie Hayes, one of whom was Green's nephew or niece, and then in the household of their son, Leroy, whom she had watched grow up and had probably helped to raise. Before this, Nancy Green had been married for thirty years and had two children, but neither they nor her husband was still alive in 1900. In that year she listed her occupation as "cook," which could have referred to her job demonstrating Aunt Jemima pancake mix or else indicated that her primary employment remained in domestic service. The latter was the case in 1910, when she reported her job as "housekeeper" in a private residence. Performing as the trademarked mammy was not her primary job by that time, if it ever had been. By 1920 Green was no longer working regularly for wages; she reported her occupation as "none."[27] Because of her role as Aunt Jemima, Nancy Green left a larger archive than most black women born into slavery who became domestic workers after the Civil War. Yet the power and the longevity of the trademark have rendered her actual historical record obscure and her full identity impossible to discover.[28]

Located in the capital city of the New South, the Atlanta Cotton States and International Exposition of 1895 displayed the same swelled chests and spectacular schemes of the Chicago fair two years earlier, if not its grand scale or enormous attendance figures. Designed to showcase the region's dramatic post-Reconstruction economic growth and potential, the Atlanta fair aimed to attract tourism, business interests, and capital investment and to position the region as a gateway to international markets farther south. Key to this construction of a modern New South was the impression of harmonious race relations sustained through benevolent white management. Just a year shy of the U.S. Supreme Court's *Plessy* decision declaring "separate" accommodations to be constitutional and potentially "equal," the Atlanta fair celebrated legal segregation as a panacea for local and national race and labor problems.[29] The figure of the faithful slave appeared in various incarnations at the fair to support this argument and to suggest historical continuities between the Old and New South. Aunt Jemima pancake mix was demonstrated there, and since Nancy Green was said to have attended every fair before her death except the one in Paris, it is likely that she was in Atlanta.[30]

Although, after the exclusions of Chicago, many thrilled at the inclusion of a Negro Building created and overseen by an African American board of managers, several black organizations and newspapers encouraged a boycott of the fair on account of segregation in the city of Atlanta broadly and in the fair's planning and execution in particular.[31] Arguably, the Negro Building could be taken as an example of supposed southern white benevolence toward blacks as much as it could a record of black achievement and progress. White fair managers could argue that the southern white man was indeed "the best friend of the Negro" when they noted the absence of such a feature at the Chicago fair.[32] Planners and the press made much of the fact that the building had been designed and built by black people, failing to note that much of the fair had been built by black labor and that predominantly black convict workers had initially cleared the grounds for the exposition. Yet all transportation, public facilities, and audience seating were strictly segregated. And while black fairgoers could enter any building on the grounds, they could find refreshments only in the Negro Building. Since it was located at the far southwestern edge of the fairgrounds at the corner of Jackson and Tenth streets, between the Midway Heights concessions and the grandstand for Buffalo Bill's Wild West Show, this meant a long walk from the rest of the attractions for African American visitors.[33] The fairground's layout complicated the aims of the Negro Building further by putting it so close to, and thus likening it with, the human sideshows of the Midway and Buffalo Bill's acts. Among the concessions made especially for Atlanta was the "Old Plantation," where visitors could watch and listen to "faithful slaves" dance, sing, and play fiddles and banjos. The Old Plantation was the only concession President Grover Cleveland visited on his official trip to the exposition, a fact later promoted in advertisements. Variations on the concession at subsequent fairs both in and outside the region claimed to be composed of actual slave cabins.[34] At every turn, fairgoers were encouraged to see a dynamic New South still connected to Old Southern traditions through plantation fantasy and white paternalism.

Representations of faithful slavery even carried into the Negro Building itself. Flanking the outside of the hall's main entrance were two reliefs, one of a black mammy and the other of the recently deceased Frederick Douglass—arguably the two most famous black figures of the day. At first glance there seemed to be a certain irony in the pairing of these two figures, the fictional faithful slave and the famous runaway slave, abolitionist, and radical activist. At least one contemporary commentator argued that this was purposeful and appropriate. In an article devoted to Booker T. Washington's celebrated appearance at the fair, a reporter described the two medallions as opposite ends of the trajectory of black progress, "representing the past and the present conditions of the Negro."[35] Notably, this vision of black progress equated the past with the faithful slavery of black women while the contemporary period was defined by manly action, remarkable individual achievement, and strength of character, a gendered historical framing that would animate a range of black activist rhetoric throughout the twentieth century. The building's 25,000-square-foot interior was divided into fourteen state exhibits, separate displays featuring fine arts, literature, and patented inventions created by African Americans, and a large restaurant. Several of the state exhibits were dominated by contributions from black institutions of industrial education, such as Booker T. Washington's own Tuskegee Institute in Alabama. The Negro Building also provided a variety of special services for black visitors necessitated by segregation at the fair and in its host city. In addition to the restaurant, these included a medical facility and an information center for those seeking overnight accommodations at establishments open to black guests.[36] In all, no site at the fair, other than the Woman's Building, would receive more visitors than the Negro Building.[37]

If the medallions at the entrance represented the two

most famous black figures of the day, the fair became best known for introducing to the nation another famous African American, Booker T. Washington. His address on opening day, eventually dubbed the "Atlanta Compromise" by critic W. E. B. Du Bois, solidified Washington's place as the leading black political voice of the early twentieth century. At the fair, Washington crafted his vision of black progress in the New South through accommodation, gradualism, and economic independence largely around the figure of the faithful slave. When he asked white southerners to "cast their buckets where they were," by which he meant to continue to rely on a black southern workforce despite the influx of white (or whitening) immigrants, Washington appealed to a nostalgic plantation history that he claimed both races shared:

> While doing this, you can be sure in the future, as in the past, that you and your families will be surrounded by the most patient, faithful, law-abiding and unresentful people that the world has seen. As we have proved our loyalty to you in the past, in nursing your children, watching by the sick-bed of your mothers and fathers, and often following them with tear-dimmed eyes to their graves, so in the future, in our humble way, we shall stand by you with a devotion that no foreigner can approach, ready to lay down our lives, if need be, in defense of yours, interlacing our industrial, commercial, civil, and religious life with yours in a way that shall make the interests of both races one.

This was followed immediately by the most famous statement of Washington's speech: "In all things that are purely social we can be as separate as the fingers, yet one as the hand in all things essential to mutual progress."[38] With his easy transition from examples of interracial intimacy to an apparent endorsement of segregation, Washington suggested a very different arc of black progression "up from slavery" from the one on display at the entrance to the Negro Building. He offered plantation nostalgia as evidence of contemporary "patience" and a lack of "resentment" among black southerners for past and present wrongs. Washington manipulated the ability of the faithful slave story to assuage white guilt in hopes of creating a space for some degree of cooperation, free from the suspicion and violence that guilt often engenders. Washington assumed the mantle of "Leader of the Race" in the year of Frederick Douglass's death through his appeals to the very same plantation fictions that Douglass had worked so hard to refute.

Bringing to mind the promotional Aunt Jemima buttons of the Chicago fair two years earlier, a proponent of Washington's vision suggested a lapel pin commemorating the speech. William J. Cansler, a prominent black teacher from Knoxville, Tennessee, asked Washington:

> Couldn't that expression of yours, "We can be as separate as the fingers, yet one as the hand in all things essential to mutual progress," be symbolized in the form of a button worn on lapel of coat as are worn by Grand Army men, Oddfellows, Masons & c: represented as an open hand, fingers extended and diverging? This could be sold on Exposition grounds at the Negro exhibit and would be bought and worn by thousands both white and colored. It would fittingly symbolize the new epoch in the Negroes history in the South, as well as immortalize the expression.[39]

Cansler's pin would testify to one's loyalty to Washington's brand of politics, as it would also serve as an income-generating souvenir of the Atlanta fair itself. It would indeed signify this "new epoch" in southern and national history in which the color line was drawn, maintained, and adapted to through stories of faithful slavery.

Notions of racial intimacy in the context of a strict hierarchy, personified in the loyal ex-slave, were central to Washington's articulations of a regionalist black politics of gradualism and accommodation. They were as much an animating force of his aspirations for the race as a strategy for wooing southern whites to the cause of black progress. In that same speech he appealed to black southerners to "cast their buckets where *they* were"—a spatial metaphor for accepting their place within existing hierarchies and simultaneously a call to remain in the South, or in their geographic place. A staunch regionalist, Washington would devote much of his political life to discouraging black migration.[40]

It is ironic that the woman who served as the very embodiment of the modern faithful slave to which Washington appealed had herself left the South for Chicago some time earlier. As Washington spoke that afternoon of the past's lessons for realizing a potentially bright southern future, it is possible that Nancy Green was elsewhere at the fair serving pancakes as Aunt Jemima. Like so many other African Americans living in or visiting Atlanta that day, both she and Washington were former slaves. For Nancy Green, the journey to Georgia would have meant a return to the region she had left. For both, the exposition meant a journey into the Old South of white imagination and fantasy. Images of the mammy and plantation legend shaped Green's and Washington's lives in profound ways. While the faithful slave narrative helped to catapult Booker T. Washington to national fame and political power, it simultaneously plunged Green into historical obscurity behind Aunt Jemima's designation as the "most famous colored woman in the world."

2 ANXIOUS PERFORMANCES

For sweet charity's sake 40 clever Tacoma [Washington] ladies blacked their comely faces with burnt cork last night and appeared on the big stage of the Ninth Street theater as negro minstrels. The social folk turned out by the hundreds to see what the belles of the town would look like when blacked up.

—*Tacoma Daily News*, 1894

WHEN THE WOMEN of the Arche Club of Chicago hired Jeanette Robinson Murphy in the early winter of 1901 to provide them with an afternoon of "plantation entertainment" and instruction in the ways of "the genuine Southern Negro," it seems likely that many did not expect the program to be quite so interactive. Murphy, a white, southern professional "reader-entertainer" who specialized in black dialect, had little trouble getting the white clubwomen to tie bandannas around their heads and shoulders in the style of an old mammy. Nor did the group hesitate to rub the left hind foot of a southern graveyard rabbit for good luck. Many grew self-conscious, however, when Murphy asked them to join her in singing a "negro lullaby" in dialect. The *Chicago Tribune* reported that by easing them into the performance with

step-by-step instructions on how to sing and move like an
enslaved old black woman, Murphy drew her reluctant lis-
teners into the act: "First Mrs. Murphy had the audience
repeat the words. Then she gave them the tune. Then she
told them to put their tongues close behind the upper teeth
and not to let go of their 'n's' until they reached the next
one." Once Murphy taught them to sound the way they believed a mammy sounded, she got them moving: "She suggested they clap their hands and stamp with one foot in syn-
copated time. At this period it was easy to imagine a minstrel
chorus on a rehearsal or a Georgia camp meeting in progress." To the left of the stage where Murphy stood was a concession operated by an unnamed black woman identified in
the *Tribune* only as the "original 'Aunt Jemima.'" The woman
served cornbread and hotcakes and wore a large gold medal
she had received at the Paris Exposition of 1900. "Her beaming smiles radiated over the hall," claimed the *Tribune*.[1] One
wonders what this woman must have thought as she watched
Murphy teach the white women's club how to perform faithful slavery in dialect.[2]

The spectacle of the Arche Club's "afternoon way down
South" was considered entertaining enough to have been reported with illustrations in the *Tribune*. It was a common
scene across the United States at the beginning of the twentieth century. White women around the country participated
in professional and amateur impersonations of enslaved black
women on stages and in living rooms, whether for historical
presentations, for shared amusement, to raise funds for favorite causes, or for pay. Since its inception in antebellum
proslavery literature, white women had a special connection
to the mammy figure. They were, in fact, the country's primary producers and consumers of the faithful slave narrative.[3] The range of needs filled by the figure of the faithful

slave—what made these women cling to mammy and to the popular nostalgia for human bondage—were as varied as the women themselves. Yet in expressing their privileges, desires for status, and anxieties through the performance of faithful slavery, members of the Arche Club were in many ways emblematic of the popular romance with mammy and the Old South.[4] This was certainly true of Jeannette Robinson Murphy, whose assertions of privilege and expertise based on her gender, race, and regional identity, combined with her need for employment, financial and otherwise, fueled this romance.

The presence of a black woman portraying Aunt Jemima marked the artifice of the white woman's performance while it generated the illusion of authenticity for the entire affair. Despite the *Tribune*'s report that the black woman was the "original Aunt Jemima," the woman working at the Arche Club meeting that afternoon was not Nancy Green, the originator of the role.[5] Neither Green's nor the unnamed woman's hired performances as enslaved mammies revealed their real names; their servile status was presumed and taken for granted.

Through their sheer scale, the Chicago and Atlanta world's fairs impressed upon visitors the gravity and importance of the things they saw, rode on, ate, heard, and dreamed about there, including representations of faithful slavery. But the power of these stories and their centrality to American modernity were more often experienced in everyday acts at home, like tucking into a stack of buttery pancakes or reading popular books.[6] A small book titled *Mammy's Letters* (1922) written by a woman from Richmond, Virginia, is representative of these more common and mundane moments of sharing and enjoying tales of the faithful slave. In her introduction, Gertrude Langhorne lamented:

Mother, Home and Mammy! They are three of the most beautiful words in the English language and the latter is now almost obsolete. I keenly regret it for those generations yet to come, who cannot learn its dearness. I never see my mammy without a tugging at my heart and a tightness in my throat. Some of the happiest days of my life ever had, or will have, were spent in the shelter of her arms and surrounded by the tender care her love always gave me. It makes one long with an unspeakable longing.[7]

Langhorne's sentimental, pathos-filled invocation of "three of the most beautiful words" sums up graphically the centrality of mammy iconography and the interracial relationships it suggested—real and imagined—to white women in the early twentieth century. *Mammy's Letters* reflected the surge in popularity of the faithful slave narrative in the 1910s and 1920s, and the prominence of white women as the narrators and keepers of these historical fictions. The text brings together the major themes of the genre: white supremacist nostalgia for antebellum paternalism and supposedly faithful slaves; the glorification of white domesticity through a black maternal figure; claims of intimate and satisfying bodily contact between black women and whites in the private sphere of the white home; and, finally, white southerners' allegedly indescribable or "unspeakable" longing for the black mammy.

Langhorne constructs her text as an archive of letters received by her during the First World War from Jerdena Jefferson, the black woman she called "Mammy." The fabricated nature of this collection and Langhorne's own role as the ultimate author of Jefferson's letters are clear. "It may be of interest to state," she begins, "that the following 'Letters' are genuine in every detail—even to the names used. Several are copies of those written me by my old ex-slave Mammy. The others are incidents related by her that I have arranged in letter form."[8] As was true generally with white-authored recollections of the enslaved mammy, it is the testimony of a white woman that is the measure of the loyalty and authenticity of a black woman. The provenance of the "letters" is admittedly questionable, but the "truth" of their claims is actually established by the confession of white authorship. Furthermore, the letters are intended to ring true, as they are all written in the same dialect that animated black voices on minstrel stages and in Plantation School literature. Langhorne chooses literally to speak for her mammy, in dialect, via the fictionalized cache of letters.

The logic of the letter as historical evidence suggests contemporary documentation, an on-the-spot record of events and, even more important, of private emotions and thoughts. The collected correspondence of ordinary people, those who are not political figures or famous in some other way, seems especially revelatory of everyday connections among individuals across time and space, and denotes intimacy between the correspondents. The act of saving letters is itself intensely sentimental, attributing to them an additional emotional value. For Langhorne and her intended audience, this was central to fashioning the voice of mammy as one of tenderness toward the white recipient of her missives. The expressions of confusion and requests for assistance from whites contained in many of the letters reflected the paternalism inherent in stories of faithful slaves. Notably, *Mammy's Letters* was not crafted as a two-way correspondence. Langhorne does not reproduce any letters from herself to Jefferson, nor does she "arrange in letter form" anything she may have said, or wished to have said. The conversation implied in the text is actually one between Langhorne and her presumed white audience. Remember the good old days and the good old Negroes, she urges her readers, for these memories soothe in the face of contemporary upheavals and the losses of the recent war.[9]

Ultimately, Langhorne presents the "letters" as a sort of totem of the physical and emotional intimacy she believes she shared with Jefferson, and that she found beyond easy description—"unspeakable," as she puts it. When white southerners struggled palpably to express the depth of their feelings for the black maternal figures and domestic workers they once knew as mammies, or conjured in fantasies of family plantation legacy, they often resorted to assertions of the "indescribable" nature of their longing. To assert the impossibility of explaining, and thus the incapability of non-southern whites to know or understand, served to shore up the boundaries of a white regional identity as well as defend against critics of past and present southern race relations.

This was certainly the case with Thomas Nelson Page, who, in his popular defense of segregation, *The Negro: The Southerner's Problem* (1904), argues similarly indescribable connections among "Mother, Home, and Mammy." The mammy "has never been adequately described," he claims, "chiefly, I fancy, because it is impossible to describe her as she was." Page continues in characteristically florid style:

> Who may picture a mother? We may dab and dab at it, but when we have done our best we know that we have stuck on a little paint, and the eternal verity stands forth like the eternal verity of the Holy Mother, outside our conception, only to be apprehended in our highest moments, and never to be truly pictured by pen or pencil. So, no one can describe what the mammy was, and only those can apprehend her who were rocked on her generous bosom, slept on her bed, fed at her table, were directed and controlled by her, watched by her unsleeping eye, and led by her precept in the way of truth, justice and humanity. She was far more than a servant. She was a member of the family in high standing.[10]

There is an easy slippage here between mother, the enslaved mammy, and that other symbol of selfless, unending, and markedly nonsexual maternal affection, the Virgin Mary. Yet in the context of the early-twentieth-century popular romance with the faithful mammy, such blurring was not at all uncommon. While Page draws no apparent distinction between his mother and his mammy, Langhorne's beloved trinity of "Mother, Home and Mammy" divides the two figures as it simultaneously connects them via the white home. Langhorne posits the cloistered spaces of white domesticity as a terrain of contact between mothers and mammies, similar in their roles as nurturers and as embodiments of nostalgia, yet separated unequivocally by race. Her wistful narrative actually says nothing more of her white, biological mother, however, and instead dwells only on the motherly attentions she received from Jefferson.

Despite long-standing protestations that the mammy was a completely nonsexual figure, there is sensuality approaching the erotic in both Page's and Langhorne's descriptions of the physical intimacy and racial role reversals in their experiences of black caretaking. This eroticism remains unmediated and undeterred by the authors' youth in the scenes they recollect. It is as adults that they construct these memories. Page was a middle-aged man when he recalled with such emotion sleeping in a black woman's bed and eating her food, and described her generous bosom, as well as her "dignity, force, kindness; her showy bed . . . the exercise of her authority, and . . . at least two 'good whippings'" administered by her.[11]

While the trope of indescribability may convey the sublimated eroticization of the black mammy's body, it was overtly intended to mark the author's elite southern class position. Like so many others, Page insisted that "among the slave-owning class, there was hardly a child who had not been rocked in a colored mammy's arms."[12] Thus, those who shared memories of mammy or claimed some affinity with a mammy figure were necessarily claiming a part of that class legacy and status. Although regional authors like Page wrote Plantation School fiction and social criticism for a national audience, southern whites commonly shared among themselves proclamations, reminiscences, and stories of their limitless affection for mammy, trading narratives of black bodies to denote class and regional belonging and to forge intraracial relationships.[13]

If the ambiguities of indescribable emotion were intended to produce class exclusivity—suggesting that those who knew just *knew* and needed no further explanation—they simultaneously marked the fundamental eroticism of the mammy construct. Langhorne's choice of the word "unspeakable" to describe her "longing" signifies the desire that slinks through the mammy narrative. A few months before *Mammy's Letters* was published, Senator Edward Pou of North Carolina had stood on the floor of the U.S. Senate and argued, as a defense of southern segregation and lynching: "There is one other thing that you men from the North cannot comprehend, that ineffable, indescribable, unspeakable love that every southern man feels for the old black nurse who took care of him in childhood. The sweetest memories of my life go back to my old 'mammy.'"[14] Circulating through these justifications of segregation and violence is a profound nostalgia for sanctioned physicality between black women and both white women and men. They express a longing for access to black women's bodies, beds, and private lives, the last now concealed from them in segregated black neighborhoods and institutions. Denied here was the fact that whites continued to claim sexual access to black people within coercive as well as consensual frameworks, while often responding to even the suggestion of black men's cross-racial desire with violence and murder.

The supposedly sexually undesirable mammy figure formed

one side of a white-authored, mutually reinforcing dual image of black women's nature. On the other side was the voraciously sexual "jezebel." Whereas the mammy was promoted in popular white representations as embodying maternal affective relationships, the "jezebel" explained the undeniable fact that sex had indeed occurred across the color line between black women and white men and continued to do so. The stereotypical "jezebel" lusted after, lured, and cajoled white men, and thus bore the responsibility for interracial sexual encounters. Deborah Gray White argues that "Southerners were able to embrace both images of black women simultaneously and to switch from one to the other depending on the context of their thought."[15] These were not two separate women. The characterizations were read onto a single black female body within the shifting contexts and needs of white supremacy.[16]

In their evocations of the romantic plantation South, Langhorne's letters are intended to forge a link between the recent experiences of the First World War and the Civil War. Through the voice of Jerdena Jefferson, a black mother who first fears that her son Efrom will be drafted into military service, then expresses her anxiety and confusion once he is indeed drafted, Langhorne resuscitates another popular faithful slave figure: the young manservant transformed into a Confederate brother-in-arms. Her narrative telescopes time, pushing the Civil War and the Great War into closer historical proximity. The thoughts on mobilization she attributes to Jefferson often recall "the other war," a vague reference that realistically should refer to the more recent Spanish-American War, yet in the context of this story necessarily brings to mind the Civil War.

Recalling the supposed legions of faithful enslaved Confederate fighters, Efrom's ex-slave parents assume that he has been pressed into military service to go into battle with "Mr.

Phil" (Phil Miller), the son of their former master, as his body servant and protector. Jefferson implores, "Plese ax Mr. Phil ter do de bes he can by him [Efrom] fur his ole Mammy's sake 'cause I so skeered."[17] Of course, Efrom was not drafted to perform these services for Phil. According to the fictionalized letters, Jefferson becomes increasingly upset over the course of the narrative because she and her husband are not sure where Efrom is, and they cannot understand why he is not with Phil. Arguably, much of the charm of these letters for Langhorne's (white) readers is that the old black woman would automatically assume, even in the 1910s, that Efrom was drafted to serve the old master's son. It is a mark not only of her deep and abiding faithfulness but also of the endurance into the twentieth century of supposed paternalist bonds of mutual obligation and care transmitted across generations.

For Langhorne, Jefferson remains as faithful to class hierarchies as she does to those of race, expressing in explicit fashion how inseparable the two were, and still remain. Through Jefferson's voice she stages a critique of the modern military as a potentially equalizing institution. *"Dar air some turrible mistakes goin' on in dis Govmint,"* Jefferson worries. "We had a letter from Efrom sayin he war real well an' in Camp Mills. Say he hav inquire evrywhar fur Mr. Phil but cant fine no news uv him. Uv cose, I knows dat 'tis a misunderstanin' cause Sterling Bolling wuz with Mr. Cocke in tother War an Major Dance an' Major Old an' Kunnel Harris as' all de rest frum here had dey niggers to look arter dem an' Efrom *wuz tuk fer Mr. Phil.*"[18] Jefferson's biggest fear, other than the danger her son may encounter as a soldier, is that he has been assigned to shine the wrong man's shoes. "He may be wid' po white trash now fur all I know."[19] Elite white concerns about the potential for military service and institutional authority to blur the lines of established social hierarchies are put into the mouths of those on the lowest rungs of those systems, the poor and people of color, in an attempt to cast them as universally shared.

Langhorne's account of one black family's supposed experience of the Great War provides a powerful counterimage to the martial experience as it was popularized by civil rights activists and black nationalists during and after the war. Black activists referred constantly to black men's military service as exemplary of black Americans' patriotism and civic commitment as well as of the failure of federal and local institutions to recognize them. African Americans were expected to perform the service of citizens while they were not acknowledged as such, and were ordered to protect U.S. interests abroad while they themselves were not protected from violence at home. Langhorne's narrative denies this association by placing black military service in the context of the largely mythical commitment of the faithful male slave to battle alongside his master or to protect the (white) home front in the absence of the white patriarch. Her book processes post–World War I sentimentality and dread by harking back to the Civil War era and a mythic construction of race relations. We white southerners know about the violence, human toll, and pain of war, Langhorne suggests, and it is all shared with black people and rendered endurable by their care and the safety of mammy's bosom.

Mammy's Letters is the sort of book that would have found its way easily into the hands of women who belonged to the United Daughters of the Confederacy (UDC). Its small booklet format lent itself to being passed from person to person at local meetings or transported easily to national conventions to share or perhaps to sell. Its subject matter was dear to the hearts, and to the social and political projects, of UDC members. From the organization's inception the

Daughters were focused on Confederate history as central to their mission of vindicating the South and glorifying the Lost Cause. This history, they believed, included stories of faithful slaves. Founded in 1894, the United Daughters of the Confederacy initially acted as an umbrella organization for chapters of the Ladies Memorial Association and various other Confederate women's groups. While the UDC ultimately pursued goals that affected a broad swath of southern culture and politics, its roots were in the memorial associations it incorporated, and much of its early work was devoted to commemoration. By the early 1900s the UDC was an exceedingly popular organization among white bourgeois and elite southern women, involving those who found other turn-of-the-century women's political organizations distasteful as well as women who participated in a wide range of progressive reform activities. Its membership increased steadily during the early twentieth century, growing from approximately 17,000 members in 1900 to 100,000 in 1918 by the UDC's count.[20] White women established local chapters throughout the South as well as beyond the region in areas as far-flung as Paris, New York City, and Helena, Montana.

While commemorative activities and public spectacles of mourning for the Confederate dead remained central to the UDC program throughout the early twentieth century, the organization pursued a much broader social and political agenda than the memorial associations that preceded it and other patriotic women's groups of the day. Of primary importance to the Daughters was both the "preservation" of a glorious memory of the Confederacy and the solidification of their own roles as the keepers and disseminators of this "truth." Rather than simply maintaining an already extant, collective understanding of the historical past, however, the Daughters' activities served to reproduce this memory as they persistently reinvented the Old South and Confederate traditions.[21] Like other turn-of-the-century women's groups, UDC members saw themselves as particularly suited to reform efforts and patriotic education.[22] To this end they not only raised monuments and orchestrated public events for Confederate Memorial Day throughout the South but also successfully campaigned to remove from southern schools textbooks they deemed hostile to the Confederacy, founded and staffed memorial homes to care for aged Confederate soldiers and widows, organized a children's auxiliary organization, the Children of the Confederacy, and sponsored historical research, among other activities.

Although a majority of UDC chapters and state organizations were (and continue to be) located in the South, the more widely dispersed nature of the organization's membership called into question the anchoring of southern identity to the land itself or to the place where one stood at any given moment. This would became more true with the passage of time and the emergence of generations of Daughters nurtured in children's auxiliaries who were not born in the South at all but continued to identify themselves, in part through their UDC membership, as southerners. Whatever members' individual geographic locations, their activities—participation in local, state, and national meetings; organizing and contributing to preservation, memorialization, and commemoration campaigns; reading organization-sanctioned historical works, fiction, and the monthly magazine *Confederate Veteran* (the national organ of a variety of Lost Cause organizations); and collaborating with the United Confederate Veterans (UCV) and the Sons of Confederate Veterans (SCV)—formed the basis of a Confederate public sphere in the twentieth century. It was within this sphere that the Daughters crafted their regional identity, a circle where they could feel, profess, and protect their "southernness."[23]

The southern identity generated here was highly exclusive,

and no one was more conscious of or committed to its exclusivity than the members of the UDC themselves. In their articulations of Confederate pride, whether through monuments to fallen military heroes and "faithful slaves" or "proper" history texts, the Daughters produced a particular form of southernness grounded in notions of white supremacy, patriarchal gender conventions, and elite privilege. Concerning the class and racial composition of the UDC's membership, the historian Anastasia Sims has noted: "Their loyalty to white supremacy was implicit; they also sharply delineated class distinctions among whites. Eligibility was based on ancestry, on an applicant's ability to document a satisfactory answer to that quintessentially Southern question, Who are your people?"[24] As in the DAR (Daughters of the American Revolution), founded four years earlier, and to which many UDC members also belonged, basing membership eligibility on ancestry was designed to facilitate class exclusivity. It was a principle that merged with popular turn-of-the-century ideas about race, blood, and eugenic science.[25] Being a southerner did not require residing in the South, since it was believed to be in one's blood—literally. Of course, a number of black southerners could trace their bloodlines to elite white Confederate pasts as well, a fact willfully ignored by the Daughters until 2002, when the first African American member was enrolled.[26] The UDC carefully policed the boundaries of its membership by defining who could *not* be a part of its honorable postbellum South: most African Americans and the poor of any race.

But maintaining these boundaries, particularly of class, was tested in the early twentieth century by the emergence of a New Southern, largely urban middle class. Women from this milieu flocked to the UDC, filling its ranks and seeking to craft for themselves through their membership planter-class associations and their identity as "southern ladies." Their status hunger drove much of the Daughters' local historical work aimed at recovering and proclaiming the collective honor of the Confederacy.[27]

The organization's historical mission took a decidedly more intense turn with the election of Mildred Lewis Rutherford to the position of historian general, a post she held from 1911 to 1915. The executive office had been created by an amendment to the UDC's constitution three years earlier, centralizing the group's historical work and thus denoting its growing importance within the organization. Rutherford's belief in regional vindication through "truthful" histories of the antebellum South and the "War Between the States" had long motivated both her volunteer work and her career as an educator. She was in many ways representative of the type of woman who gravitated toward the UDC. Born in the summer of 1851 to William R. and Laura Battaile Roots Cobb Rutherford, Mildred Rutherford graduated from the Lucy Cobb Institute in Athens, Georgia, in 1868. She went on to become a teacher of literature at the school and its principal from 1880 to 1898. Her organizational work was extensive, as was her record of publication. She served as the president of the Athens, Georgia, Ladies Memorial Association, was chairman of the YWCA for the Gulf States, and president of the Federated Mission Union. Rutherford was elected for life to the office of state historian of the Georgia division of the UDC before she went on to become historian general of the entire organization. In 1907 she published textbooks on English, American, and French literature as well as *The South in History and Literature*.[28] So while Rutherford's background and associations were typical of those of average UDC members, she was far from average, surpassing most in her ambition and success.[29] Rutherford was singular not only in her work but also, in an organization that usually identified married women only by their husbands' names—as Mrs. Jefferson Davis, for example—she also stood out in her lifelong decision not to marry. She was always listed as Miss Mildred Lewis Rutherford.

Upon assuming the office of historian general, Rutherford distributed in pamphlet form an open letter to state and chapter historians detailing her historical mission and seeking to ensure that it would be carried out according to her exacting standards. In it Rutherford expressed thanks for her election to office, calling it "the highest gift that is in their [the UDC members'] power to bestow, so I regard it." If the office of historian general was the greatest gift, the work she was to organize was, to her, surely the most important. "I rejoice that you have a part with me in this historical work—the most vital work of our organization," she declared. Never one to shy away from the spotlight, Rutherford also submitted a copy of her pamphlet to the *Confederate Veteran*.[30] Its publication in this venue served the dual purpose of reaching more of the UDC's membership while publicizing Rutherford's election and ambition to the larger sphere of Confederate organizations. The theme of Rutherford's tenure in office generally was to be the collection of the "*unwritten* history of our beloved South." Bemoaning that much of the Daughters' historical work to date had been confined to reiterating topics and arguments available in existing histories of the region and the war, Rutherford called upon her legions to gather the relics and narratives of the quickly vanishing generation who had experienced Civil War battles and the plantation South firsthand. Rutherford urged, "What we wish is history—the historical spot where an event took place must be accurately located, the date accurately given, and no 'think so' must be recorded as fact."[31] While her desire was for "history," or to her fact, not supposition or speculation, a subtle change in intonation suggests something very different: what we wish for *is*, or becomes, history. And that is indeed what characterized most of the work the Daughters performed, something that becomes especially clear in the detailed and abundant "histories" of faithful slaves which they produced. These white women pined after the faithful black mammy, a desire arising from their resistance to black freedom struggles in the South and beyond.

For Rutherford, the measure of "truth" was its ability to withstand scrutiny, a need she felt on behalf of the Confederacy, her region, and her class. To this end, the bulk of her pamphlet is devoted to appropriate topics and submission formats. Rutherford sought to strengthen the Daughters' historical methods because she believed this was necessary if they were to be taken seriously both as women and as keepers of the past. Over the years, UDC members would take great pride in their historical accomplishments, shaping the southern public school curriculums for decades, encouraging original research among children and college students, publishing their own work, and contributing to the general historical narrative of the region. These efforts deeply informed the treatment of the South, the Civil War, and Reconstruction in the professional historiography of the early twentieth century. One organizational history of the UDC notes, for example, "The greatest single piece of work [under Charlotte Osborne Woodbury's term as historian general, 1925–1927] was the collecting of material on the reconstruction period and forwarding it to Mr. Claude G. Bowers for his book, *The Tragic Era*."[32]

The subjects in need of investigation outlined by Rutherford included veterans' "Reminiscences," "Sketches of Women," "Daughters of the Confederacy" (by which she meant histories of local chapters), "Books by Southern Authors," and "Stories of Faithful Slaves." The list made clear which areas Rutherford believed were as yet "unwritten," which chiefly involved the contributions of southern women past and present and the history of faithful slavery. Collected now at the Museum of the Confederacy in Richmond, Virginia, the city that is also home to the national headquarters of the UDC, the extensive scrapbooks that resulted from Rutherford's campaign are a lasting memorial to her work and ambition, and a vast record of Lost Cause thought in the early twentieth century. Her papers, filled with articles and reminiscences presented by members to their local chapters, further attest to the way she inspired others with her belief in the redemptive power of "truthful" history and the imperative of "preservation."

Rutherford's criteria for the collection of faithful slave stories indicate the already wide popularity of the mammy narrative in this period. In keeping with her thematic concern for the less well documented "truths" of the Confederacy, she argued, "Sketches not only of the *old mammy* of the South should be preserved as history, but of the many faithful slaves to whose care the women and children were confided when our brave men were at the front, and of those true to their former owners after the war closed."[33] These narratives were critical to the UDC's larger project of challenging dominant portrayals of slavery as brutal and arguments that the Civil War had been fought only to protect the institution. One of Rutherford's most popular and widely referenced pamphlets, "Wrongs of History Righted," was devoted largely to this purpose under the heading "Was Slavery a Crime and the Slaveholder a Criminal?" Presenting an argument very similar to Ulrich B. Phillips's "plantation school" thesis in *American Negro Slavery* (1918), Rutherford cast southern slavery as a paternal, civilizing institution, concluding that "slavery . . . was no crime. In all the history of the world no peasantry was ever better cared for, more contented, or happier. These wrongs must be righted and the Southern slaveholder defended as soon as possible."[34] What better defense than the stories of slaves who were loyal in their "service" and remained so after emancipation?

In a telling shift, the scrapbook volume on this subject ultimately was titled "Tributes to Faithful Slaves" rather than, as originally planned, "Stories of Faithful Slaves." The name change served a dual function, on the one hand marking its contents as homage to and recollections of actual "faithful slaves"—as facts, that is, rather than mere "stories." At the same time, as a memorial volume the scrapbook makes clear that Rutherford and others believed the days of black people's faithfulness to whites and white supremacy were over, that they had been replaced by racial strife and troubling assertions of equality. Notably, a number of the clippings it contains are obituaries of faithful ex-slaves from southern newspapers and the *Confederate Veteran*. Composed by whites for white audiences, these eulogies were deeply political in their assumptions about the passage of a utopian racial hierarchy. Despite Rutherford's original request that she not be inundated with mammy narratives, much of the scrapbook is devoted to the highly vaunted figure, and Rutherford's papers spill over with additional mammy reminiscences and stories that did not find their way into the scrapbook.

A story by Elizabeth Coffee Sheldon illustrates the process by which the narratives were typically collected for the scrapbook. "Black Mammy and Her White Baby" was submitted to Rutherford by the historian of Brunswick, Georgia's, Clement Evans Chapter in October 1913. A note at the end establishes Sheldon's elite Confederate genealogy, identifying her as "the daughter of Hill Bryan Coffee and Mary Church, and . . . granddaughter of General John Coffee." The narrative itself, which is crafted in the third person, opens: "When little Elizabeth, age 7, was told by her mama, that the negroes were free, her first question was, 'Does that mean my dear black mammy?' When her mama assured her that it included all of the colored race, she burst into tears, and running out of the room, was soon in her black mammy's lap, crying, as if her little heart would break." Notably, the theme of the tale, a child's devastation upon learning of emancipation and her fear that this meant her "mammy" was "free to go away from" her, carries an unspoken recognition of the coercion that organized relationships between enslaved domestic caretakers and their young charges. The mammy's response quickly puts to rest the girl's fears: "Go away from you chile? Me go' lef you? Nebber; Nebber." In the adult Elizabeth's recollection of her "experience," mammy loved her "white baby" too dearly to accept her freedom; her loyalty to the child and the white home was far too abiding. Sheldon concludes with a scene in which the black woman speaks to another domestic slave, Lindy, instructing her as it were in the attributes of faithful service and love for white babies: "See dat chile? She is the sweetest ever born in this wild world. Her pa can't spoil her, she jist can't be spoilt. Ebery blessed mornin I eat the sugar out of her tea cup. It is the sweetest sugar I ebber eat, cause dem baby lips of her's makes it sweeter. Leave dat chile? Nebber. Nebber. No freedom for dis ole nigger if I have to give up my white baby."[35] This passage puts a startling spin on the abject longing usually attributed to whites in stories of mammy when Sheldon depicts the black woman as so hungry in her love for a white child that she literally eats her waste in the form of sugared residue, so sweet because it has touched those white baby lips.

The wish that underlay the accounts of faithful slaves constructed and consumed by the Daughters was that nothing could have been more precious to enslaved black people than their white charges. The intimacy these white women craved, and the lost love of enslaved women they mourned in the face of twentieth-century struggles for civil and economic justice, bespeak a kind of surprised bewilderment, no less sincere for its obvious complicity in the violence of attempts by whites to maintain the old racial hierarchies. These faithful slave stories constitute a register of the Daughters' doubts and private fears and their need for reassurance that their beloved South was truly precious to the women they called "Mammy."

As UDC members crafted their mammy narratives to share with local chapters, to preserve in division scrapbooks, or to publish in the *Confederate Veteran*, they devoted much time to getting mammy's voice, imagined as a thick-tongued, soothing croon, "just right." The women's memories of the past, shaped by popular stories of faithful slavery, mingled with their contemporary experiences of segregation and racialized domestic service. This is seen in the way UDC members relayed their perceptions of black southern speech in written dialect tropes patterned after examples ranging from Plantation School fiction to Aunt Jemima magazine ads.

Among Mildred Lewis Rutherford's collected papers is an edited manuscript, "The Old Slave's Lament," which stands as a kind of archive of the construction of the voice of the mammy. While the author is not identified, the typed document is heavily edited in Rutherford's hand. The entire piece is written in the first person, in the voice of an old mammy, wistful for plantation days. Throughout, Rutherford has crossed out a number of words and replaced them with dialect forms: "came" becomes "cum" and "the" is rendered as "de," and the phrase "dar is the very place," already partially in dialect, is replaced with "dar is de bery place." In a notable substantive change, the oft-cited physical intimacy of breast-feeding is edited out of the text altogether. In the sentence "My freedom—Yas—*I got dat*; But it seems a thing a part. An it don't fill up de yearnin of my waery, empty heart Dat is longing for de sight of dem dear chillun dat I nussed an de old house dat sheltered me all de morning of my days," the word "nussed" is crossed out and "raised" penciled in next to it.[36]

As they sought to present on the page the "authentic" voice of the mammy, UDC authors performed a kind of racial masquerade—an epistolary blackface. This element of performance became embodied more literally when some of the women read their reminiscences and essays at local chapter meetings or historical evenings, giving a voice and manner to the black mammy figures they described. When Mrs. James K. Gibson of Stanton, Tennessee, presented her narrative "Our Faithful Slaves" to her local chapter, she folded dialect passages composed by herself and references to the work of Joel Chandler Harris and Thomas Nelson Page into a longer narrative contrasting her childhood memories of race relations with commentary on the more troublesome and disappointing contemporary southern black people. Of Page's work she argues that "his description is not overdrawn, for from many of our homes" came the faithful slaves he detailed in his fiction. On the copy of the paper she forwarded to Rutherford, Gibson noted that her reading was followed by her own rendition of the song "Massa's in the Cold, Cold Ground."[37]

While UDC members' faithful mammy narratives were shaped in form and content by regional and national literatures, commercial culture, and depictions on film and radio, they were also heavily influenced by the racial masquerade performances of other white women. The early twentieth century afforded members of the UDC, and Americans all across the country, numerous opportunities to witness white actors and lecturers perform blackness both with and without the help of black greasepaint or burnt cork. Urban vaudeville stages continued to be heavily populated by blackface performers well into the twentieth century, as was the early American cinema.[38] Less well known today but probably much more familiar to women like those in the UDC was the continued centrality of racial masquerade and dialect reading in rhetorical training and parlor performance, local speaker venues, and the enormously popular national lyceum or Chautauqua circuits of the 1910s and 1920s. In sharp contrast to the vaudeville theater, where blackface minstrelsy flourished and respectable white women of the elite and middle classes were (or claimed to be) loath to go, this culture of public and semi-public oratory encouraged women's attendance and participation as educational, edifying, and an appropriate expression of their status.[39] Part of the energy and novelty of white women's amateur minstrelsy for charity or pleasure, like the Arche Club in turn-of-the-century Chicago, derived from the fact that it constituted the crossing of a class barrier and a thrilling dip into low culture.

Saved among the papers of UDC member Janet Randolph is a promotional pamphlet for an "impersonator" from Richmond, Virginia, named Mary E. Bell. It is possible either that Bell solicited Randolph, understanding UDC meetings and social functions to be natural occasions for her entertainment, or that Randolph witnessed Bell's impersonations and saved her promotional material. Bell is pictured in formal attire on the front of the pamphlet, which describes her performance: "Stories of the Old South, the Crooning Lullaby's [sic] of the Old Negro Mammies with Many Amusing Anecdotes of a Later Generation of Negroes, make up an Hour or more of Delightful Pastime." Mary Bell sang and recited these stories in a performance she called "The Old Black Mammy." Rather than list the songs and tales or the popular authors Bell recited, however, the two-page pamphlet is devoted to a description of the mammy and Bell's reasons for impersonating the figure. Bell explains that her performances

MRS. MARY E. BELL

Impersonator

Stories of the Old South, the Crooning
Lullaby's of the Old Negro Mammies
with Many Amusing Anecdotes of a
Later Generation of Negroes, make up
an Hour or more of Delightful Pastime

Address for dates: **Box 217** **Richmond, Va.**

"Mrs. Mary E. Bell, Impersonator." (Photo courtesy of The Museum of the Confederacy, Richmond, Virginia.)

serve an educational purpose as they entertain. "I have often wished that the younger generation could know what this old creature was to us, of the South," she begins. But alas, "the present has no parallel," and "coming generations will know of her only through . . . writings . . . Her like will never be seen again."[40]

Mary Bell makes a case for her ability to bring the "like" of Mammy into the parlors and the social functions of Virginia's white elite, to the very locations where black domestic workers continued to toil but, as their employers so often bemoaned, could not—because they would not—be the mammy figure's "parallel." As evidence of the fine likeness Bell produced, the promotional pamphlet contains a series of testimonials from famous Old Dominion writers such as Thomas Nelson Page, Ellen Glasgow, Mary Johnston, and James Branch Cabell. Also listed are Mark Twain and his friend, the author, critic, and editor William Dean Howells, and T. Hoge Tyler, the governor of Virginia. Presumably all had witnessed Bell's performances. The testimonials give a sense of what Bell's impersonation entailed. She did not wear blackface makeup, although she did seek to embody the black mammy through gesture and manner as well as in language and accent. Cabell attests that Bell "caught to a marvel, both in gesture and in intonation, the peculiarities of the old time 'house darkey,'" and declares her "among the very best of our negro impersonators." W. Gordon McCabe of the University of Virginia concurred: "Every nuance of negro accent, gesture and trick of thought, she reproduces with absolute fidelity." Howells similarly praises Bell's portrayal of the faithful slave in what he calls her "delicate and faithful art."[41]

These testimonials served a variety of functions as promotional tools. Designed primarily to solicit bookings for Bell, they presented her as being an expert in the manner and speech of the black mammy because she was of the class to have been raised by one. In the opening testimonial, Polk Miller, himself one of the most famous white southern impersonators of black dialect of the day, asserts:

> I have known Mrs. Mary Bell for nearly fifty years, and although I was well aware of the fact that she was raised under that old civilization when the negro mammies "bossed the household" and loved the children of "Ole Marster" and "Ole Mistis" as her own, I had no idea that she could so perfectly impersonate them until a few weeks ago, when we induced her to come to Bon Air and give us an evening of story and song in the negro dialect. It brought back memories of a happy past to us all who lived under that old regime, and to the young people it was an amusing and educational pastime. Those who fail to hear Mrs. Bell will miss a great treat.[42]

With each point, Mary Bell's status as a fine southern lady is enforced as the source of her special knowledge of black life and sound. Similarly, her audience's elite identity is asserted in their shared recognition and knowing laughter while watching Bell's performance. Bell's own description of the mammy whom she impersonates pivots on the figure's role in coding and protecting the status of the white family: "How intense was her pride in her 'white fokes.' How tender, how constant was her love for her white 'chil'un.' How lordly, how sovereign her contempt for all those who, according to her ideals, were not 'quality fokes'! She was the self-appointed guardian of the dignity, pride, and honor of 'de fambly'! . . . Many a man and woman, born and reared in the south, and whom the world called 'great,' knelt at black Mammy's knee . . ." Bell's portrait-style head shot on the cover of the pamphlet depicts her in fancy dress, the neckline of her gown pinned smartly with a brooch. Bell is advertising her services as an entertainer, to work in others' homes and at meetings and social functions as an artist of black dialect and an "expert" in Old Southern folkways. The fact of her public work and any question this might raise concerning her own status is erased. In the complicated nexus of refinement, whiteness, and labor, Mary Bell assumes the role of the black mammy to reinforce her own status as a lady.

In this way Bell is emblematic of a larger function of the mammy figure in the early twentieth century. The antebellum minstrel show had "reproduced and revitalized a set of class values," Eric Lott argues. "It was through 'blackness' that class was staged." In other words, the minstrel theater of the antebellum period served to shore up and affirm the working-class identity of performers and audiences as it defined them racially as white.[43] Bell's work, and the fact that it was made to seem very *unlike* work, reveals the continuing importance of racial masquerade to the constitution of class identity nearly one hundred years later and in a very different context. Mammy's "blackness" was a staging ground for the construction of class and regional identities for the white female performers who professed to embody it *better than* contemporary black women. In their portrayals they claimed an elite status based on specialized racial knowledge that could only come from connections to the slave-owning past. Detailed accounts of their personal history and refinement as well as their claims to be popular educators served to soften or mask the fact that they were workers performing for pay.[44]

Advertisements for dialect readers and impersonators in the *Confederate Veteran* suggest that Bell was only one of a number of women who performed within the Confederate public sphere of meetings, public events, publications, and social networks. An advertisement for Jeanette Robinson Murphy that ran in the *Veteran* three years before her work with the Arche Club in Chicago promotes an evening of "Negro Dialect and Slave Songs." The ad touts her success among "New York's most exclusive society," and notes that this Kentuckian was "a Southern woman by birth and breeding."[45] Another advertisement, this one for Louise A. Williams, titled "Preserving Amiability of Black Mammy," refers to the Georgia woman's performance in Nashville, noting that "in spite of hot weather" it was well attended "by a highly representative class." It quotes a review from the *Nashville Banner*:

> And now and again while she read there floated out over the audience a bar of real old-time plantation melody—not the imitation kind that has become so plentiful and even popular, but the genuine sort, the sort that has never been written and never can be, the sort that can be learned only from hearing a credulous black mammy or a tale-telling uncle of the olden times, the sort that has about it a quaintness, a sense of something not belonging to this age or place—something that fills the unfamiliar listener with a sensation of pity.[46]

At the suggestion of the *Veteran*'s editor, Williams traveled outside the city to the Confederate Soldiers' Home to present her performance and remind the residents of the "real old-time plantation."

Members of the UDC leadership, locally and nationally, lent their endorsement and Old Southern authentication to a number of southern female dialect performers, or "lecturers," on the popular Chautauqua circuit. Founded by a Methodist minister in the 1870s, Chautauqua originated in the Northeast but grew by the turn of the century to encompass rural and then urban communities around the country. Advertised in advance and organized much like the tour of a circus or fair, Chautauqua programs were composed largely of lectures and presentations devoted to Protestant social gospel, individual and community improvement, and current events. Populist and, later, Progressive politicians and activists were favorite draws. William Jennings Bryan, for instance, was a regular headliner. The promise of uplifting and wholesome entertainment drew large middle-class audiences.

As central booking agencies came to dominate the circuit and programs became more secular, a wider range of theatrical entertainment was made available. Although promoters drew a careful line between the Chautauqua circuit and potentially vice-ridden urban vaudeville, the boundary between the two blurred as several performers worked both.[47] During its Jubilee Anniversary year, 1924, which would also be the peak of Chautauqua before it faded out during the Great Depression, almost 40 million people attended its entertainments somewhere in the country—10 million more people than had visited the Chicago and Atlanta expositions combined.[48]

Like Mary Bell, Jeanette Robinson Murphy, and Louise Williams, many other women who portrayed the mammy figure in performances, readings, and lectures traded on their southern backgrounds and claims to elite status to legitimate their acts. Helen Waggoner, who was billed as a "reader-entertainer," boasted of "the accuracy of her negro dialect" in her 1924 promotional literature: "'I imbibed it,' says Miss Waggoner, 'from my old colored mammy. She is one of my earliest recollections, and I just naturally grew up knowing how to talk like the colored folks.'"[49] Waggoner's suggestion that she drank in black culture from her "mammy" implies that she was nursed by a black woman. Her alleged upbringing informed her decision not to appear in blackface, for to do so might have hidden her celebrated delicate beauty and "indefinable charm of gentle breeding." Waggoner's impersonation was amazing, the promotional literature suggests, because this young southern beauty brings "to life" in voice and manner her very antithesis in popular culture, the black mammy.

Emily Farrow Gregory, another mammy performer and a southern transplant to New York City, was giving dialect readings as educational evenings before YMCAs and similar Progressive organizations in the Northeast, Midwest, and upper South. The title of her talk was "Tales and Songs of the Old Plantation—told—'As only a Southerner can tell them.'"[50] Gregory explains that she had put together her "simple, natural talk on the old time customs of the Southern negroes (the foster parents of the children of the South)" because she recognized the "demand for something new and original, something cultural in its influence, with an educational value, at the same time amusing and entertaining." She goes on to assure potential audiences that the "lecture is changed and adjusted to meet the needs of the organization for which it is given." Among the many organizations and institutions Gregory had already educated and entertained were women's clubs in Massachusetts, New Jersey, and New York and educational institutions including the University of Missouri, a New Jersey public school system, and the Pratt Institute in Brooklyn, New York.

In the midst of the Great Migration of black southerners northward, as cities in the Midwest and Northeast swelled with populations of new migrants, Gregory chose to present herself as an itinerant white southern educator. Audiences witnessed her impersonations and absorbed her "lessons" in the fantasies of the Old South—portrayals of easy race relations, comfortable hierarchies, and contented labor—as they daily confronted the changing racial landscape of their communities and nation. As often as audience members and reviewer testimonials praised Gregory's "perfection of dialect and intonation" and the "naturalness" of her presentation of "the real Southern 'darkey,'" they also noted what they assumed to be her elite class position and white feminine refinement. A passage from the Brockton, Massachusetts, *Daily News* review of her presentation to the women's club there noted, "Mrs. Gregory is of charming personality, rather tall and of stately carriage, and with that cordiality of address innate with the Southerner." Gregory's regional identity, despite her New York City address, and her class are scripted onto her "stately" body through her ability to make that body "become" the black mammy, removing any stigma that her job as a performer may have carried. Gregory's identity as a worker for wages is downplayed in the assertion that she was born to her expertise and felt impelled to share it.

Audiences and reviewers claimed that performers such as Bell, Waggoner, and Gregory brought to life before their eyes the "real" old-time faithful mammy. For them, these women possessed a special physical ability to inhabit the black female body which commentators consistently described as "natural." It would seem that in this respect the artifice of "blacking up" might actually have inhibited this impression rather than marking carefully the whiteness of the performer, for the two most important ways to authenticate white knowledge of the black mammy—regional identity and elite class status—were themselves scripted onto the refined white southern female body.

But some women did choose to wear blackface makeup. As the United States officially entered the First World War, Mrs. John McRaven was traveling the circuit appearing as a faithful slave mammy in a dramatic play titled *Mammy*, by Mrs. Bernie Babcock. It detailed the horrors of war and the glory of the plantation South, now gone. Unlike the readings of Waggoner and Gregory, McRaven's act was billed explicitly as a stage play, which helps to explain her appearance in blackface. A UDC chapter historian and poet laureate of the Trans-Mississippi division of the United Confederate Veterans claimed in the promotional literature: "'Mammy' stands unique and alone as the greatest drama of the Southland. It is a graphic picture of the last days of the Old South, true to life (as thousands can testify), and brings back recollections of our own Mammy to each of us who has ever been so fortunate as to have known one of these faithful and affectionate beings." Cordelia Powell Odenheimer, the president general of the UDC at the time, lent her support: "I do love your [Babcock's] 'Mammy.' She is so human, true, and noble—is just the real Mammy."[51] The performer herself, McRaven, is pictured twice in the pamphlet. The front cover is filled with a large, dramatic headshot of the actress, a mass of curls crowning her head, under the tag "More than a Success—a Sensation." One opens the brochure to find McRaven transformed, pictured in full blackface makeup and a tight headscarf under the boldface name "Mammy." The page layout reiterates the racial crossing described by the brochure and photos, as the blackface image and bold title "Mammy" are joined within a heavy decorative border. Surrounded by laurel wreaths, the image is placed above a scene from the play depicting the mammy character's death. In this way the promotional literature underscores the passing of the faithful slave in contemporary times and the death of idyllic race relations.

Cordelia Powell Odenheimer herself decided to black up a few years later as an amateur performer. In a series of letters exchanged between Odenheimer, now the former president general of the UDC, and Janet Randolph in February and March 1923, Odenheimer made reference to a performance as mammy she had given in blackface at a charity function: "A few days before the Convention I gave one of my 'Old Mammy' monologues out at Dr. Pembroke Thom's place for the benefit of the Welfare Society."[52] In a subsequent letter she elaborated: "At the entertainment, I was a blacked face, colored Mammy, I had sung the old darkey hymns, gotten religion, in true Zion in the Wilderness style, done the Mobile Buck, danced the Juba, auctioned off leftovers and done everything in my power to make the affair a success."[53]

Odenheimer's performance brings our discussion of white women's racial masquerades as mammies full circle. As a well-

"MORE THAN A SUCCESS—A SENSATION"

MRS. JOHN McRAVEN
Premier Presentation of the Drama
"MAMMY"

" 'Good' is not the word for Mrs. McRaven in 'Mammy.' She is wonderful."

"Her dialect is perfect."

"A sob-show and a laugh-fest in one, is Mrs. McRaven's interpretation of 'Mammy.' "

"In the tragedy scenes Mrs. McRaven grips the heart until it aches. In the comedy scenes her dialect and negro impersonation is irresistible."

"Out of its sobs and smiles comes one of the most appealing pleas for peace ever made."

What Five Generals Say

"I heard with unusual interest M[r]s. McRaven's wonderful interpretation [of] the extraordinary production, 'Ma[m]my,' so thrilling, so true to life, so p[a]thetic. She seemed to be inspired. [I] have never listened to her equal on a[ny] stage, anywhere—New York, Chicag[o,] Saint Louis, Memphis, New Orlean[s,] Galveston, or any other city, and I ha[ve] had the pleasure of hearing the greate[st] that ever trod the boards in Americ[a.] So I say, without qualification, I nev[er] knew Mrs. McRaven surpassed by a[ny] reader. She is wonderful!"—*Gen. [F.] H. Haynes, Officer Staff, 1861-1865.*

"I think Mrs. McRaven's renditi[on] of 'Mammy' is wonderful. I, myse[lf] was never so affected by the recital [or] presentation of any subject, nor have [I] ever seen an audience so 'carrie[d] away.' "—*Gen. J. R. Gibbons.*

"The drama is to life true and pe[r]fect, as I know by personal experienc[e.] It is very graphic, touching and beau[ti]ful, with characters true to life. Mr[s.] McRaven is wonderful. I do not s[ee] how it could be more perfect. The[re] is nothing to offend either side of th[e] veterans, for or against the Union. Onl[y] the deep heart-beats for suffering h[u]manity are touched. God bless the a[u]thor and she who so beautifully giv[es] the drama."—*Gen. B. W. Green.*

"The splendid drama, 'Mammy,' [is] far superior to any production I hav[e] ever listened to on this line. It shoul[d] draw an appreciative audience any[-] where."—*Gen. James F. Smith.*

"I hope you will excuse me if I seer[n] too enthusiastic, but I wish to say th[at] the interpretation of Mrs. Babcock['s] drama, 'Mammy,' by Mrs. John Mc[-] Raven, is superior to anything of th[e] kind I have ever heard."—*Gen. Jona[-] than Kellogg.*

MAMMY

From **THE PASSING OF MAMMY**

Copyright 1915 by Neale Publishing Co.

From the Man Who, as a Baby, was Cradled in Mammy's Arms

"As I sat there listening to the clear, yet sympathetic voice of Mrs. McRaven, I was taken up in the spirit and lost sight of the surroundings. . . . A half century of time vanished and I was a child again, on the old plantation where I was born. Gus was home from college and Mammy was crooning the child songs and scolding the picaninnies. The beautiful mother was there, torn between duty to her country and love for her handsome first-born boy, who was leaving her—possibly forever. Father was there, with his dignity and bravery, cheering on the boy and soothing mother. The great giant negro George was there, showing his royal blood through his black skin (George was the son of an African king), pleading of father that he be allowed to go with "Mars Gus" to the war. . . . Then George and Gus were gone, and father, taking down his old Mexican sword, was gone. Mammy was left to comfort and protect mother and the little children. . . Time passes. George comes home with the last letter, written just before the fatal Chancellorsville. The dark days come when Mammy seemed to be the center post in the home, with the sick mother and little children clinging to her. . . And the last dark days—the terrible finale—I awake! Where am I? . . Was this young woman giving a reading? No, no! A wizard had come and with magic wand had swept aside fifty years and had called back the long ago dead and they were with me again, not in spirit only, but in the flesh. . . To both North and South the wonderful presentation of "Mammy" by this gifted daughter of the South, Mrs. McRaven, will be a revelation—a true picture of a Southern home, a society that has passed away, and a condition that will come no more."

—*John M. Bracey.*

mmy—It doesn't hu't—not much, Missy. e time hab come. I didn't tell you, li'l , but las' night de shadder angels wuz a-n,' an' I heered dem callin', callin', calli-de moonlight. I wuz skeered hit wuz e Jedge dey wuz arter, but it were yo'r ol' Mammy. She am gwine pass on.

s. *Denton*—You shall not die, Mammy. not let you. O Mammy, what can I do ou? I must do something!

mmy—Dar am one t'ing I hab allus wanted. s. *Denton*—What, Mammy? You shall anything.

mmy (*smiling, closes her eyes, breathes 'y for a moment, opens her eyes with a start*) w fas' de shuttle fly! I put de weddin' h on yo'r mammy. I wuz de fust to hol' n my a'ms. I nussed you at my breas'. ssed you fo' yo'r weddin'. I wuz fust to Mars Gus in my a'ms—dat bressed, bres-hile! I nussed him an' de odders. When white mammy wen' off wid de shadder an-

gels, she say to me, "Lub her—lub her fer me, Mammy." An' Missy, dar hab not bin a day, neider 'n hour, not a minute I hab not lubed you. Now de en' hab come. I'se gwine to pass on an' I wants—I wants one t'ing—jes one.

Mrs. Denton (*sobbing*)—Yes, Mammy, yes. What is it?

Mammy—I wants my grabe on de hillside, jes' 'long de foot ob where dey's gwine to lay you, and close by whar Mars Gus gwine be put when de wa' am done. I want to be allus close by you, Missy.

A little later, after Mammy has said farewell and received a message from Judge Denton to be delivered to Gus, she rouses from a moment of unconsciousness and, with the loom of her old mistress in mind, says, "De shuttle—hit fly—so fas', weabin'. You mus' hurry—we mus' all hurry! Li'l' Missy—I'se gwine on. Goodbye, my da'lin, da'lin chile goodbye."

Mrs. John McRaven in "Mammy." (Photos courtesy of the Redpath Chautauqua Bureau Collection, University of Iowa Libraries, Iowa City, Iowa.)

known figure in Washington, D.C., and Virginia society and onetime holder of the highest national office in the UDC, Odenheimer possessed an elite status and regional authority that were unquestioned. Influenced not only by national and local narratives of the faithful mammy but also by her experience of watching other white women perform as mammies, Odenheimer blacked up both to entertain and to raise funds from benefactors of the Welfare Society. Undoubtedly, much of the entertainment value for them lay in the spectacle of a fine southern lady dancing the Juba in blackface. On a deeper level, however, Odenheimer's performance of faithful slavery signaled to her audience their own white supremacy by linking them to a history of planter-class paternalism. She thus encouraged their charitable giving as a responsibility of their class and a natural extension of the plantation legacy, confirming for them in the process that they did indeed belong to that tradition.[54]

In positioning themselves as the preservationists of the faithful slave's role in Confederate history, the women of the UDC also preserved, or at least promoted, white elite class status. For many rank-and-file Daughters, and for the masses of Americans who witnessed black impersonators' performances or displayed Aunt Jemima syrup dispensers on their kitchen tables, class status could be the source of anxiety. Claiming a connection to a mammy, no matter how tenuous or commodified, was soothing to whites. The mammy narrative confirmed not only their racial superiority but also their desires for higher rank and social worth.[55] But inside the women's teary paeans to mammy lurked fears about their own position in society.

This intersection of nostalgia and status anxiety reflected in the mammy figure was abundantly clear to black critics. They pointed to it in their challenges to the UDC's 1920s campaign for a national mammy memorial in Washington,

D.C., which coincided with Odenheimer's blackface performance for the Welfare Society. In a historical rejoinder to the
memorial scheme, Jessie W. Parkhurst of the Tuskegee Institute argued that the mammy was "an imaginary figure created in the minds of those who never possessed a 'Mammy.'"[56]
On the eve of the monument bill's passage, James Weldon
Johnson similarly pointed to the white panic broadcast by the
campaign:

> There is another phase to this "Black Mammy" tradition
> which most people are not cognizant of. How many peo-
> ple realize that the claim of having had a "Black Mammy"
> has long been the greatest claim that one can make to being
> a Southern aristocrat. Curious, isn't it, that every Southern
> white person who wishes to have it recognized that he or she
> belongs to the "true," "original," "first-family" aristocracy
> must lay claim to having been nursed at the breast of a "Black
> Mammy," and so the "Black Mammy" has come to be the
> symbol of Southern aristocracy.

As for the women who sought to build the mammy memorial
and their supporters he mused, "Perhaps it may be that the
idea of erecting a bronze monument at Washington has behind it a desire on the part of many of these outsiders to
share in the claim to aristocracy through a share in this symbolic 'Black Mammy.'"[57]

3 THE LINE BETWEEN MOTHER AND MAMMY

You can't take me back. I love my mother and the whole world cannot part us. If my own mother on her dying bed thought it alright for Mother Jackson to care for me, why should those people in Chicago interfere? I just won't let them take me away. I won't.

—Marjorie Delbridge, 1917

IN LATE DECEMBER 1916 a Chicago juvenile court judge removed a fourteen-year-old white girl, Marjorie Delbridge, from the care of her adoptive mother, an African American woman named Camilla Jackson. Citing racial difference as the only cause, the judge ruled that the black woman, whom he called the girl's "mammy," could not be Marjorie's legal guardian. Having raised her since infancy, Camilla Jackson was the only mother Marjorie had ever known. Reports vary as to how young Marjorie's home life first came to the attention of the authorities. Once it did, however, the court's persistence in seeking to remove her from Jackson's custody—and, perhaps more important, from the black neighborhood where the teenager lived—was rivaled only by the zeal with which local members of the Southern Women's Club rushed to claim responsibility for the girl's future. None charged that Jackson and Delbridge did not love each other, nor was there any evidence of neglect, abuse, or inability to provide for the child. Jackson's prominent black attorneys, one of whom would go on to become an assistant district attorney and candidate for Chicago city alderman, challenged the court's actions on the grounds that racial difference had no legal bearing on custody. They argued that court officers were motivated by a "sickly sentimentality" concerning race; this was an apt phrase that encompassed the case's animating faithful slave narrative, the profound racism apparent in it, and the surprising persistence of the authorities in its pursuit.[1]

This was not the first time an American court had separated a black mother and the white girl she had raised from birth by arguing that a "mammy" could not bring up a white child in her own home. In March 1911 a New York City judge removed an eight-year-old "white girl, with long golden curls and big blue eyes," from the custody of Jane Collins, whom the *New York Times* described as "a black mammy of the old type." The judge explained to Collins that while there was "no doubt that you treat her kindly, clothe her well, and that she is happy with you," he could not possibly restore the child, Margaret Clemens, to her custody because Collins was black. Collins had pleaded with the judge, challenged the notion that racial difference could negate love and a good home, and, ultimately, broke down in grief. She was markedly different from Camilla Jackson, however, in her quick capitulation to her adopted daughter's removal. She publicly affirmed the court's rationale; as one newspaper headline put it two days later, "Black Mammy Gives Up Child—She Wanted Little Girl She Raised to Be with White Folk." Camilla Jackson, in sharp contrast, would never concede to the Chicago juvenile court's decision and would go to great lengths to keep her daughter.[2]

The Marjorie Delbridge case became a tabloid media event in Chicago as its twists and turns were reported breathlessly in the press over several months. Like the better-known Leopold and Loeb and Rhinelander cases of the 1920s, this legal drama was sensational and gripping to readers, lucrative for papers, and widely revealing. It illuminated graphically the racial constraints on the ideas of sexuality, domesticity, and motherhood that lay at the heart of early-twentieth-century mammy narratives. In a court of law, Jackson and Delbridge were confronted with the fiction of faithful slavery and the limits of white tolerance for interracial maternal intimacy. Coming in the midst of the Great Migration of black southerners to northern cities, both the case itself and the publicity it generated were motivated by increasing popular and institutional concerns about race relations and Chicago's supposed "Negro problem." These concerns coalesced in Progressive anti-vice crusades, which focused on the city's expanding "Black Belt" as the source of prostitution, crime, and interracial entertainments. This is where Marjorie lived.

The story of the relationship between Camilla Jackson and Marjorie Delbridge might have been understood as an account of the everyday crossings of the color line that were particularly common among working people and the poor—crossings that worried vice reformers, juvenile authorities, and the police in Chicago. In his autobiography *Along This Way* (1933), James Weldon Johnson described a childhood marked by the quotidian realities of interracial contact in his Jacksonville, Florida, neighborhood. When he was born in 1871, his mother was too sick to nurse him. A white friend and neighbor who lived one block over and who had also recently given birth nursed Johnson alongside her own infant until his mother was well enough to feed him herself. "So it appears that in the land of black mammies I had a white one," wrote Johnson. He and this woman maintained a special bond until her death, and he always made sure to visit her whenever he went home. "I do not intend to boast about a white mammy," he wrote, "for I have perceived bad taste in those Southern white people who are continually boasting about their black mammies . . . Of course, many of the white people who boast of having had black mammies are romancing."[3] The Marjorie Delbridge custody case makes clear that while many "romanced" about the mammy figure, there was a sharp limit to the acceptability of a black woman's maternal devotion to whites, at which point the state stepped in to police the color line between the "mother" and the "mammy."

According to James G. Cotter, one of Camilla Jackson's attorneys, "the Juvenile court got control of the girl by unusual actions." A female court officer pretending to be a missionary and Sunday school teacher had befriended Jackson and Delbridge.[4] Gaining the adoptive mother's trust, the woman was able to take Marjorie to the courthouse under the ruse of escorting her to school. A custody hearing was held, in which court officers represented both the state and Marjorie Delbridge. Jackson was not represented at all and was only made aware of the juvenile court proceedings after the county had negated her guardianship. The *Chicago Daily News* reported that "'Mammy's' wrath and grief caused a fine storm in the Juvenile court when she learned the nature of the proceedings." She promptly engaged the services of the prominent black legal firm of Cotter and De Armond to challenge the decision.[5]

The white-owned press never clearly explained how this interracial family first came to the notice of the authorities. The *Daily News* suggested that the state became aware of the family when Camilla Jackson applied to the county for assistance. Jackson was one among thousands of black "washerwomen" in Chicago, and her work may not have provided enough income to support her family.[6] Jackson was not the only working adult in her household, however. Her husband, James Jackson, was a carpenter. Despite the fact that he had been married to Camilla Jackson for at least forty-six years, for reasons that remain unclear James Jackson was not mentioned once by juvenile authorities, the courts, or the press during the custody battle. A silence reigned over Marjorie's entire adoptive family, which included several siblings as well as her father. They were rendered invisible by the court and the press, which managed to isolate Camilla Jackson from her husband and other children and link her only to Marjorie. Court officials and news reporters thus helped perpetuate the notion that she was the girl's "mammy" and not her true mother. This had not been the case in the 1910 census, in which the Jackson family was not recognized by the federal government or local census takers as being interracial at all. Except for the boarders in their home, everyone was listed under the last name of Jackson. Marjorie, age eight, was reported to be a "mulatto" who had been born in Pennsylvania.[7]

Black readers of the *Chicago Defender* knew that Cook County authorities had been working to separate Marjorie from her black adoptive family for months. Responding to a string of reports from "white people and some meddlesome ones of the Race" that a white girl was living with a black family on the South Side, juvenile authorities had demanded the previous August that Jackson relinquish Marjorie. When Jackson appeared in court with her lawyers instead of her adopted daughter, they dropped the case. Two months later, however, Marjorie was detained briefly in a home for girls. She had been swept into a juvenile system increasingly concerned with vice, the sexuality of young, working-class women, and the possibility of interracial contacts in South Side neighborhoods.[8]

Without question, it was the mere existence of this relationship, and not the substance of it, that caused the greatest concern among authorities. Contrary to the family's account given to census takers in 1910, Camilla Jackson testified that she had been Marjorie's primary guardian—her mother—since the girl was a week old. Although elements of this biography would be called into question later, throughout much of the case it was agreed that Marjorie had been born in Atlanta, where her birth mother, called both Zenubla and Zemula Delbridge in the press, was a stage actress and traveling performer. When her company moved on from Atlanta, she left Marjorie behind with Jackson, to whom she sent a little money each month until her death when her daughter was seven years old. At that point an "uncle" began sending money each month and assured Jackson that she was to continue raising Marjorie. Jackson moved her family to Chicago, where the man continued to send money. At the time of the court proceedings, however, Jackson had not heard from him for a year, another factor that could have precipitated an application to the county for assistance.[9]

From the outset, white-owned Chicago dailies described Camilla Jackson as Marjorie's "mammy," not her adoptive "mother." The papers' refusal to use the parental designation reiterated the juvenile court's fundamental assertion that racial difference was just cause for negating custody. As the story stretched over the next five months and readers became familiar with the legal drama's lead actors, white-owned papers would often dispense with Jackson's name altogether, referring to her only as "Mammy." In this context the term not only invoked a romantic, regionalized image of a faithful slave but also simultaneously marked the mother-child relationship Jackson and Delbridge claimed as being more the familiar interracial relationship between a black servant and her white charge.

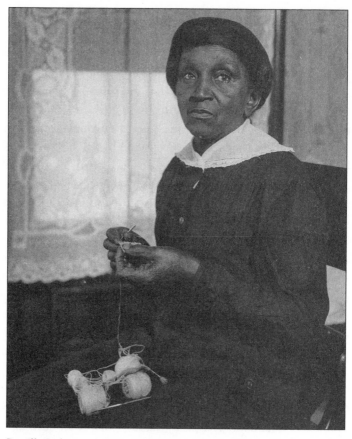

Camilla Jackson, 1917. (Glass negative, DN-0067703, *Chicago Daily News.* Photo courtesy of the Chicago Historical Society.)

The Delbridge case makes clear that the deeply held beliefs in the special relationships between black women and white children and adults which defined them as instances of faithfulness did not extend to all contexts or to all relationships. This was especially true if they occurred within black families and domestic spaces. Faithful slave narratives emerged from a long history of white denials of the legitimacy of black families and their emotional bonds under slavery. When celebrating the figure of the black mother, whites

Marjorie Delbridge, January 24, 1917. (Glass negative, DN-0067485, *Chicago Daily News*. Photo courtesy of the Chicago Historical Society.)

never referred to her own family, a deliberate silence that allowed them to ignore the coercion that helped make possible this intimate relationship between black female caretakers and their white charges. It also showed a fundamental lack of concern for black women's private emotions, their families, and the maternal work they performed outside the white domestic sphere. This absence of concern was never nonchalant or careless; instead it revealed an overriding white desire not to perceive black women as belonging to any other family at all.

After the Civil War, those who promoted sentimental narratives of the mammy located black motherhood solely within the white home, in contrast to an earlier emphasis on the economic value of black mothers who reproduced the slave labor force. By the nineteenth century, slavery in the United States depended on black women's reproductive labors to perpetuate it. In turn, the domestic slave trade relied on the broad devaluation of black families so that it could continue to divide them. Popular understandings of the family as an agglomeration of adults and children connected physically, through sentiment, and by the law, as well as through lines of gendered, generational, sexual, and economic power, were highly racialized. This resulted in the perception of the value of black motherhood as something apart from care and nurture.[10] The system of slavery placed a monetary and labor value on black women's production of more laboring black bodies. When black women's work was appropriated by the white household, their care-giving labor was reframed as motherly instinct and love in the figure of the mammy, thus not as work at all. The emotional traits that defined maternal affection fell outside the realm of black women's relationships with black children in this framework. The black mammy figure became a powerful icon of motherly affection and care, but this was not held to be an inherent attribute, innate to black women. Rather, promoters of the mammy narrative believed these traits to be the product of the supposedly civilizing environs of white domestic space. In popular narratives, close association with whites enabled the rapid, more enduring assimilation of black people to white norms.

The custody battle over Marjorie Delbridge was driven by early-twentieth-century concerns that this was true in the reverse as well. The state's interest in Marjorie's living arrangements drew its urgency from a circular logic linking biological and cultural explanations of racial difference. Eugenic concerns with heredity and bloodlines ran headlong into Progressive reform arguments that urban poverty and vice were the result of environmental factors and thus remediable. Juvenile authorities and the Cook County courts sought to remove Marjorie from her black adoptive home because they feared that she was already acting, or was culturally, "too black." Their underlying worry seems to have been that this would lead to interracial romantic relationships, resulting in the biological mixing of racial characteristics in her children. The *Chicago Tribune*'s first story, run with a photograph of Marjorie posed in her winter coat and hat, hands clasped beneath her chin, made clear not only the connotations of faithful slavery that would animate the entire legal controversy but also the linkage of biological and cultural definitions of race. The headline read, "'Mammy's Girl'— Taken by Juvenile Court from Faithful Colored Woman to Whom She Had Been Intrusted [*sic*] by Dying Mother." The paper noted that the court intended to locate one of Marjorie's blood relatives or else "place her in a white home," both options presumed to be equally suitable and equally superior to leaving the fourteen-year-old in Jackson's home within Chicago's Black Belt.[11]

A key facet of the press's and the court's framing of this relationship as one of mammy and child rather than as an adoptive family was the southern origins of the pair. Subsequent reports would elaborate on the context of Zemula Delbridge's request that Jackson care for her daughter. They painted the entire situation in the high gloss of status and Old Southern gentility that was the hallmark of the mammy narrative, considerably increasing the melodramatic and the marketable tensions of the legal story. Zemula Delbridge was said to have explained to Jackson that she and her sister had been brought up with a mammy and that she "wished her child to have the same privilege of rearing."[12] This served to refocus a story that had borne no mark of being about people of significant privilege or elite status, while the regional dressing transformed a relatively mundane if potentially sordid tale of a young, single actress giving birth and leaving her child behind to continue her travels and career. Zemula Delbridge's profession alone provided a possible explanation for her behavior, confirming popular notions of the debauched status of the public women of vaudeville theater. References to a refined southern past and a mammy changed things, however, much like the similar claims of Negro impersonators and dialect readers, with whom Delbridge might have shared a stage. More than rehabilitating Zemula Delbridge's character, however, this narrative was all about casting her daughter Marjorie as a girl perilously close to racial ruin and in dire need of saving, the danger of her fall made all the more tragic by her elite southern heritage.

The Marjorie Delbridge custody battle and the larger conversations about race, environment, and sexuality it engendered occurred at the height of the Great Migration. With the outbreak of war in 1914, the flow of European immigrants into Chicago to work in the city's stockyards, processing plants, and factories virtually stopped. Within two years, industries making war materiel for Europe and the United States' own escalating military preparations generated enormous numbers of industrial jobs in northern cities, many of them unskilled and ideal for workers with no industrial experience. Economic conditions, labor agents, and news reports helped pull black southerners northward, as reverberations from the war heralded a new range of possibilities for those seeking relief from poverty, segregation, and violence in the South. Between 1910 and 1920, over fifty thousand blacks arrived in Chicago from southern states, mostly from the Deep South, a majority arriving between 1916 and 1918. Several thousand more moved through Chicago, often staying for brief periods before heading on to other cities such as Detroit. These networks of black relocation and affiliation in Illinois, Michigan, and Indiana would come to play a central part in the events of the Delbridge custody struggle, ultimately reaching into Canada.[13]

The same Chicago newspapers that covered the case reported daily on the rapid growth of the Black Belt. The city's three major white-owned papers dealt with the migration extensively, usually in alarmed tones reflecting racism, fear, and regional stereotypes. Decrying the Midwest's growing "Negro problem" in articles that tended to focus on vice, crime, violence, and disease, the papers fed the worries of their readers with stories that often overstated the actual numbers of black arrivals.[14] The *Daily News* seems to have been more sympathetic to black migrants and more positive in its depictions of African Americans than the two other major dailies, a generalization that holds true for coverage of the Jackson-Delbridge case as well.[15] News reports consistently printed the home addresses of the case's principal figures, locating them within a contested and shifting geography of residential segregation and the rapid expansion of the Black Belt. While the Jackson family's arrival predated the onset of the Great Migration by at least four years, they were still considered newcomers to the city. They lived at 3226 Calumet Avenue between Thirty-second and Thirty-third streets, not far from the Twenty-ninth Street beach where the Chicago Race Riot would break out two years after the custody battle's conclusion.

One early item about the case reflects the *Tribune*'s desire to reverse the black migratory flow. In an article headlined "'Yankees Ain't Quality Folks,' Says Mammy," Camilla Jackson is said to have felt that "the north is no place for an 'ole black mammy an' her own white baby.' So 'Mammy'

Camilla Jackson is 'gwine south' . . . Mammy Camilla is very bitter. And she longs for her southland."[16] While the paper reports that Jackson planned to leave now that her daughter had been taken from her, she herself says nothing of the sort in the article. Jackson would continue to live with her husband and her family in Chicago for the rest of her life.[17] Throughout the case, white-owned papers used dialect whenever they quoted Jackson directly, which enhanced their description of her as a faithful mammy. On paper, at least, she sounded like one. In its first story about the case, the *Daily News* described Jackson, bent over her washtub "with heavy heart," angrily discussing the decision: "Fo'teen years . . . I'se had her, and nobody said nuthin.' Then these pesky cou't people come bustin' round and say I ain't good enough to raise white chillun. Ma'jorie's just as good white folks as anybody, even if she was brought up by a black mammy."[18]

The court's only cause for removing Marjorie from her adopted home was the race of her mother and the majority black population of her neighborhood. At no point was Jackson charged with anything else that might have led to the removal of her daughter. "A coterie of members of the juvenile court and 'school ma'rms' according to mammy's attorneys, have developed a sickly sentimentality as to the surroundings of the young girl Marjorie without regard to justice and right," reported the *Chicago Tribune*. "The law acknowledges no such sentimentality for the races, they say."[19] The first of many attempts by Jackson's lawyers to have the decision thrown out on these grounds was dismissed by the judge, although he did set another hearing at which Jackson could petition the court to be named the rightful and legal guardian. In the meantime, Marjorie was to remain in the custody of a juvenile facility located far away from Jackson's house and the Black Belt. Granted a brief visit with Jackson,

Marjorie refused to return to the girls' home and had to be collected by authorities.[20]

James Cotter and Chester De Armond indeed believed that racial sentimentality was driving the fervent interest shown in the case by Assistant State's Attorney Robert M. Hogan, lead council for the county. Infuriated by an interview the lawyers had given to the *Chicago Defender* in which they had said just that, Hogan filed a contempt charge claiming that Jackson's attorneys were insulting the court and its officers.[21] Seeming pleased with its role in tweaking Hogan and the fact that the charge was dismissed, the *Defender* editorialized that "the state wanted to keep the color line out of the fight, and only insert it in places where it would benefit them."[22]

Despite Jackson's lawyers' arguments concerning the unconstitutionality of the decision and their vows to follow the case to the Illinois Supreme Court, Judge Charles Bowles did not overturn the juvenile court's original ruling ordering the removal of Delbridge from Jackson's care. Alongside its headline "Taken from Mammy" the *Tribune* depicted a nostalgic scene with a photo montage of Jackson and Delbridge labeled "Marjorie Delbridge and 'Mammy.'" Next to the photographs was an illustration of a stereotypical aged mammy figure wearing a shawl and headscarf, her hand resting upon the shoulder of a smiling blond girl of seven or eight; neither figure resembled Jackson or Delbridge in any way. The accompanying article evinces more sympathy for the plight of both than the paper had previously shown, although the illustration casts the case as the separation of a faithful slave and ward, not mother and child. In his ruling the judge stated that a child is not property to be transferred at will. "The mother's act was worthless and in no way binding," he ruled, "as a child could not be 'given' as can a chattel."[23] The *Defender* made this legal logic of enslavement even more clear in its report, noting that the judge had said, "No mother could give away her child like it was a chattel or property."[24]

Newspapers juxtaposed reports of Jackson's and Delbridge's sorrow over the court's decision with the testimony of court officers who had argued for their separation. They described the two clutching each other in the hallway outside the courtroom and weeping. "Marjorie cried and said she didn't want to go and said she would rather live with her 'Mammy' than anywhere else in the world—even in a palace . . . Camilla Jackson, who is the 'mammy,' also wept and begged the court not to do what it had done."[25] Juvenile authorities were forced to admit that other than race, there was nothing "wrong" with Marjorie's adoptive home or her upbringing. They "said that Marjorie was well cared for physically and well instructed under the old 'mammy's' care, and they admitted they were principally concerned because the child was too happy with her colored guardian. 'She has acquired a happy, carefree, humorous disposition that will not do at all,' said one of the officers severely. 'She isn't serious a minute. She has no realization of life or the gravity of things that make it up."[26] According to the *Daily News*, the same person continued, "She's just like the little colored children she runs around with so much."[27] The *Tribune* argued that one had only to look at the pathetic scene in the courthouse corridor to see that the court had succeeded in making sure that "some of life's bitterness had at last found Marjorie and her old 'mammy' also."[28] Judge Bowles was firm in his ruling and announced that the court would determine where Marjorie was to live permanently, and with whom, the following week.

The *Defender*, finding in this space between the ruling and its ultimate implementation room for changing the court's decision, contested the finality with which the white-owned papers had reported the outcome. "The Defender's interest in the case is, as in all cases, that justice be given Mrs. Jackson, and the child not be removed simply on account of the woman not being white . . . If the child is taken and put in a white family habeas corpus proceedings will be started. It will be a fight, fight, fight until the constitutionality of the Juvenile court act is proved in this state."[29] The paper also noted that steps had been taken by both black and white people to raise money for an appeal. Although there seemed to be a significant outpouring of sympathy and offers of help from people across the racial and social spectrum of Chicago, within days Jackson and her lawyers were telling papers that it was doubtful they would be able to afford to continue their legal struggle for long.[30]

The juvenile court's desire to see Marjorie appear more serious and conscious of reality was indicative of its expectations for a white girl reaching maturity. Although the *Tribune* had depicted her as a child, the court's interest in the case was prompted by Marjorie's status as a teenager, who could soon become, or perhaps already was, sexually active. Camilla Jackson suggested as much when she noted in the immediate aftermath of the court's ruling, "Maybe these white folks is a-figerin' a white husband won't come aseekin' mah li'l Marjorie in a colored folks home."[31] Not spoken but implied here was the possibility that a black suitor might.

The state's attorney's office, which pursued the Delbridge case with such tenacity, was at the same time attempting to crack down on South Side clubs with interracial clienteles, commonly known as Black and Tan resorts. These clubs represented one of the most notorious targets of Chicago's Progressive reform organizations, such as the Committee of Fifteen and the Juvenile Protection Agency, which also sought to close or regulate brothels, saloons, gambling and billiard parlors, and taxi dance halls. City Progressives had successfully shut down Chicago's red-light district in 1912, scattering its inhabitants and establishments, which regrouped quickly in the Black Belt, where they were left alone by police as long as they stayed out of white neighborhoods. The presence of vice within the Black Belt meanwhile reinforced white supremacist notions of black immorality and hypersexuality, which also shaped popular responses to the Great Migration. The Delbridge case was informed by these intermingled concerns. In the months leading up to the girl's removal from Jackson's custody, the Committee of Fifteen had identified eight brothels along Thirty-first Street, within two blocks of her house.[32]

Among those who had taken a great interest in Marjorie's welfare were a Mr. and Mrs. Louis Brock, who lived in the Hyde Park section of Chicago. Racial tensions were escalating in their neighborhood, which bordered the rapidly expanding Black Belt.[33] During the summer of 1917, the homes of several new black residents and the offices of agents who had rented or sold properties to them near Hyde Park would be firebombed.[34] Rather than send Marjorie back to the girls' home to await news of her fate, the judge placed her with the Brocks at the couple's request. For all of his assertions that a child was not chattel to be passed from person to person, Judge Bowles's action was deeply contradictory. He entrusted Delbridge to strangers who had simply appeared in his courtroom asking for her, and who did not know her or have any legal claim to her. The press suggested that the white couple, who apparently had no children of their own, might wish to adopt Marjorie, but also reported Mrs. Brock's comment: "'The Southern Woman's club, of which I am a member, will meet Wednesday night . . . [T]he question of what to do with Marjorie is to be discussed."[35]

Judge Bowles clearly agreed with the *Daily News* that with the appearance of Mrs. Brock, a white southern woman,

Marjorie's prospects had turned much brighter. "I haven't adopted her," Mrs. Brock explained. "I have only taken her home with me to see what can be done. Tonight we will discuss the matter at the Southern Women's club. My idea is to place her in some real nice boarding school in the south, surrounding her with the nicest children. While she is at school the club can be on the lookout for a home for her and perhaps for her mammy. It will thus be easy to solve all the problems and at the same time make a fine woman of Marjorie."[36] What Marjorie was most in need of, according to the court—and Mrs. Brock—was a change of environment. Inherent in this was the idea that, even better than living with white southerners in Chicago, Marjorie might be best served, and best poised to become "a fine woman," if she were returned to the South, far from Chicago and her connections there.

While the judge's disposition of Marjorie disproved his own claim that a child could not just be given to anyone as property, the person most treated like chattel in this drama was Camilla Jackson. Beyond calling her "Mammy," Mrs. Brock's expressed hope that a place could be found for her with Marjorie suggests that Jackson was somehow connected to the girl as a form of property, as if she could be moved around at others' will and did not have a home, family, and community of her own in Chicago. In Mrs. Brock's view, Marjorie's place was to define Jackson's and not the other way around, as things had stood before the court's ruling. Her hope that the girl's relationship to "her Mammy" might be sustained by keeping them together in another location was reiterated in other accounts of the Southern Women's Club. Several members claimed to have had mammies as children, and as a group they believed that although Jackson had done "splendid work in rearing" Marjorie, "her environment could no longer benefit" the girl.[37]

Daily News readers had already been shown the presumed

Marjorie Delbridge in the Brocks' home, 1917. (Glass negative, DN-0067585, *Chicago Daily News.* Photo courtesy of the Chicago Historical Society.)

benefits of a new environment. The paper ran a photo taken at the Brocks', captioned "Marjorie Delbridge in a New Home," which depicted her posed in a neatly pressed, new-looking dress, seated on a low carpet-draped platform. Next to Marjorie sits a baby carriage, which is presumably meant for the large doll that rests in her lap. In her hands she holds an open book; two more lie at her knee. Together these objects signify that propriety, abundance, refinement, and learning are to be gained within white domestic space. The carriage itself, which was mostly cropped out of the photo when it ran in the paper, carries a double message as a prop. It frames Marjorie as younger than she actually was while signaling the fate that might have befallen her had she stayed with Jackson. The photo reassures the viewer that rather than being a young mother to a black man's baby, Marjorie is safely ensconced in white domesticity and childhood. The caption beneath the photo reads "White Girl, Ward of Colored 'Mammy' Since Infancy, Happy To-day in Altered Environment as Protégé and Prospective Foster Daughter of Mrs. Louis Brock." Certain elements of the picture contradict this assertion of happiness, however. This is particularly true of the doll, which is lying against Marjorie's arm at an odd angle. Its placement makes the staging of the scene obvious; the pose appears wholly inauthentic, and suggests visually that Marjorie was not at play or even really connected to these things. Less easily quantified, but clear in contrast to earlier photos, Marjorie's face looks strained and her smile pinched. She does not exude the happiness or "brightness" in her new surroundings that the article describes.[38]

Despite this glowing account of the potential for Marjorie's life with the Brocks, all was not well among the members of the Southern Women's Club. The couple's decision to go to the courtroom and take the girl home with them was seen by some as presumptuous and by others as publicity-hungry and opportunistic. The Wednesday evening club meeting grew contentious as the women argued over Mrs. Brock's behavior and Marjorie's future. Brock squared off against a Mrs. Bailey, who had described to the press earlier her plan to take on Marjorie's education as a "club project." This included involving the United Daughters of the Confederacy in selecting an appropriate school. Bailey's husband accused Brock of rushing to the courthouse before the club meeting so that she might "seize the limelight." Brock, aghast, replied that she had had no such motivation but "thought only of the child's future," adding that she was appalled at the low sum the club intended for Marjorie's tuition. If the club decided to spend more on the girl's schooling than she and her husband could afford alone, Mrs. Brock concluded, "I gladly will let [Marjorie] go."[39] The *Defender* editorialized that if a boarding school was to be the solution, Mrs. Jackson should have a say in where Marjorie went, and that it should be a girls' school in the Northeast.[40] But before anything could be sorted out, even before the court could make a final determination as to where Marjorie Delbridge should live and with whom, she vanished.

In the chaos that followed Marjorie's disappearance, abduction, or departure, depending on who was telling the story, accusations flew. Several new figures emerged, national borders were crossed, and authorities combed black communities not just in Chicago but all around the region. "The girl's disappearance has electrified a search from more angles probably than would that of any other Chicago child except from a family of great wealth," declared the *Tribune*.[41] While much about the disappearance was mysterious and contested, all agreed on the basic facts of Marjorie's activity until the moment on the evening of Friday, January 26, 1917, when she disappeared. It was also generally believed that whatever the circumstances, Marjorie had probably left the Brocks' willingly. Two questions remained, however, which titillated newspaper readers, fanned the outrage of court authorities, and haunted those who cared for her: Where was Marjorie Delbridge? And with whom did she leave, if anyone?

Having removed Marjorie from Jackson's care but reserving final judgment in the case, the presiding judge had set a hearing for the morning of Saturday, January 27. Early the evening before, Camilla Jackson visited Marjorie at the Brocks' house, with the couple's permission, to bring her a coat to wear to court the next day and to talk. As the two sat together in the parlor, a fundraising event and rally to protest their separation was getting under way at the Dream-land Hall, not far from the house on Calumet they had once shared. When Jackson got up to leave at 7:30, Marjorie asked the Brocks if she could walk her to the front door of the apartment building, which was three floors down. The couple agreed. They did not become suspicious until about ten minutes had passed and Marjorie had still not returned. By that time she and Camilla Jackson were gone. The Brocks immediately assumed that they had left together and called the police—and the *Tribune*. They charged that Marjorie had been "abducted," a claim the *Tribune* reiterated in its front-page headline, "Marjorie Delbridge and 'Mammy' Gone—Negress Calls in Motor and Kidnaps Girl." No one—not the Brocks, the press, or the police—suggested that Marjorie had not gone willingly, however. In its first report of her disappearance, the *Defender* reminded readers that Marjorie had vowed that no matter where the courts sent her, she would do whatever it took to get back to her mother, Camilla Jackson.[42]

As terms like "Negress" and "kidnapper" joined "Mammy" in the white press's vocabulary describing Jackson, the *Defender* editorialized on the problem of nomenclature. In an editorial under the headline "Mammy," the paper urged its readers to boycott any other newspaper that used the demeaning label to refer to black women, making a pointed reference to recent reports about Camilla Jackson. The *Defender* added that the same went for "wench" and "Negress," too: "To the many readers of the Defender and especially to the young men and women, we want you to know and feel that the paper or person or persons who refer to you and yours as 'Mammy' offers you one of the gravest insults that any living mortal can offer another, and it should be resented even if it should cost one their life." The editorialist likened the "mammy" to the enslaved "wench" who was sexually exploited by white men, saying the only difference between the two was that "the mammy waited on his wife and nursed her [the wife's] child along with the child that the 'mammy' bore for her master . . . Mrs. Jackson, the woman in the limelight with the Marjory [*sic*] Delbridge case, is not a mammy, and avers that she has never bore a (white) child for her master or any white man in her life."[43]

In the first hours of Marjorie's disappearance, the Brocks sent for the police, canvassed their neighborhood to find out if anyone had seen anything suspicious, and "called the *Tribune* and told them the circumstances and asked the newspaper's help."[44] That paper subsequently devoted several column inches to the story, much of it focused on the plight and sorrow of the Brocks. Mr. Brock had gone directly to Camilla Jackson's home that night assuming Marjorie would be there, and continued to go periodically to demand the return of the girl. "I haven't slept since Marjorie was taken away," sighed Mrs. Brock "wearily," according to the *Tribune*, and her husband was so upset, she said two days later, that he had lost fifteen pounds.[45] Police could not locate Camilla Jackson for questioning, but her lawyers insisted that she was at home, having taken to her bed with worry over Marjorie's disappearance. The description of Marjorie released by the police to aid Chicagoans in spotting the missing girl combined her vital statistics with subjective information that revealed their assessments of the white public's assumptions concerning Marjorie's background. Delbridge, the police said, "is 14 years old, five feet two inches tall, and weighs 117 pounds. In her speech there is practically no hint of association with Negroes. She has black curly hair, which reaches to her shoulders, rosy cheeks, and black shining eyes. When she smiles, a frequent occurrence, she half closes her eyes." The statement goes on to describe the blue serge dress and gray coat that Marjorie had been wearing when she disappeared.[46]

With the search under way, Judge Bowles continued the case for a week and announced that he was holding Jackson's attorneys responsible for producing the girl. They replied that they could not because they knew nothing of her whereabouts. Meanwhile, Hogan prepared contempt charges against Jackson, her granddaughter Willa Mae Powell, and her attorneys Cotter and De Armond for refusing to tell the court what he believed they knew. The inclusion of Powell is notable because this was the first time that any source made reference to other members of Jackson's family. What became clear as the story of Marjorie's disappearance unfolded was that Jackson had a large network of friends and kin in Chicago and the surrounding area, especially in Detroit, where it was revealed much later that she had a son. These networks followed the geography of the Great Migration. Notably, James Jackson and the fact of their marriage were still never mentioned, while Powell's sudden appearance in the story only emphasizes the complete lack of interest on the part of the press or court officers in Jackson's family as a whole. The only member of her household that the authorities and the newspapers cared about was Marjorie, at least until it seemed that others might have been involved in a conspiracy to kidnap her.[47]

After two days, the police were no closer to locating Marjorie Delbridge but had narrowed a dozen theories about her disappearance down to three. It was possible, they believed, that Marjorie had run away on her own, that Jackson had lured her away and was hiding her among friends, or that an outsider to the case who had been following it in the papers had taken her with the hope of eventually reuniting her with Jackson. To this set of theories Jackson kept adding another. She argued that it was someone from the Southern Women's Club who had taken Marjorie from the Brocks'. "I believe the women of that club know where Marjorie is," she said, "for I saw two white women and a man on the corner . . . Maybe one of them's got my baby. I'm nearly dead." Contradicting her story, a neighbor of the Brocks' who lived in their building said that she had seen Delbridge receiving instructions from Jackson on the front stoop. The neighbor had not heard their conversation but said that Jackson pointed south, and that Marjorie nodded and then walked in that direction while Jackson walked the opposite way.[48]

Like Jackson's kinship network, the geography of the search and of suspicion also traced the spread of black migration, moving quickly beyond the confines of Chicago's Black Belt. Police said that in addition to searching all of the apartments along Calumet Avenue in the three blocks around Jackson's home, they had sent teams to East Chicago and Gary, Indiana, "where there are large colored populations, on the possibility the child may have been spirited across the state line and hidden."[49] As the search expanded, no one would answer the door or the telephone at Camilla Jackson's house. Her lawyers released word that Jackson had been made very ill with worry over Marjorie's well-being and that she was in the care of a physician.[50] Two days later the racialized edge of suspicion sharpened. "In the realm of possibilities discussed by agents of the private and public interests seeking the girl was the theory that the missing ward was secreted in some Negro home in the 'black belt' where her every movement was known to Mrs. Camilla Jackson, the 'mammy,'" reported the *Tribune*.[51] Brock, who to this point had been so friendly and forthcoming with the press, and whose first call after phoning the police when Marjorie disappeared had been to that paper, expressed anger that several of the "detectives" she had spoken to had actually been reporters misrepresenting themselves and that this had hindered efforts to find the girl.[52]

The Brocks were adept at more than using the press.

"I have had Marjorie's pictures reproduced on slides," Mrs. Brock told the *Tribune*, "which are now showing in the moving picture houses with the printed request that anyone knowing of her whereabouts will communicate with me."[53] The public display of these slides as moviegoers settled into their seats spotlights the links between news and entertainment that drove the tabloid story. It suggested that the Brocks were indeed Marjorie's rightful guardians, casting the white couple, not Camilla Jackson, as the parents who had lost a child. This facet of the search anticipates the intersection of publicity, danger, and perceptions of childhood in the contemporary "have-you-seen-me?" visual culture of television ads, mass mailings, and milk carton photos.

The real and the reel intersected again in an account given by Mrs. Brock of a shared experience at the movies that might have prompted some of Marjorie's distress. Just days after the court severed her relationship with Jackson, Brock took Marjorie to see D. W. Griffith's *Intolerance*, his blockbuster follow-up to *Birth of a Nation*. Perhaps she did not realize that the film involved the story of a young woman whose baby is taken away from her when she is deemed unfit by the state because of a series of assumptions, misunderstandings, and injustices grounded in stereotypes about the white urban poor. According to the *Tribune:*

> Mrs. Brock accidentally gave the key to what may prove the psychological disturbance that sent Marjorie a fugitive from her home. "I took Marjorie to see *Intolerance* one day last week," said Mrs. Brock. "She was entranced by the picture, but during the scenes that showed the activity of social workers and Juvenile court officers in tearing the little mother's baby away from her she reached a pitch of excitement that amazed me." "'That's Miss So-and-So!' she would exclaim. 'That is Judge So-and-So!' And throughout those scenes she gave the actors the names of persons and officials who played

a part in her own appearance as a child going through the mill of justice. I have been wondering whether the little girl has not brooded over the similarity of her case to that in the play."[54]

It is likely that upon reading this, many who had seen the film pondered the uncanny similarities, including the fact that Griffith depicted the female reformers who set the drama in motion as villains. It would not have been a huge leap to consider Mrs. Brock and her fellow members of the Southern Women's Club in this same context.[55]

When Jackson was still in seclusion and Marjorie was still nowhere to be found after four days, the court took measures that redefined the young woman as a culprit in the "crime" of her own disappearance rather than as the victim of a possible kidnapping. Hogan was granted a warrant for Marjorie's arrest on the basis of his argument that she had likely left the Brocks' of her own accord and was thus in defiance of a court order. Hogan claimed that he had sought the warrant only so that police could bring Marjorie in right away if they found her. Leaving aside the question of whether this was a case of simple expedience, a desire to punish Marjorie when she was caught, or a combination of the two, the warrant meant that Marjorie was no longer the object of concern in a custody struggle; instead it criminalized her wish to stay with her black adoptive mother. The next day the search for Marjorie was halted briefly when police arrested the wrong girl.[56]

Perhaps everyone had it wrong, argued the *Tribune*, when the paper reported the next day that "Marjorie May Be Part Negro, Woman Thinks."[57] A Mrs. Lavinia McCashen, formerly of Galveston, Texas, claimed to authorities that she had rented a home to a black family named Delbridge. She believed that she had seen Camilla Jackson there and that Jackson's son was Marjorie's father and was married to the girl's mother. This would make Jackson her grandmother, not her "mammy." McCashen, taken to confront Jackson, told her, "I would take an oath . . . that you resemble the woman who came to my house with an apparently white child in Galveston." Camilla Jackson and her lawyers denied that she had ever been in Galveston and insisted that Marjorie was "pure white."[58] Hardly surprised by a claim that Marjorie was not really white, the *Defender* noted that a dramatic shift in interest for the welfare of the girl would occur if the charge were proven: "As one would drop an overheated poker . . . so will the daily press and likewise the dear public drop . . . Marjorie Delbridge, and all those connected with her [if there is] one grain of truth that this poor little 'white' girl has one drop [of black] blood coursing through her veins."[59] Quickly dismissed by the court and by police, the "accusation" hung about the Delbridge case until its ultimate resolution some months later.

In an attempt to thwart contempt charges, but still refusing to bring Jackson to court, Cotter and De Armond entered a motion to change the venue of the hearing on the grounds that the judge and assistant state's attorney were both driven by bias, by their "sickly sentimentality" concerning race. They argued in addition that the court had no legal jurisdiction over the case at this point, since "Marjorie was no longer a ward of the court, having been removed from the court's jurisdiction when she became a ward of Mrs. Brock." Furthermore, "the girl ran away of her own volition and was not kidnapped and consequently no crime was committed."[60] The court brushed aside these arguments, resisted Hogan's bluster that Jackson should be arrested at once, and ordered that she appear the following morning to "prove that she did not kidnap Marjorie" or else face jail time.[61] Marjorie had been gone for a week.

The next day's papers revealed that Hogan and police had wiretapped Jackson's phone and had heard conversations between De Armond and, they thought, one of Jackson's daughters which led them to believe that the two were involved in hiding Marjorie somewhere in Chicago. Armed with this information, Hogan claimed that if Jackson and her lawyers said one more time in court that they knew nothing of Marjorie's whereabouts, he would charge them all with perjury, adding: "I am going to find Marjorie if it is the last act of my official career . . . If I do not find her, and that is within the next day or two, somebody is going to jail or possibly the penitentiary. I am convinced by my investigation that there has been a conspiracy to conceal the girl, who, despite anything to the contrary is still a ward of the Juvenile court . . . There has been enough fooling with the court."[62] This "fooling" would continue for the next several days, however. Accusing Jackson and her lawyers of "playing possum" with her claims of poor health, Judge Bowles had her examined by a court-appointed doctor.[63] According to the *Tribune*, the doctor found Jackson to be "in a nervous condition, but added that it was his opinion that it would do her good to get out of the house," and so declared her fit to appear in court.[64] The *Defender* cast this incident in a different light, saying that although the court's own doctor had found her to be ill, Hogan demanded that she show up anyway and that Judge Bowles had agreed, warning that she would be arrested if she failed to appear.[65]

Surrounded on the front page of the *Daily News* by wartime articles urging Chicagoans to "Hoist Your Flag!" and instructing the city's young men "Where to Enlist" was another item, "'Mammy' Jackson on Stand." The paper reported that she had "tottered" into court and in a "weak" voice denied having taken Marjorie or having tried to induce her to leave the Brock home.[66] The *Tribune* followed up with a story the next day that included some of the questioning. All of Jackson's testimony was relayed by the paper in dialect: "I don't know where my baby is . . . I wisht I did. If I knowed I'd shore go to her, no matter whar she was." Judge Bowles asked Jackson if Marjorie had ever talked about running away. Jackson replied yes, and reminded the court that Marjorie had run away from the girls' home back in December: "Yes, suh, she did . . . After she had run away from the Juvenile Protective home she come straight home and said to me: 'Mammy, no matter what they do to me, I'll run away and come back to my old mammy. I just had to come home.' I said: 'They'll lock you up for this, chile.' And she said she didn't care what they did." She sobbed that all of her friends were looking for Marjorie and that she was terribly worried because she believed "somebody is holdin' her against her will." Judge Bowles was not swayed. "Mrs. Jackson had better find Marjorie if she knows what is good for her," he said. "Otherwise somebody may go to jail."[67]

Two and a half weeks after she first went missing, Marjorie Delbridge was located in Detroit but disappeared again before she could be taken into custody. She sent a letter to Camilla Jackson, which Jackson later produced for the press:

> Dear mother: I am safe and well. I thought not best to let you know where I was until my case was settled in the court. But, dear mother, I waited as long as I can, but court or no court, I am telling you that I am safe and well and with friends of yours and mine. I do long to see you once more. I have cried for you day and night. Get on the train and come down and get me. I have been to Canada and back again. Come and get me and take me back to Canada, away from the courts. I am leaving here tonight for Canada with our friends, but when you get here the people will give you our Canadian address. So come right away. Hurry at once. Your dear girlie, Marjorie Delbridge.[68]

Chicago newspapers ran front-page banner headlines and devoted several column inches to the new twists in the search, often swinging between accusations on the one hand and sympathy for Marjorie's plight and her desire to stay with her adoptive mother on the other. The *Daily News* likened her flight to a runaway slave narrative. The paper reported that she was being moved from house to house and back and forth across the Canadian border between Detroit and Windsor, Ontario, just one step ahead of the police. "Colored people are aiding her fight against removal to the home of her white guardians," the paper noted, "and in so doing have disclosed an 'underground railway' not much different from the one used by negro slaves in escaping north to free territory . . . She is at present a runaway from the home of Mr. and Mrs. Louis Brock and the Juvenile Court."[69] She had been located in the home of an older black couple, Mr. and Mrs. Enoch Taylor. Mrs. Taylor was said to be a friend of Camilla Jackson's, though she denied knowing her to the police. Warned before she could be taken into custody, Marjorie was believed to have slipped away via this "underground railroad."

For the first time in the case, newspaper readers were able to hear from Marjorie herself in an extensive interview she gave before disappearing again. Sounding remarkably self-possessed, she was careful to make clear that Jackson was her adoptive mother, not her "mammy," and charged the courts with putting her in far more danger than she ever could have been before by locking her up with "bad girls" and treating her like a criminal. Marjorie vowed that if she could not be with Jackson, she would run off to Canada before she would risk being placed in juvenile detention again. As she sat on a piano bench and explained the circumstances of her departure, Marjorie ate candy and commented on the amount of weight she had gained while on the run. In what may have been a nod to the *Defender*'s urging its readers not to call Jackson or any other black woman "Mammy" or suffer anyone who did, Marjorie began her story: "It was mighty funny and exciting how I left Chicago. I was just finishing my supper when mother came. I don't like the name 'mammy.' I always call my mother—mother."[70]

Marjorie explained how she came to be in Detroit, starting with the night of her disappearance when she walked Jackson to the front door of the Brocks' building. Once out of the apartment, Marjorie said, she began to cry and pleaded with Jackson to take her home with her. Jackson, also crying, said she wished she could take her, but left, telling her sadly, "I'll see you in court, baby, in the morning." Marjorie watched her head north and, still in tears, turned to go back inside when she saw two cars parked at the south side of the building with their lights on and heard someone call her name three times. A woman stuck her head out of one of the car's windows and beckoned Marjorie, who paused, but then ran up to the vehicle. When she got closer, she "saw two ladies. They were white. One opened the door and said 'Get in, Marjorie. I am a friend of your mother. We won't hurt you. We only want to take you away from the court so you'll see your mother again.'" Marjorie climbed into the car, and the two women began speaking to each other in a "peculiar language"—French. As they drove off, Marjorie believed that they were headed to the home she had shared with Jackson and the rest of her family, but she soon realized they were leaving the city. They drove to the train station in Hammond, Indiana, where one of the women, Helene, asked her driver to purchase two train tickets, one "lady's" and one for a child. When the train arrived and she and Helene began to get out of the car, the other woman, whose name Marjorie said she did not know, referred to Helene as her sister, kissed Marjorie on the cheek, and told her to mind. By the next morning the two were at Helene's home in Canada. "I won't tell you what town it is" in, she said, presumably because she planned to go there again and hide.[71]

Marjorie spent much of the interview detailing her confinement in the girls' home and challenging the state's interest in her sexuality. If anyone was endangering her morals, she insisted, it was the juvenile authorities:

> Why, if my own mother thought it all right for me to live with mother I don't see why others should interfere. I have done nothing wrong. Neither has mother. I have been in the Juvenile Detention Home twice. It is a horrid place. I would stay forever [in Canada] before I would go there again. It is just like being in jail. They locked me up behind bars, and I had to wear a uniform just like bad prisoners. They even made me scrub the floor from 6:30 until 10:30 every morning. It was scrub, scrub. They sent me there last October. They tried to say I got a postal card from a boy, and they said I wrote a letter to him. They said his initials were "A. F. W." I did receive a card, but I never answered it. Why, I don't know any boys with those initials. I don't care for boys. I am only 14. I don't care for anybody but mother. I have no confidence in anybody but my mother. They would keep me in the detention home as if I was bad a week or ten days at a time and then send me to another home. Everywhere I was sent they would place me with bad girls. These were very disorderly. Why, they used some language there that I never had heard in my life before. You cannot blame me for not wanting to go back there.

Marjorie insisted that Jackson had nothing to do with her escape and was upset that "they" were blaming her for it. "I wish mother was here. She is my mother, and I don't care what anyone says. I only wish I was of age." In a touching reference to her birth mother, Marjorie told the reporter: "I am going to be an actress—not a movie, but a real one. You look at me and you can see my mother."[72]

In response to her interviewer's questions, Marjorie could not clarify any of the family relationships of those around her or connected to her. While "Aunt Helene" had told Marjorie that she had known her since she was a little girl, Marjorie did not recognize her. She did know that she had two older brothers but had never met them. The man who sent money and had been referred to up to this point only as "Uncle" she called "Mr. Davis." Within days he was identified as Henry Davis, "a Canadian [who was] supposed to be in South America" at the time of Marjorie's discovery in Detroit. Marjorie said that she had not seen him in several years, but when pressed to say exactly where and when she had last seen him, she could not be specific. Nor could she clarify his relationship to her, her birth mother, or Camilla Jackson. The *Tribune* concluded that the child's parentage and family ties remained "as deep a mystery as ever," and that Jackson was the only person who might hold the key.[73]

Despite all of the reports of an extensive "underground railroad" and Marjorie's international mobility, Detroit police took her into custody a day later when they found her hiding in an upstairs room of the Taylors' house. She was put in a Detroit juvenile detention facility, the very kind of place where she hated to be, and was allowed no visitors. As Hogan sped to Detroit to start extradition proceedings, Jackson's lawyers filed another writ of habeas corpus asking that the Detroit court refuse to return Marjorie to the custody of the Chicago authorities. They also asked that the judge restore guardianship to Camilla Jackson.[74]

Meanwhile, another story of Marjorie's disappearance was being pieced together in papers by Hogan. Marjorie's interview in Detroit had detailed "a dubious story of her abduction . . . [most likely] concocted by the persons the child is now seeking to shield," he argued. "I have believed from the first that Marjorie's abduction from Mrs. Brock's apartment was a carefully framed conspiracy. I have said in open court that I had evidence which led me to believe that Mrs. Jackson and her lawyers . . . knew where the child was being hidden."

Hogan and his team thought that Jackson and her attorneys had allowed Marjorie to be discovered in Detroit after they had provided her with a cover story that would exonerate them, which she recited in her long interview before going back into hiding. They also considered Marjorie's letter part of the wider plot to shield those responsible.[75] In their attempts to disprove Marjorie's account of running away, Chicago investigators tried to track down "Aunt Helene." While they were not convinced that she existed, police were sure that if they found her, she would turn out to be a black woman. James Cotter responded with another theory, arguing that Helene was certainly white and that it was likely that she was Marjorie's "real," or biological, aunt. He now claimed that it was Marjorie's birth family that had attempted to kidnap her: "Marjorie's mother, Temula [sic] Delbridge, an actress, was of a fine family in the south. Her mother's people tried several times to get Marjorie away from Mrs. Jackson. Henry Davis, a wealthy uncle, offered Mrs. Jackson $2000 if she would surrender the girl." This was the first time anyone connected to Camilla Jackson had suggested that Marjorie's extended birth family was actively seeking her. Adding to the confusion, "Uncle" Davis, originally said to have been sending money for Marjorie's upkeep, was now named among those family members trying to kidnap her.[76]

Camilla Jackson's and Marjorie Delbridge's hopes for a legal reunification were again dashed when a Detroit judge denied the habeas corpus petition and found that the Chicago juvenile court did have jurisdiction in the case. "I want to say to all parties interested in this case that the paramount issue is the welfare of the child," he scolded. "The orderly, legal and right thing to do is to bring her before the court of her own state, which is equipped to do what is best for her. This proceeding is dismissed. The child is turned over to the detention home in Detroit, with instructions to bring about her speedy return to Chicago."[77] Upon hearing the ruling, Jackson burst into tears, and in the words of the *Daily News*, a devastated Marjorie "threw her arms about the old darkey's neck" and sobbed. They clutched each other so fiercely that court officers had to pry them apart before Marjorie could be led away.[78]

Marjorie appeared again in a Chicago court on Monday, February 19, where she was declared a "delinquent" and ordered to be placed "in the home of some white family."[79] During this hearing Hogan introduced yet another version of Marjorie's "abduction" that she had affirmed in an affidavit. Marjorie now said that she had hidden in Chicago for six days in a house that was only a block away from her home with Jackson on Calumet Avenue. She stayed with a woman she first called "Miss Shaw," but who was later identified as Sadie De Armond Muse, the daughter of Chester De Armond and a law student. Marjorie described her as "a light-colored Negress [who] knows lots about law because she is going to be a lawyer. She dresses fine and she is very intelligent." In her statement to police Marjorie named Camilla Jackson, James Cotter, Chester De Armond, and Sadie De Armond Muse as those who had planned and implemented her escape from the Brocks. She said that Jackson had visited her at the Brocks' apartment that night not to bring her a coat but to tell Marjorie that a car was waiting to take her away. When she got to the vehicle, Cotter was alone at the wheel. There were no Canadian sisters with a hired driver waiting for her. Cotter drove her to Muse's house, where she stayed for almost a week until she was driven in disguise to Hammond, Indiana, where she and Muse caught a train to Detroit. Marjorie made no mention of any trips across the border into Canada. Cotter denied the story, saying that it was now "the third version she has given since being found in Detroit. I cannot believe the girl made it of her own volition. If she said the things attributed to her, her tale is preposterous. I was not in the cab in waiting at Mrs. Brock's residence; I did not take her to Mrs. Muse's home; I did not drive her to Hammond, and I had absolutely nothing to do with her escape from the city."[80]

The final hearing on the girl's fate occurred a week later. Judge Bowles granted custody of Marjorie to the "child placing department"—meaning to the county—until she was twenty-one years old. Jackson's lawyers made one last effort to return Marjorie to her home by filing another writ of habeas corpus. When this was denied, on February 28, 1917, the Marjorie Delbridge custody case was closed—or so juvenile authorities and most Chicago newspapers believed.[81]

For two months there was no news of Marjorie Delbridge or Camilla Jackson. In the midst of war, continued increases in black migration to and through Chicago, and local labor conflicts, among other things, it is likely that Chicagoans no longer gave much thought to Marjorie or her "mammy." But on May 2, 1917, the *Tribune* reported in ecstatic front-page coverage that Marjorie's birth relatives had been located. And not only were they white, but they were also rich and southern and longed to have her at home with them in Alabama. It looked as if at least one migrant from the South was set to return. Although the paper never fully explained its role in finding the family, it was the *Tribune* that notified Marjorie of their existence. The front-page headline, "Marjorie Joyous at News of Kin; Sends Her Love," was followed by a bold subhead that got to the very heart of the custody case: "Says She Will Not Live with Negroes—Mrs. Jackson Denies." Calling from Alabama, the *Tribune* reporter reached Marjorie at an unnamed juvenile institution, told her about the family, and said her actual last name was Weatherly. While both of her parents were dead, the reporter said that her grandfather on her mother's side, a W. W. Leak, was eager to meet his granddaughter. Although Marjorie was described by the reporter as "so excited that at times she could hardly articulate," she did manage to gush enthusiastically, "'O, isn't that fine? Isn't that fine?' . . . 'Mrs. Jackson (she doesn't call her "mother" now) has often told me that the Leaks and the Weatherlys were relatives, but I did not know where they were and she didn't either, or at least she never told me if she did. And to think that I may some time see them! O, I do so want to see them!'"[82]

Also surprised by this news, Chicago juvenile authorities were cautiously optimistic about what it meant for Marjorie's future. Mary Bartelme, who by 1922 would be the assistant to the judge before whom all cases of girls' delinquency in Chicago were tried, said that no decisions would be made until she had written to Leak and assessed the situation.[83] While Bartelme hoped that this revelation might mean "a home for the poor little thing at last," she qualified her statement by noting that Marjorie was doing "so well" at her Chicago school and she did not want the girl's progress thwarted. This mention of Marjorie's progress was inextricably connected to questions of race and to her new insistence that she no longer wished to live with black people. When asked how she liked her school and if she would be interested in leaving it to go to Alabama, Marjorie replied: "Oh, the school is fine and I like everyone here. I don't even want to see Mrs. Jackson or live with colored people again. But I do want to see my own people. I send my love to them." Following her comment that she no longer wished to see or speak with Jackson, Marjorie's reference to her "own people" had a double connotation, referring most directly to her biological family but suggesting her own race as well. Bartelme instructed the *Tribune* to keep Marjorie's institutional residence in Chicago confidential now that she was being thrust back into the tabloid limelight. "It is considered best that she should be freed from the annoyance of telephone calls and visitors who might flock to the school to see the child whose romantic history has gone the length and breadth of the country."[84]

With the discovery of a new family came an entirely new biography for Marjorie. While the man who claimed to be her grandfather was not quoted in the story, it did include comments from other Leak family members. They said that Marjorie's mother, Lillian Leak, "was a belle of Montgomery until she was won by George Weatherly," the brother of a prominent attorney and politician in Birmingham. Her marriage to Weatherly proved the belle's undoing. It was so bad, the relatives claimed, that Lillian felt she had no choice but to leave. Estranged from her father, W. W. Leak, Lillian Weatherly "arranged for the care of her infant daughter" and went to Florida, where she subsequently died. Apparently she never turned for help to any of the family members who now detailed her unfortunate marriage and final days to the *Tribune*. With whom she left her daughter was not specified in the article, and Camilla Jackson was not mentioned. Marjorie's father, George Weatherly, died shortly after his wife. Speaking with her attorneys present, Jackson denied adamantly that these two families were in any way related to Marjorie: "The true secret is with me. I know everything. There is not a moment in Marjorie's life I don't know . . . Mrs. Zemula Delbridge, Marjorie's mother, gave me the baby. Marjorie's folks don't want her. She's mine. Her mother gave her to me, and I'll fight for her as long as I have got a penny. Her father is not dead. But her mother died in Tampa, Florida. All of Marjorie's people live in Georgia. I never heard her mother speak of the Leaks or the Weatherlys." In an attempt to dispel the narratives of Old Southern gentility that had from the start clung so tenaciously to this legal drama and framed Jackson as a faithful slave, she concluded provocatively by saying of Marjorie's birth mother's family, "They were people of no standing and I know all about them."[85]

Despite Camilla Jackson's protestations, a few weeks later Tilford Leak, supposed cousin of the girl the press now called Marjorie Delbridge Weatherly, came to Chicago to pick her up and take her back to Montgomery. The *Tribune* ran two pictures of a smiling Marjorie, suitcase in hand, ready to board the train. The headline read, "She's On Her Way to Home of Sunshine and Roses," and elaborated in a subhead, "For Years a Waif without Knowledge of Her Relatives, This Girl Is Being Taken Back into the Family Circle by Her Cousin," who is pictured alongside her in one photo. Calling Marjorie a "waif" suggested that she was an orphan. Although most readers would have been very familiar with her case, this served to write out of the picture fourteen years—most of her young lifetime—of being raised in a black family by Camilla Jackson, the woman she had insisted was her only mother just three months earlier. The paper did not print a comment from Tilford Leak or relay any parting words from Marjorie but ran only a short article by Mrs. Louis Brock, who practically oozed vindication. Brock said that she had been called a dear friend in "a letter . . . written by little Marjorie 'Delbridge,' who from now on will be known as Marjorie Leak Weatherly. It did my heart good to read it and I am the happiest woman in Chicago today because this child has been claimed by her people and has come into her own. The person who remarked that mine was 'misplaced sympathy' should have seen the tears of gratitude in the eyes of this kind man who is speeding south with Marjorie. Sympathy for a little child is never misplaced."[86] Like Marjorie's reference to her "own people," Brock's assertion that the girl had been claimed by "her people" highlighted the racial dimension of that common southern question intended to locate family, status, and place: "Who are your people?" Or, to put it in terms of the faithful slave narrative, it showed that being "*like* one of the family" was still very far indeed from *being* family.

The *Tribune* reported again about a tearful Marjorie, only now, the paper said, hers were fat "tears of unrestrained joy" when she met her grandfather in Montgomery. "Marjorie, who has been taken into the Leak family as one of its own, will be given every advantage that the social and the financial prestige of her cousins affords."[87] Mrs. Brock was not the only person to claim vindication with this outcome of the custody case. Several months later, in an article describing his ongoing attempts to have James Cotter and Chester De Armond disbarred, Robert Hogan announced that he, too, had heard from Marjorie: "Assistant State's Attorney Robert E. Hogan yesterday received a letter from Marjorie, who is attending a convent in the south. She said she was happy to be with her relatives and now perceived that the efforts made by the juvenile court were resulting in a far better life than she had enjoyed before the trouble."[88]

Marjorie's return to the South, where she was safely ensconced within the sphere of white domesticity and authority, away from urban corruption, and vowing to stay among her "own people," brought the faithful slave narrative to an almost unbelievable fairy-tale ending. While many Chicago readers found this conclusion most satisfactory, and the *Tribune*, which seems to have been largely responsible for it, covered her return extensively, there was no comparable story of Marjorie's homecoming in the Montgomery or Birmingham newspapers. Presumably, neither the Weatherlys nor the Leaks were interested in publicizing their connections to a Chicago scandal or Lillian's decision to give her daughter to a black family to raise.

This resolution, which conformed so neatly to narra-

tives of southern glamour and faithful slavery, was never confirmed as anything more than a story scripted to suit popular
prejudice and racial stereotype. There is no way to tell from
available sources whether Marjorie was actually related to the
Weatherlys and the Leaks. Camilla Jackson insisted that she
was not. Whatever the facts, the Leak family did take her in.
Marjorie Weatherly, age seventeen, was listed as a dependent
cousin in the Montgomery household of Tilford Leak in the
1920 census. Camilla and James Jackson had moved to a different home in Chicago by then. A decade later, just a few
years before Camilla Jackson's death, it appears that her husband had died. She was living with her granddaughter Willa
Mae and her family. Marjorie's trail in the documentation
dissipates after 1920. Perhaps she married and changed her
last name, or maybe she no longer believed that she was kin
to the family she had lived with in Alabama. More than one
Marjorie Delbridge turns up in state records, but it is impossible to know if any of them is our Marjorie, or possibly her
daughter, and in most cases it seems unlikely. One wonders if
Marjorie in her adulthood ever contacted Camilla Jackson or
if she chose to keep to her "own people," as she had promised
as a teenager on her way to a new life in the Deep South. Did
Jackson ever speak to her or hear of her again? In her last
years at her granddaughter's house, Camilla Jackson lived
next door to a couple with a daughter named Marjorie who
was about the same age Jackson's own Marjorie had been
when she told census takers twenty years earlier that the girl
was her "mulatto" child. Camilla Jackson must have thought
of those times and of her loss often when she saw the little
neighbor girl and heard her parents call her name.[89]

4 MONUMENTAL POWER

*Save a few years of the Reconstruction, the national
capital has been to the Negro a scene of sorrow. Even
at this very hour the ghost of the slave power is stalking about seeking to perpetuate the aged master-and-
slave scheme of society.*

—Neval H. Thomas, 1923

IN 1922 THE DEDICATION of the Lincoln Memorial before a segregated audience in Washington, D.C., occurred against the
backdrop of the fourth year of heated congressional debates
over the need for federal anti-lynching legislation. In that
same year another national memorial campaign was begun
by a local division of the United Daughters of the Confederacy who sought to tell their own version of this history and
define its contemporary lessons. Drawing upon relationships
they had cultivated with senators, congressmen, and journalists, the women embarked on, and nearly succeeded in, an attempt to get a monument to the "faithful colored mammies
of the South" erected in the shadow of Lincoln's memorial.[1]

While nostalgia for the Old South had long been a part of
the national culture, it was invested with a new urgency in
the contexts of black migration, labor unrest, and the terrible
violence of urban race riots that threatened to become an ep-

idemic in the late 1910s. White Americans worried endlessly about the national "Negro problem," blaming blacks and radicals for the turmoil and grasping for solutions. Some found solace in a retreat to an imagined history of beneficent antebellum slavery and southern gentility, a time when hierarchies were clear, whites were good stewards of their land and their laborers, and black people loved them. In the haze of the plantation myth, the faithful slave smiled warmly back at whites and offered comfort. The women of the UDC, however, believed that the Old South had more to offer than a soothing memory or a fleeting escape from reality. In this past they saw answers to the "Negro problem" and a way to end the violence and political upheavals of the present.

The United States Senate agreed with the women on the value of a national memorial to faithful slaves and authorized a land grant for the statue in 1923. Wide protest and fierce controversy followed as predominantly African American organizations and individuals intensified their campaign to ensure that no such monument would stand within the capital's city limits. While the desire to erect a national mammy memorial reflected the pervasiveness of faithful slave narratives in the early twentieth century, the decision to carve it in stone and cast it in bronze was of a fundamentally different magnitude, a fact recognized by supporters and critics alike. This was not a commercial or entertainment-driven use of the mammy figure, which had been common for decades, but an obviously political effort to legitimize this distorted version of the southern past. It looked as if the ultimate representative of the faithful slave—the mammy—would join the pantheon of heroic figures and historic events memorialized in the capital because they defined the character and promise of the nation.

At base, the mammy memorial controversy was a contest over *representation* in all of its meanings. The stakes were high because this kind of public representation of black women would have such a significant impact on conceptions of national citizenship, the substance of equal protection, and black civil rights. The mammy monument clearly marked the confluence of these cultural and political meanings of representation. The erection of a national memorial would confer civic legitimacy on its builders and patrons and imbue the monument's message and iconography with a kind of official "truth."[2] The authorization of this truth by the federal government would in turn connote the illegitimacy of other civic assertions and challenges to the faithful slave narrative. The campaign and the controversy surrounding the proposed memorial revealed sharply competing political strategies and ideologies that were freighted heavily with popular conceptions of slavery and the plantation South. They underscored the ways in which the faithful slave narrative had always been a nuanced civic discourse of aspiration and containment.

The United Daughters of the Confederacy strove to define the public authority of white women by commemorating the hierarchies of the Old South. Writing of the UDC's extensive commemorative activities in an organizational history published in the 1930s, former president general (1911–1913) Rassie Hoskins White asserted the special importance of public monuments to the group's social and political agendas. The Daughters devoted so much time, labor, and money to these endeavors, White explained, because "they knew monuments would speak more quickly, impressively, and lastingly to the eye than the written or printed word."[3] She expanded on the importance of attracting such attention: "[UDC] chapters, State Divisions, and the general organization have done remarkable work in other lines, unseen work, but it is this *visible* work—great monuments and memorials—that has brought the organization publicity and acclaim for these thirty-five years of work, for they have spoken and will speak to a world indifferent to that vast amount of work which is invisible."[4]

Largely owing to the efforts of the United Daughters of the Confederacy, and the Ladies Memorial Associations that preceded its formation in the nineteenth century, grand monuments and smaller statues to the Confederacy and the Lost Cause proliferated across the southern landscape from 1880 through the 1930s. While this period marked the heyday of monument building in the South, public sculpture and memorial campaigns would remain central to the UDC's mission. These statues attested to much more than the heroism of Confederate political and military leaders or the valor of the common soldier. Inscriptions that included the names of UDC chapters responsible for erecting the monuments ensured that the women's labors for the Confederacy would be remembered beyond the unveiling ceremonies. Every statue was a representation of the fundraising and political effort it had taken to get it built, marking the process literally and for posterity in granite, marble, and bronze.[5]

The location of these monuments in civic spaces, on courthouse lawns, and in town squares or parks was equally important to the UDC's crafting of a public role for its members. By the 1920s there were few southern towns that did not have at least one Confederate monument, made possible by the persistence of these women and the new economy of a growing commemoration industry. The *Confederate Veteran*, for instance, was filled with advertisements for catalog order companies offering readymade statues of soldiers and promoting the services of numerous quarries and foundries to the commemorative organizations that were fast becoming important customers. It was now economically feasible for even the smallest hamlet to erect its own statue, in turn making it a civic requirement that each of them do so.[6] These ads mark the expansion of funeral monument companies into the growing public sculpture trade and the movement of the memorialization of common soldiers out of local cemeteries and into the center of town. This shift in locale also changed the meaning of the memorials, which now honored living as well as deceased veterans.[7] And as the living veteran saw his own valor celebrated in the town memorial, so too did the members of the organization or collective that had built it. In the South, more often than not, this was the United Daughters of the Confederacy.

Arguably, it was this trend toward commemorating common lives and collective honor that gave rise to the desire to broaden the pantheon of virtuous Lost Cause subjects worthy of monuments. But even as the commemoration of the average soldier became the unquestioned and necessary expression of local and regional civic pride, the inclusion of other figures such as white women and "faithful slaves" was contested and, particularly in the case of enslaved people, generated much debate. The 1922–23 drive for a national mammy monument was the culmination of nearly twenty years of discussion within the UDC about erecting some kind of memorial to the loyal slaves of southern mythology. These debates joined other calls for such a memorial from Confederate veterans, southern legislators, and regional boosters.[8]

Debates within the UDC over the idea first intensified in late 1904 and 1905 in a series of exchanges printed in the *Confederate Veteran*. In September 1904, Mrs. G. Gilliland Aston of Asheville, North Carolina, made a public plea for a monument, which was endorsed by Mrs. Fred A. Olds, president of the North Carolina division. In an open letter to the UDC, United Confederate Veterans (UCV), and "all the women of the South," Aston argued that the UCV campaign to erect a monument to southern women should be redirected to fund a memorial to "faithful slaves." Aston compared white southern women's sacrifices for the Confederate war effort with what she saw as the potentially questionable support of enslaved people for the same cause. White women, she said, had endured the struggle "for the sacred ties of kindred and country." But "how different with the faithful slaves! They did it for love of masters, mistresses and their children. How nobly did they perform their tasks! Their devotion to their owners, their faithfulness in performing their labors and caring for us during these terribly disastrous years, and their kindness at the surrender, while we were powerless and helpless, have never been surpassed or equaled."[9]

In making this claim, Aston revealed a certain ambivalence about the nature of the owner–faithful slave relationship, generally described by the UDC as benevolent and noncoercive. While white women on the home front could be assumed to support the Confederacy, her letter implies, the actions of the enslaved were "different" because they appeared to work against their own interests to an astounding degree. Slaves who remained loyal when they had the opportunity to free themselves or to attack those who held them in bondage must have made their choice out of genuine love for their masters. This, Aston declared, was a loyalty worthy of commemoration. Typical of the faithful slave narrative in general, the humanity and agency of enslaved people is referred to only in terms of their presumed "faithfulness" to and "kindness" toward whites.

Building a monument to faithful slaves would not negate the monument's commemoration of white southern womanhood. In keeping with the Daughters' desire to make their own work visible, Aston proposed an inscription for the statue that would highlight their own activism and graciousness: "Given by the Confederate Veterans as a memorial to the women of the South, and given by them in memory of the faithfulness of our former servants." Such an inscription would celebrate white womanhood, as the UCV had originally intended, while foregrounding contemporary white women's activism and public agency in rededicating the work to enslaved people. Implicit in this inscription was the fact that for Aston, like so many other white Southerners, the "women of the South" did not include enslaved black women. Indeed, slavery itself would be written out of the monument entirely as "faithful slaves" were redesignated "former servants."[10]

While Aston's plan garnered the support of her state division leadership, others found it highly inappropriate. In November 1904, Mrs. W. Carleton Adams of Memphis, Tennessee, denounced the proposal, writing: "This is not the time for erecting monuments to the old slave—if there will ever be a time. Our country is already black with their living presence. Shall there be a black monument erected in every southern city or state, when there is not a State in the South not in mourning for some beautiful woman whose life has been strangled out by some black fiend?" Here Adams countered Aston's assertion of black people's historic selfless love for southern whites with the presumed contemporary sexual threat posed by black men, the core of white supremacist defenses of segregation and violence against African Americans. If this were not enough, Adams concluded that the "negro of this generation would not appreciate any monument not smacking of social equality. The North would not understand the sentiment." In other words, seeing modern black freedom struggles as disloyal, Adams did not believe that African Americans deserved to be placed in the monumental pantheon of southern heroes. And even if they were, white northerners would be incapable of comprehending the meaning of such an act.[11]

Another Memphis Daughter, Mary M. Solari, challenged

Adams in the pages of the *Confederate Veteran* while offering her own vision for a monument. Although Solari did not reject Adams's focus on the present, she was concerned less with the "faithful slaves" of the past than with the impact a monument might have on future generations of African Americans. "To those slaves who watched the fireside, tilled the soil, helped spin, weave, and make raiment for the master and sons on the battlefield," Solari wrote, "to those slaves who protected and provided for the families at home is due a monument that will tell the story to coming generations that cannot be taught the lesson of self-sacrifice and devotion of the slave in any other way." Bemoaning the loss of what she believed to be the civilizing function of slavery, Solari hoped that a monument to faithfulness might serve the same purpose for African Americans living under southern apartheid. This belief in the capacity of public sculpture to forge new relationships of affinity and power, rather than simply memorialize times past, would become the organizing principle of the national mammy memorial drive of the 1920s. Beyond its capacity to instruct African Americans, Solari insisted, this kind of commemoration had much to teach white southerners as well: "If a time is ever ripe for a noble deed, now is that time, for the grand, courteous southern slave owner is fast passing away; and to erect the monument would be to hand down to posterity an open book, in which our southern children can learn that every negro is no 'black fiend.'" Solari countered Adams's racist venom with an alternative white supremacist illusion of race relations founded on paternalistic benevolence and maternal fantasy. Again foreshadowing the 1920s monument drive, Solari concluded her call for a faithful slave memorial with a paean to mammies. White northerners' reception of the memorial would be negative, but she cared little: "The North would not understand the sentiment. Of course not."[12]

In the context of this debate in the pages of the *Confederate Veteran*, another proposal to construct a memorial to faithful slaves was put forward by women from the Tennessee division at the UDC's annual convention in 1907.[13] The measure failed, however, as members voted to table the resolution. As Rassie Hoskins White would observe nearly thirty years later, "The organization was not ready for the work then and postponed consideration of it."[14] Given the contentious debates leading up to the 1907 convention, her assertion does not appear to refer to the organization's ability to raise funds for some kind of memorial or commission a design. Rather it may describe the inability of members to conceive of the "value" of such a commemoration at the time. The UDC could achieve no consensus on the need for a monument to enslaved black people. Another call for a faithful slave memorial would be made at the 1912 convention, but it never materialized. Ten years later, changes in the social and political landscapes of the South and the nation at large would elicit radically different responses to the prospect of commemorating "faithful mammies."[15]

The near success of the 1922–23 memorial campaign and the motivations of those who championed it can be traced back to several events, both national and local, in the early years of the twentieth century. The election of Woodrow Wilson to the presidency in 1912 was one central aspect of the modern "southernization" of Washington, D.C., culturally, politically, and socially. The fact that Wilson's presidency was drenched in the rhetoric of national white reconciliation and surrounded by spectacles of reunification staged throughout the capital and the country belied the fact that a distinctly southern sensibility had always characterized the city. The election of a southern president swelled the population of white southerners in the District and in the federal government and brought to the fore a longstanding conversation about the regional character of the capital. Carved out of two slave states, Maryland and Virginia, and itself the location of a thriving slave market until 1850 and a district where slavery was legal until 1862, Washington, D.C., had long been steeped in the economic and social structures of the slave South. After the Civil War it continued to be home to a largely southern-born population, which included increasing numbers of black migrants seeking political representation, relief from white surveillance and labor coercion in the rural South, and the better jobs and social mobility available in an urban center with established black institutions, the legacy of a significant free black population. By the early twentieth century, with one third of its population African American and a hardening de facto and de jure network of segregation intended to contain this population, Washington, D.C., looked very much like the rest of the urban South.[16]

Wilson's election deepened significantly the southern character of the city, both socially and politically. Himself a relocated southerner who had been elected on the promise of a "New Freedom" for Americans, Wilson introduced legally segregated federal workplaces, severely restricted federal appointments of black officials, and expanded, through his sanction and activism, levels of segregation in public spaces, entertainment, and housing in the city. That Wilson was widely understood to be a southerner despite his long career as a history professor and college president in Pennsylvania, Connecticut, and New Jersey, and the fact that he was the governor of New Jersey when he ran for the presidency, was itself a testament to the malleability of regional identity. From the moment he assumed office, the city's mainstream, white-owned press cast Wilson as the consummate southerner, particularly the *Washington Post*, still the leading local newspaper. Wilson's southernness was also assumed in the black press, which reported his policies as a clear indication of his regional sentiments.

Commonly the *Post* framed the president's southern ties as family ties, both immediate and extended. And perhaps no members of his "family" other than his first wife, Ellen Axson Wilson, signified his regionalism and the elite southern domesticity of his household more than the cast of black domestic employees who were often described by the press as the president's "family servants," some even as "Mammy." Engaging popular notions of faithful slavery, these stories promulgated a kind of regional glamour swirling about the southern-born and southern-identified president. This air of refinement, paternalism, and privilege required the presence of affectionate, jovial black domestic workers to make it seem authentic. This was exemplified in a story run by the *Post* not long after the Wilsons first moved into the White House. Ideas of whiteness, southern gentility, and budding femininity combine in this portrait of the relationship of the Wilsons' toddler niece, Josephine, with her black caretaker, "Mammy Nannie." The long feature opens by setting a tranquil scene: "The White House Baby [Josephine] was asleep, for it was nap time, and she lay cuddled up to her white bunny rabbit in the little bed that served for another White House baby a long time ago." The tableau becomes regionally specific only with the inclusion of a black domestic worker: "Josephine glories in the possession of a real colored mammy, who was also her mother's nurse, and on sunny afternoons she can be seen, with her little cousins, attended by the faithful Mammy Nannie playing on the White House terrace."[17] Romanticized conceptions of slavery and ownership are reinforced here by the assertion that "Mammy Nannie" had "belonged" to Josephine's mother. Furthermore, in marveling that this woman was a "real colored mammy," the reporter identifies this particular possession as one available only to the most elite southern families, such as the First Family, an access to black labor that went far beyond purchasing a box of pancake mix, displaying a knick-knack, or paying for child care. "Mammy Nannie's" status as a hired employee is the central fact elided in the *Post's* description of a *real mammy* on the White House terrace.

"Mammy Nannie" was not the only black woman in the Wilson household whose labor, wages, and personal life were hidden behind the faithful mammy moniker. Late in the first year of his administration the city was abuzz over preparations for the wedding of Wilson's second daughter, Jessie. An article detailing plans and highlights of the guest list concluded, under the subhead "Family Servants to Be Witnesses":

> Four guests at the wedding whose names will not appear in the society columns, but who, nevertheless, will witness the ceremony with more than ordinary pride, will be the four negro family servants of the Wilsons, who will come from the South to see it. These servants were honored guests at the Inauguration, and mammy, the nurse of Miss Jessie Wilson, will be there, too, to "see her chile step off," as she quaintly puts it. These humble guests will view the scene from the corridor.[18]

Glamorous southern domesticity is marked here by those who "will view the scene from the corridor," a startling manifestation of the idea that the center is defined by its periphery. The unnamed "mammy's" statement, rendered in dialect, is "quaint" in her claims of maternal interest in the president's daughter but powerful in veiling any suggestion of a wage-labor relationship to the young woman. While it was ultimately the president's southern gentility that was expressed in these White House mammy stories, it was nevertheless asserted by way of the relationships of white women in his household to these mammy figures.

Another group of white southern women who assumed a central place in the capital during the Wilson years were the members of the D.C. division of the UDC. They, too, would come to define themselves through the figure of the enslaved black mammy as they sought to shape the character of the city and the nation. Within days of Wilson's election in 1912, the UDC held its national convention in Washington, the first time the city would host the Daughters' yearly meeting. The convention's highpoint, and the reason for its location outside the old Confederacy, was the laying of the cornerstone for the Confederate Monument at Arlington National Cemetery, which would be completed two years later.[19] In a nod to their overlapping membership and as a show of national hospitality, the Daughters of the American Revolution offered the use of their headquarters, Memorial Continental Hall, for many of the events, including opening ceremonies. The unofficial theme of the evening, indeed of the entire convention and cornerstone ceremony, was sectional reconciliation through national patriotism, martial glory, and southern pride. The hall was draped with alternating American and Confederate flags, and the Marine Band played "The Star-Spangled Banner" and "Dixie." The highlight of the evening occurred when outgoing president William H. Taft mounted the speakers' podium, stood beneath a Confederate flag, and looked out across a room crowded with Daughters to give a prophetic address. With Woodrow Wilson on his way into the White House, Taft noted, "Southern opinion will naturally have greater influence, and the South greater proportionate representation in the Cabinet, in Congress, and in other high official stations."[20] While Taft focused on changes to his own office and the political environment, the women in his audience had grander plans for southern influence in the city and the nation, in which they, who had not been able to vote for Wilson, would have a direct hand.

In terms of national clout, the Arlington Confederate Monument was considered by the Daughters to be one of their most important achievements. As they listened to the president that evening, it was still being sculpted in Italy by Moses Jacob Ezekiel, a Confederate veteran from Richmond, Virginia. Completed and unveiled in 1914, the monument stands over thirty-two feet high and remains one of the tallest memorials in the cemetery. Among its several tiers and allegorical characters are thirty-two life-sized reliefs in various groups encircling the monument's center. In his memoirs Ezekiel referred to these as "scenes which I think show without any description how intensely and how seriously the men and women of every station in life had responded to the call to arms."[21] The scenes include soldiers, a blacksmith and his wife, a minister with his wife and young son, and a belle wrapping a sash about the waist of her soldier beau. Settled among these representations of Confederate military service and white southern family life—the Lost Cause pillars of martial honor and charmed domesticity—are two figural groups depicting faithful slavery. One part of the frieze shows an enslaved black man marching into battle alongside his master, loyal to the man and to the Confederacy. A separate grouping next to this one depicts a white soldier taking leave of his children. Colonel Hilary Herbert, who chaired the executive committee of the Arlington Confederate Monument Association, on which Thomas Nelson Page sat, described this portion of the statue in a commemorative text:

> And there is another story told here, illustrating the kindly relations that existed all over the South between the master and slave—a story that cannot be too often repeated to generations in which "Uncle Tom's Cabin" survives and is still manufacturing false ideas as to the South and slavery in the "fifties" . . . [T]o the right of the young soldier and his body-servant is an officer, kissing his child in the arms of an old negro "mammy." Another child holds onto the skirts of "mammy" and is crying, perhaps without knowing why.[22]

While Ezekiel believed his central scenes to be so self-evidently affecting that they required no explanation, Her-

Confederate Monument, Arlington National Cemetery, detail.
(Photo courtesy of Edwin H. Remsberg.)

bert devoted much of his text to interpreting their meaning. In the case of the monument's faithful domestic slave narrative, however, his explication is subverted by the sculpture itself. The physical intimacy and familiarity depicted between the enslaved woman and the soldier runs counter to stereotypical assertions that the mammy figure was an elderly, asexual surrogate mother. In spite of itself, this monumental scene might easily be read as revealing the possible shared biological parentage of these two children by the enslaved woman and the white Confederate departing for war. Although Herbert describes the figure as an "old Negro mammy," nothing about her seems particularly elderly. In body shape, dress, and features, she looks very similar in age to the blacksmith's wife in the scene to the immediate right. The constant refrain of "old mammy" to describe the image typifies the denial that grounds the faithful slave narrative and informs white supremacist ways of seeing—or, in this case, of not seeing.[23]

The Daughters, who uncharacteristically had given Ezekiel complete control over his design and provided no input on any aspect of it, were thrilled with the memorial. Like the famed Gettysburg Reunion the year before, the 1914 unveiling was heralded as a celebration of national unity, as denoted in the *Washington Post*'s headline "Gray and Blue Join—Unite in Unveiling Great Confederate Monument."[24] Ezekiel was similarly proud of his Confederate service, his artistic achievement, and its location at Arlington, so much so that prior to his death in 1917 he left instructions for his own burial at its base. It is possible that the monument helped intensify the desire of some Daughters to see a memorial to mammy erected within the city limits of the capital.

As Taft had predicted, these years were described officially by the organization as a time when the South regained its national power and influence. A source of special interest and pride to the Daughters was the president's marriage to Ellen Axson Wilson. Among Mildred Lewis Rutherford's scrapbooks, largely constructed during these years, the volume titled *The South of Today* was devoted almost entirely to Wilson and the First Lady. And while she was the First Lady of the nation, for UDC members, Ellen Wilson was also the First Southern Lady. In an essay included in the scrapbook, "The Women of the New South," South Carolinian Agatha D'Aubigne remarked: "Who but a Southern woman upholds the standard of the New South in the Capital of the Nation? Mrs. Wilson is a woman of great charm of manner, as handsome as any other Southern woman of our day, and an artist both with pen and brush."[25] An established painter as well as a political wife, Ellen Axson grew up and was educated in Rome, Georgia, where she met Woodrow Wilson in 1883 while he was visiting the community to do legal work. They married soon after, and she assumed a central role in his journey to the White House. Notably, prior to the Democratic National Convention in 1912, Ellen Wilson campaigned extensively in Georgia to spotlight the candidate's ties to that state and to assert his southernness. She has also been implicated in the set of policy decisions that were for many the clearest indicator of the president's regional identity: his aggressive commitment to segregation. At the same time, displaying a combination of white supremacist assumptions and paternalistic concern, she was a leading champion of legislation to set minimum housing standards for the alley dwellings of Washington that were home to much of the black working population of the city. Ellen Wilson died in the summer of 1914. The infamous White House screening of D. W. Griffith's *Birth of a Nation*, after which the president was said to have exclaimed, "It is like writing history with lightning. And my only regret is that it is all so terribly true," occurred in part because he was still in mourning and felt it inappropriate to attend a theater.[26] Gracious, attractive, and variously talented, Ellen Wilson was a model of the sort of poise and subtle influence many UDC members sought to achieve themselves. The year after her death, Woodrow Wilson married another southern-born Washingtonian, Edith Bolling Galt.

The issue of influence was always a tricky one for the Daughters, as their struggles over public monuments suggested. Broadly put, they understood themselves to be a preservation group with an expansive social agenda informed by Progressivism but tied always to the project of protecting and promoting Confederate honor. At the same time, however, this was an enormous and far-flung organization made up of individual women who shared a set of commitments but often disagreed on methods and priorities. Trickiest of all, perhaps, was the inherent contradiction embedded in their claims to public authority that were founded on their self-fashioned role as the epitome of southern ladyhood. The UDC's organizational commitment to a pervasive, albeit romanticized, patriarchy and rigid social hierarchy was often confounded by their own activism and must have been individually discomfiting for some. One result of this contradiction was the professed affinity of many for exercising a more indirect influence within the political realm.

While all Daughters were not anti–woman suffrage, most who spoke out on the subject were.[27] In her essay on New Southern women, D'Aubigne follows her praise for the First Lady with a statement of qualified resistance to the ballot: "Shall I say ought of the future of the Women of the New South? Shall I breathe suffrage for women? Nay, let the future care for itself, and be sure that when suffrage is given the woman of the New South, she will know how to use it."[28] Believing the national franchise for women to be inevitable,

D'Aubigne suggests that a lady does not agitate for the vote, but will be ready—and, it seems, happy—to use it once she has it. Rarely equivocal on any matter, Rutherford had detailed the power of indirection and the responsibilities of the Daughters to their families, communities, and nation in a clear denunciation of the vote for women a few years earlier. At the convention in Washington, D.C., in 1912, having nearly completed her first year as historian general, Rutherford detailed the year's work and took the occasion of her platform to speak to the issue of women's power and suffrage:

> Now you say, "What can we do?" What can we do? Anything in the world we wish to do. If there is a power that is placed in any hands, it is the power that is placed in the Southern woman in her home. [applause] That power is great enough to direct legislative bodies—and that, too, without demanding the ballot. [applause] As you are, so is your child, and as you think, so will your husband think. [laughter and applause] That is if you are the right kind of mother and wife and hold the confidence of your husband and children. Your children are to be the future leaders of this land.[29]

Rutherford's commitment to traditional gender roles, which she understood to be the bedrock of Confederate honor and the UDC's mission, was unwavering. Although she herself eschewed the roles of both wife and mother, she rarely hesitated to promote them as the ideal path for other Daughters. At the same time, the fact that she felt the need to address the issue of women's activism and the vote suggests that not all women in the organization shared her sentiments.

Within months of the UDC's convention and Rutherford's popular argument against the ballot for women, the national fight for woman suffrage took a radical turn and became far more visible in the nation's capital. As of 1912, activists had succeeded in winning the vote for women in nine states, all in the West, through a strategy of state-by-state organizing.

Given the decades of work by feminists of various activist philosophies, many were discouraged by the slow pace of change. Two women so disheartened were Alice Paul and Lucy Burns, who, as leaders of the Congressional Committee of the National American Woman Suffrage Association (NAWSA), urged the organization to abandon the state-based strategy to work for a federal constitutional amendment. Although their committee was organized to lobby for congressional action on the Hill, Paul and Burns were dissatisfied with behind-the-scenes persuasion and decided to take the movement to the streets of Washington, D.C., in a spectacular display of protest. Staging it to coincide with Wilson's inauguration on March 3, 1913, they coordinated the Woman Suffrage Procession and Pageant, a march on Washington by thousands of women demanding the vote. Marginalized by the NAWSA leadership for their direct activist tactics, Paul and Burns left the organization shortly after to form what would become the National Woman's Party (NWP). In January 1917 the NWP initiated a standing picket in front of the White House, where the women were harassed by onlookers and police and denounced by NAWSA. After refusing repeated orders to cease their protest, the women were arrested and imprisoned in Virginia. Paul organized some of her fellow inmates in a hunger strike, and sought recognition for the women as political prisoners. Many in the country were shocked at the conditions of the women's imprisonment and the physically punishing force-feeding endured by hunger strikers. Arguably, much of this compassion was sparked by the spectacle of elite and middle-class white women's bodies being brutalized by the state.[30]

Although the NWP and UDC shared a concern with making themselves seen, marches, pickets, imprisonment, and hunger strikes constituted very different strategies of visibility from those practiced by the Daughters. UDC members sought representation as fine southern ladies, with the specific responsibility to preserve a version of Confederate "tradition" that required protecting racial, class, and gender hierarchies. While the NWP pushed black women and their activism out of sight, hoping to maintain the tenuous commitments of white southerners to their cause, the UDC pushed one black woman to the forefront. Members of the D.C. division would come to see their cause as best represented in the person of the faithful mammy.

As the Daughters and their comrades thrilled at Wilson's election, the District of Columbia's black population, like many African Americans around the country, worried—and with good reason. With the first twentieth-century southern presidency came the "whitening" of a number of traditionally black-held federal appointments, the codification of racial segregation in federal offices and institutions, and the hardening of the de facto segregation that had long been a fact of social, economic, and political life in the city. Despite black hopes, activism, and numerous presidential campaign promises, this trend would not only go unchanged but actually worsen under the subsequent Republican administrations of Warren G. Harding and Calvin Coolidge. These changes affected in various and contested ways the thriving communities of black elites and working people with long histories in the city as it continued to draw southern-born migrants, whether they made it their first stop or their final destination in the Great Migration. Washington, D.C., a southern city with certain characteristics both comforting and disturbing to migrants, was also the national city—uniquely so. This fact motivated diverse residents to engage in political activities and emboldened them with their proximity to seats of national power. Washington as a location shaped black politics and broadcast the struggles of African Americans for desegregation, just workplaces (which were often federal buildings), and better housing. On top of segregation's effects on the day-to-day realities of life in the city, a segregated national capital was particularly galling and carried symbolic weight beyond its borders.

Black political activism in the city was expanding and becoming more visibly radical in this period. Wilson's election derailed some of the limited access and authority that Booker T. Washington's Tuskegee Machine had accumulated within the federal government. An insurgent NAACP (National Association for the Advancement of Colored People) wrested increasing numbers of the black elite away from his style of accommodation and gradualism to a more radical integrationist activism aimed at bringing about legal transformation. This trend only intensified after Washington's death in 1915. In that same year Carter G. Woodson founded his Association for the Study of Negro Life and History, which aimed to provide an institutional framework to support black scholarship and the study of black people in an effort to counter the racist narratives that dominated professional scholarship as well as popular histories like *Birth of a Nation*. The city was also a significant power base for the National Association of Colored Women, and home to much of its leadership, including the founding president, Mary Church Terrell. The majority of black Washingtonians were not part of this elite, however. Among those who populated the city's expansive alley dwellings, some belonged to the NAACP, women's clubs, and other organizations, or at least closely monitored their activities through the pages of black-owned newspapers. For many, membership in black churches shaped not only their spiritual lives but also their social and political commitments. Still others participated in none of these things, marginalized from or uninterested in elite black institutions and organizations, and perhaps bristling overtly at the politics of "uplift" that infused them.[31]

The Great Migration and the twenty-five race riots that

ripped through cities across the United States during the summer of 1919 dramatically influenced the political culture of the 1920s, including the national mammy memorial campaign. Confined to no single region, riots erupted north, south, east, and west, from Omaha to Chicago and New York City to Knoxville. Similarly wide ranging, the summer's casualties were not limited by race, gender, or generation. Notable, and either terrifying or empowering depending upon where one stood, was the fact that while instigated by white mobs, many of the riots entailed significant black resistance. They were quelled by martial law and state violence disproportionately turned against black populations, who were largely held responsible, while communists, anarchists, and the black press were all blamed, together or individually, for inciting the violence. James Weldon Johnson called the period "Red Summer," a reference to the terror and bloodshed of that time, and a still compelling label.[32]

Washington, D.C., was among the cities to explode into rioting during that brutal summer of 1919, just days after martial law had quelled racial violence in Longview, Texas. The riot was in part instigated by the *Washington Post*, which had been running a bombastic series on a supposed wave of black crimes against white women in the city. These reports fanned the fear and hatred of white readers as they were run alongside stories of riots in other cities and red scare revelations of "Bolshevism" in the capital. After the report of a sixth incident, on the night of Saturday, July 19, a number of white sailors, soldiers, and marines gathered near the White House vowing to exact revenge on the city's black population. Moving southwest and pulling in more white men along the way, the mob attacked black men, women, and children at random, often pulling them off streetcars. The violence escalated and continued for two more days, as at least a thousand white civilians joined the servicemen rampaging in the streets while black residents mounted a loosely coordinated effort at armed resistance. It ended only when police cordoned off the downtown area and instituted martial law with the help of a federal cavalry detachment. With several dead and many more wounded, press reports the next day dwelled primarily on black violence, claiming that the "serious conflicts" had started when "the negroes began in the early evening to take vengeance for the assaults on their race . . . As the evening progressed the crowds of negroes grew, [and] knives and guns appeared." The *Post* headlined only white police casualties and Negroes run "amuck."[33]

With the eyes of the nation on Washington, it seemed to many that this riot had been somehow unique, and perhaps more terrible, in its images of federal troops policing the grounds of the Mall, the Capitol, and the White House, in the specter of "race war" in the capital city, and in the reportedly widespread armed resistance of black Washingtonians. James Weldon Johnson, investigating the riot for the NAACP, called for hearings on the conduct of soldiers, police, and the white-owned press, warning that additional violence appeared tragically inevitable. "Riots Elsewhere, Forecast by Negro—Colored Men Will Hereafter Protect Themselves, Says J. W. Johnson" blared the ominous *Post* headline within days of the riot's conclusion. Johnson predicted with sadness and defiance: "I am afraid we will have riots elsewhere as a result of those here [in D.C.] . . . When they come they will be serious. The colored men will not run away and hide as they have done on previous occasions of that kind. The experience here has demonstrated clearly that the colored man will no longer submit to being beaten without cause."[34] Two days later Chicago broke out in what became the most infamous riot of the summer.[35]

As in the rest of the country, Red Summer seemed to herald a turning point in Washington, D.C.'s, racial politics.

Three years later, however, the mammy memorial bill was working its way through Congress and the press. Meanwhile, conditions had become far worse for the city's black population. In his contribution to a series in *The Messenger* on African American life around the nation titled "These 'Colored' United States," Neval H. Thomas, an executive committee member of the NAACP and soon to be second president of the D.C. chapter, detailed the joys, sorrows, and struggles of black Washington. Looking back on the recent war, Thomas noted that 43 percent of all those who had been called to serve from the District were African American, although black residents composed only 29 percent of the city's population. This figure was characteristic of the U.S. military's disproportionate reliance on people of color and the working class that persists to this day. He pointedly juxtaposed these statistics with another set: on the basis of their proportion of the population, black Washingtonians should have held 320 positions on the police force and 663 in the fire department but, as of October 1923, could claim only 36 and 17, respectively. By this time public spaces and entertainments were generally segregated, federal appointments had not returned to pre–Wilson administration numbers, and a wave of neighborhood-level attempts at residential segregation fostered by the collusion of white resident associations and real estate brokers was under way. The "ghost of the slave power," Thomas concluded, was "stalking about" the city, "seeking to perpetuate the aged master-and-slave scheme of society."[36]

While in Rassie Hoskin White's estimation the UDC had not previously been "ready" for a monument to faithful slaves, by the early 1920s members of the Washington, D.C., division were hungry to construct a public representation of faithful servitude with the explicit hope of perpetuating "the aged master-and-slave scheme of society." Unsettled by the

turbulent years of black migration, racial violence, labor unrest, and far-ranging radical protest that surrounded the
Great War, the Daughters conceived a plan that combined
their ladylike commitments to indirect influence with their
belief in the white southern woman's unique ability to address the "Negro problem." With the terrible violence and
black resistance of Red Summer fresh in their minds, the
Jefferson Davis Chapter of Washington, D.C., proposed the
national mammy memorial in 1922. Its commemoration
campaign drew upon the mammy figure's popularity and the
salience of the regional narrative to promote a version of
southern segregation as a national answer to the "problem."
The wide appeal of mammy imagery, with its connotations of
maternal tenderness, domestic labor, and untroubled hierarchy, was central to the Daughters' concept of an intimate, affectionate form of segregation. Far from calling for total separation, and in distinct contradiction to the lived experience
of southern apartheid, the Daughters' model of segregation
was based on an idealized notion of interracial amity expressed through the figure of the enslaved mammy. In popular representation, mammy had been so faithful because she
was content with her enslavement and sanctioned white supremacy. In the Daughters' view, mammy did not just serve
but was happy to, and felt genuine affection, even uncondi-
tional maternal love, for her white masters and charges. For
supporters of a monument, she embodied the best potential
for interracial relations.

Of course, the mammy image was actually representative
of an intimate breach in segregation that permitted the passage of black women as domestic workers into the homes and
emotional lives of white people. The maintenance of white
privilege and black subordination through segregation not
only absorbed this seeming contradiction but even flourished
because of it. By legislating against black ownership of homes

in the same neighborhoods as whites, and against black access to the same commercial venues and public accommodations, segregationists sought to eliminate quotidian enactments of social and political equality. The presence of black workers in subordinate positions in white homes served a similar function.[37] The mammy figure, now personified by the domestic employee, carried the literal and symbolic burden of marking segregation's racial hierarchy, as well as denoting those interracial relationships and proximities that were gratifying to whites.

In proposing a monument plan that harked back to widely recognizable, heartwarming fictions of Old Southern paternalism and happy, faithful mammies, the UDC sought to contain African Americans politically, socially, economically, and geographically. Through the figure of the mammy, the UDC promoted this vision of a mutually beneficial, national segregation defined by "affection." In the context of escalating black migration out of the South and attendant white fears of a regional labor crisis, the UDC's mammy narratives characterized slavery, and the South generally, as a paternalistic, interracial utopia. In this way the Daughters hoped to stem the flow of African Americans out of the region, as they sought simultaneously to mold the racial terrain of the entire country in the South's image. Washington, D.C., the heart of the national civic culture as well as a discrete, increasingly segregated urban space, stood at the literal and metaphorical center of these aims.

The fact that this assertion of deep affection bore very little resemblance to the violence, coerced labor, and thwarted aspirations of both black *and* white people that characterized and sustained southern apartheid signaled no lack of sincerity in the monument proponents' claims. It is this facet of the campaign that is perhaps most difficult to understand. The constant, obvious manifestations of the facts, from mass migration out of the region, lynchings, and race riots to the perceived "insolence" or resistance of African Americans, were all blamed on the inherent failings of black people themselves and on the results of "outside" agitation. If affectionate segregation failed, it was ultimately the fault of blacks, not of the system or of white supremacy. As the Daughters sought to build a memorial to the faithful mammies of the past, they hoped that the public representation of white benevolence and mutual affection between the races might change the behavior of contemporary black people. It would make clear their place, and would keep them there. One monument advocate urged, "If the negroes of the present generation and generations to follow, measure up [to mammy] in citizenship, character, intellect, dependability, industry and godly living, they, as well as the white people of this country, will have a right to feel that they are doing mighty well," perversely equating the rhetoric of rights and black citizenship with the domestic labor of slavery.[38]

Like popular as well as scholarly claims that slavery had served a civilizing function for people of African descent, the commemoration of faithful slavery and black acceptance of white supremacy could, the women hoped, bring order to twentieth-century black populations.[39] Order would be achieved once again through the institution of slavery, this time by way of cultural memory and representation. While the monument seemed largely intended to instruct contemporary black populations, it would necessarily carry a message for white viewers about their own responsibilities in a paternalistic relationship. In the estimation of the UDC and its supporters, all would benefit from such a memorial.

Within this frame of white responsibility, the UDC had a particular understanding of the public role of white women. The terrain of white women's citizenship had changed considerably since Rutherford and others had championed the strategy of indirect influence and the NWP had taken its fight for suffrage to the streets of Washington. The national mammy memorial campaign followed shortly after the passage of the Nineteenth Amendment, which granted the vote to women. The right so many in the UDC had eschewed was now theirs, making the politics of indirection and their support of traditional gender hierarchies less clear cut but no less important.

Embedded within the proposed monument to faithful black service in white southern households was a series of politicized narratives concerning southern domesticity and southern history. As an argument for white authority over black lives, the mutual benefits of segregation, and the expulsion of black people from civic activity, the mammy memorial also asserted a vision of a benevolent white public that included women as well as men. The racialization of the domestic sphere as the appropriate place for black labor and white women's authority held tremendous potential for white women to recast their own citizenship. Many Daughters believed, as Louisa Poppenheim argued in one of her contributions to Rutherford's scrapbooks, that it was "to the patient teachings and personal training of the Southern woman [that were] due the civilization and Christianizing of the Negro in America."[40] The mammy memorial campaign suggested that this responsibility had not ended with emancipation. In commemorating mammy, the UDC retained the maternal, feminine construction of domesticity through which Progressive women's organizations had long articulated a gendered foundation for political power in the United States, while at the same time distancing white womanhood from the actual labor of housework. The power of white women which derived from the southern plantation idyll necessarily included the management of black labor that made this type of domesticity possible. This shifted the register of women's traditional

Progressive activism, justified through motherhood and domestic responsibility.[41] The Daughters sought to realign the gendered dichotomy of public and private space into one bifurcated along racial lines—by means of segregation—which nonetheless maintained the domestic foundations that justified their public activities.[42]

Thus, not only is it not surprising that the version of motherhood the UDC sought to valorize in public sculpture was the surrogate maternalism of black women, it was perhaps their most obvious choice at the time. The mammy figure cemented the Daughters' elite status within the public realm as southern ladies and confirmed their authority over black labor and behavior, which in turn formed the basis of their claims to an especially knowledgeable public responsibility to tackle the "Negro problem." Read against Rassie Hoskins White's claims for the power of monuments to make visible the work of the white women of the UDC, the mammy commemoration campaign of 1922–23 marks an attempt to carry that logic to its most extreme conclusion. Of course, the work such a monument would make most visible was that of enslaved black women, and by extension the labors of contemporary black domestic workers throughout the country.[43] Black women's monumental labors, both literal and figurative, blunted the contradiction of the UDC members' reverence for the patriarchal tradition that confined them as gender inequality was displaced by racial segregation and elite white southern identifications.

The mammy memorial campaign centered on an explicitly national vision yet was tied fundamentally to the local experiences of the white Washington women who championed it. The years surrounding World War I witnessed a swell in the UDC's District of Columbia division membership rolls as women's patriotism drew them to martially defined organizations and domestic politics enhanced the allure of Confederate "tradition." Between 1917 and 1922 the division grew from 483 members to 1,523; 534 new members joined in the latter year alone. The division was particularly proud that 93 of these women were between the ages of eighteen and twenty-five: a new generation of Daughters was filling the ranks. At the request of the women of the Jefferson Davis Chapter, which was itself a product of this growth, Senator John Sharp Williams of Mississippi introduced legislation to make a congressional land grant for their monument in early December 1922. He moved that the bill be referred to the Committee on the Library, on which he sat. Senator Williams had enjoyed a long association with the UDC in Washington, and the successful passage of the mammy memorial bill would be the last piece of legislation of his thirty-year congressional career.[44]

After it was reported favorably out of committee, the mammy memorial bill was heard by the full Senate on February 28, 1923, with seventy-seven members present:

> *Be it enacted, etc.;* That the Chief of Engineers, United States Army, be, and he is hereby, authorized and directed to select a suitable site and to grant permission to the Jefferson Davis Chapter No. 1650, United Daughters of the Confederacy, for the erection as a gift to the people of the United States on public grounds of the United States in the city of Washington D.C., other than those of the Capitol, the Library of Congress, Potomac Park and the White House, a monument in memory of the faithful slave mammies of the South: *Provided:* That the site chosen and the design of the memorial shall be approved by the Joint Committee on the Library, after procuring the advice of the Commission of Fine Arts; that the monument shall be erected under the supervision of the Chief of Engineers; and that the United States shall be put to no expense in or by the erection of said monument.[45]

After a short discussion, the bill was passed by voice vote, which means that no record exists of the numbers pro or con or of the votes cast by individual senators. It is clear from the *Congressional Record* that at least one senator did not support the bill, although his objections were to Williams himself and not to the idea of a monument to faithful slavery.[46] With Senate passage the bill was referred to the House Committee on the Library to begin the next step in the process toward enactment. It fared quite differently in the House, however, and would never find its way out of committee. This inaction, shaped by the controversy that Senate passage had elicited, would ultimately spell the end of the national mammy memorial.

In early January, Charles M. Stedman, a Democratic representative from North Carolina, had introduced a bill identical to Williams's Senate measure. The day after it was referred to committee, Stedman gave a lengthy statement to the body at large. He began by asserting the importance of a mammy memorial to the nation, as well as to his own region. The urge to commemorate great deeds and battles was a fundamental aspect of the human condition, he claimed:

> But you will search the history of all ages in vain for record of any people who have erected a monument to another race or to any class of that race dwelling among them to perpetuate the memory of qualities which entitle them to remembrance and gratitude. The bill introduced in the House should find a responsive echo in the hearts of citizens of this great Republic. They are all Americans, whether they dwell in New England, in the far South, or on our Western plains.

Stedman's patriotic vision of altruism on the part of those working for a memorial to faithful slavery explicitly drew African Americans outside the category of "all Americans." He carefully included whites of all regions, however, as he imagined a unified white citizenry forged through the valorization of faithful slaves. Despite this nod to unification, Stedman devoted most of his speech to extolling the virtues of antebellum southern civilization. Mammies played a central, supportive role in this past, he explained, thus making the romanticized relationship stand in for slavery as a whole and eliding the brutalities of the system: "They desired no change in their condition of life. No class of any race of people held in bondage could be found anywhere who lived more free from care and distress. The very few who are left look back to those days as the happy golden hours of their lives." Here freedom is redefined as the freedom from care supposedly provided by paternalism. Stedman concluded his speech—to great applause—with an estimation of the monument's meaning to those who would encounter it: "The traveler, as he passes by, will recall that epoch of southern civilization, when men were brave and women gentle and true, whose history has ever been and ever will be an inspiration to the people of every land who honor fidelity and loyalty, whether an attribute of the great and mighty or the low and humble."[47]

The women of the UDC needed southern congressmen to champion their cause logistically and philosophically, given their commitments to indirect influence and power defined by gender. These men's investment in the project and in the fantasy of faithful slavery differed from theirs, however. To Congressman Stedman, the mammy memorial would represent, above all, a glorious white South populated by brave men and their gentle women.

Contemporary newspaper reports suggest that sculptors in the Washington area began submitting proposals to the UDC shortly after the Senate bill's passage. It is unclear from these accounts whether the submissions arrived unsolicited, if the Daughters opened a formal or semi-formal competition, or if they had one model or sculptor in mind all along.[48] Adding to the confusion is the fact that at least two different groups of Daughters accepted submissions, each believing it had the

authority to select a design. All of this was further complicated by the fact that the Sixty-seventh Congress had already
adjourned, leaving the mammy monument stranded in committee. It seemed unlikely to many that the bill would make
its way through another Congress anytime soon, a fact reported with hopeful relief by at least one black newspaper in
its assessment of one of the designs.[49]

That summer the *Washington Post* published an image of
the model that was most likely to have become the memorial
had it been erected. George Julian Zolnay, a popular sculptor
of Confederate memorials, planned a design that was in some
ways distinct from the monument imagined by critics. Rather
than a freestanding sculpture of the mammy atop a pedestal or an obelisk, Zolnay proposed a small fountain, draped
in sculpted bunting, and backed by an architectural space
flanked on either side by columns.[50] In the model, a mammy
figure sits within the niche, cradling an infant and gazing at
a young girl who stands beside her with her small hands in
the woman's lap. Seated on the ground beside the mammy
figure is another child who looks on. Inexplicably, the *Post*'s
photo caption and credit report that the fountain was to be
erected on Massachusetts Avenue near Sheridan Circle, despite the fact that no site was ever selected for the memorial,
and none would be anytime soon. In late August the black
weekly *New York Amsterdam News* attempted to dispel this
misunderstanding, reporting: "Another error largely current
is to the effect that a site has been selected by Congress. Such
a bill passed the Senate, but no action was taken by the
House . . . If the House maintains its attitude, the location
of the monument may be indefinitely deferred," which ultimately turned out to be the case.[51]

Another layer of controversy and confusion began to
unfold a few days after the *Post* ran the photo of Zolnay's
model when another sculptor, Ulric S. J. (Stonewall Jackson)

Dunbar, claimed that Zolnay had stolen his design. "My idea, my idea! It is stolen," he reportedly exclaimed while "tearing at his short gray hair."[52] Dunbar accused Zolnay of having seen a model for a mammy memorial he had begun sixteen years earlier for an ultimately failed campaign in Tennessee during a visit to his Washington studio.[53] Dunbar said that when he heard of the Senate's passage of the mammy monument bill, he crafted a new base for his model and was prepared to submit it. But alas, Zolnay's design, very similar to Dunbar's in his estimation, appeared in the press before he could do so. Illustrating the article was an image of Dunbar, sculpting tool in hand, embracing his model, enabling *Post* readers to draw their own comparisons and conclusions. The tone of the article, including the assertion that "to the layman" the models "seem radically different" and its mention that Dunbar had twice before accused the winners of Confederate memorial competitions in Virginia of stealing his work, suggested that his accusation was false.

Far more interesting than the controversy, however, is the explication Dunbar gave of his own proposal and of Zolnay's. In making his case the sculptor noted: "'Why, look how the mammy is holding the white baby in my statue and doing the same in his. See the treatment of the pickaninnies, trying to have their mother pay attention to them instead of devoting all of her time to the white children. It is the same idea, and mine was modeled sixteen years ago."[54] In the absence of a statement from Zolnay, it is not at all clear that the seated children next to his mammy figure are supposed to be her biological black children. Nor is it obvious in the small, admittedly grainy photo of Dunbar's relief that the two children flanking the mammy are black. But we know from this controversy not only that Dunbar intended his monument to celebrate the faithful slave's supposed love for the white baby but also that this was to be indicated by the absence of similar care for her own children. It was this very fact of coerced and disproportionate mothering that would be decried by critics of the monument.

Two days later this particular battle was put to rest and the issue of authorship rendered moot when it was reported that Zolnay's model was indeed the one that had been chosen, and had been from the very beginning. Following fast on the heels of Dunbar's accusation, and no doubt necessitated by it, the *Post* reported Zolnay's selection, noting that at least two other Washington, D.C., sculptors in addition to Dunbar had been disappointed in the process, including an unnamed man whose design had been chosen by another committee which in the end did not have the authority to do so. "As a matter of fact," the *Post* noted, "Mrs. Jane W. Blackburn Moran, chairman of the present committee, never had in mind any other sculptor but George Julian Zolnay, so she told The Post writer several weeks ago, when seen at her residence. 'I never considered any other sculptor but Mr. Zolnay,' said Mrs. Moran, 'because I know his work and like it, and besides his wife is a Southern woman.'" Moran added that she intended Zolnay's memorial to be called *The Fountain of Truth*.[55]

The notion that generations of Americans of all races would see a national memorial to mammy and understand the figure as the embodiment of the "Truth" about slavery and about who could be a laudable black American was far more than many could bear. As news of the proposal became public, black activists, journalists, and editors in Washington led the way in challenging the campaign. Facilitated by the black press, and relying on the newspapers' ability to generate national publicity, these protests emerged before the Senate bill was ever passed.

The earliest challenge from the largest-circulation black

weekly in the capital, the *Washington Tribune*, started subtly. In January 1923, while the memorial land grant bill was still in Senate committee, the paper began reprinting the text of *Emancipation and the Freed in American Sculpture: A Study in Interpretation* (1916), written by the *Tribune* publishers' father, Freeman Henry Morris Murray. The timing of this reprint is far too suggestive to be a simple coincidence. In his introduction to the study, Murray had argued for a keen critical vision in the face of public commemoration:

> When we look at a work of art, especially when "we" [black people] look at one in which Black Folk appear—or do not appear when they should—we should ask: what does it mean? What does it suggest? What impression is it likely to make on those who view it? What will be the effect on present-day problems, of its obvious and also of its insidious teachings? In short, we should endeavor to "interpret" it; and should try to interpret it from our own particular viewpoint.[56]

Murray asserted the political and social power of monuments and counseled vigilance in examining their potential effects. A month later a front-page headline urged *Tribune* readers to "Voice Protest against 'Mammy' Statue."[57] By pairing its coverage of the monument campaign with this analytical study of artistic representation, the *Tribune* sought to provide readers with the conceptual tools for understanding the grave consequences of such a commemoration and for formulating protest. During this same week the *Baltimore Afro-American* encouraged its readers to write their senators, not just to register their outrage but "to insist on a roll call so that the public will know how every senator votes."[58]

Much of the *Washington Tribune*'s continuing fight against the monument dwelled on the inappropriateness of its location within the city's boundaries, as well as its national impact. Both elements came together in its coverage of a statement issued by the Civic Center of Affiliated Associations of the District of Columbia. The *Tribune* listed a range of "insults" or attacks on black citizenship culminating in the efforts to memorialize the mammy figure by "the ones who deny their [the mammies'] descendants educational facilities, humiliate them in public conveyances, Jim Crow them in public places, deny them the rights of suffrage of American citizens and finally insult their race by proposing a statue to commemorate servitude in the Capital City of the Nation."[59] The paper continued the theme of civic and civil outrage by depicting a model submitted by an unnamed "white woman, now of Birmingham, Ala., but formerly of Washington, D.C.," under the heading "The Proposed Insult." The image of a standing black mammy figure cradling a white baby in her arms and the accompanying article appeared on the front page under a large banner headline, "Model of Mammy Statue Insults Race."[60]

Another early challenge, which reached beyond the black public sphere to generate protest within one of the largest-circulation white-owned dailies in the country, came from Neval Thomas. Before the monument bill could reach the floor of the Senate for a vote, Thomas issued a public plea for its defeat. In early February he sent an open letter to the *Washington Evening Star* (which had already published its editorial support for the campaign), the *New York World*, the Senate leadership, and the United Daughters of the Confederacy urging that the proposed federal land grant for the monument be turned down. "Democracy is the monument that the noble 'black mammy' wants erected to her," he exclaimed, "and not this marble shaft which can only be a symbol of servitude to teach white and black alike that the menial callings are the Negro's place in the scheme of things."[61]

With his juxtaposition of democracy, on the one hand, to servitude and segregation, on the other, Thomas cut directly to the heart of the controversy manifest in the commemoration struggle. At that point, however, his letter did not reflect the official position of the District of Columbia branch of the NAACP or the national leadership. Shelby Jeames Davidson, the executive secretary of the branch, felt that the organization's reputation among its critics for elitism and a northern bias had it backed into a corner where the monument was concerned. In a letter to James Weldon Johnson at the national office in New York, Davidson reported: "We are standing still with reference to any immediate protest because our organization having been styled by some of the enemies as 'high browed' this might give opportunity for them to try to prove to the illiterate Negroes of the South and nearby that our antagonism was directed against them as a class and because of the difference in our status."[62] Revealing his own investments in the same regional and class distinctions that he feared would be mobilized against the NAACP, Davidson seems to have had little faith in the ability of recent migrants and black southerners to recognize when they were being manipulated. He asked Johnson what the best approach would be, to which Johnson replied: "We [the national office] are sending out as a release extracts from Neval Thomas's letter to the *Star* on this matter. I think the only angle we can take on it is to point out that the monument is all very well, but that it is a mockery to erect a monument to the 'Black Mammy' and at the same time Jim Crow, disfranchise and lynch her sons. I do not think we can take the position of trying to prohibit the erection of the monument."[63]

As Freeman Henry Morris Murray had written, public sculpture was not merely reflective of the people and culture that erected it but also productive of new publics and power relationships—the "scheme of things," in Thomas's words. This was clear in the black press's assessment of designs that would appear in the coming months, particularly Dunbar's.

After the Zolnay–Dunbar controversy had been publicized by the *Washington Post*, the *Chicago Defender* reproduced the photo of Dunbar cradling his model. Shifting its register significantly, the black weekly ran the photograph under the headline "A Disgraceful Statue."[64] Dunbar's model imagined its own public through the inclusion of two audience figures at the sculpture's base, an adult male kneeling before a small standing child. While these were important to denote scale, this "public" was fearfully similar to the "scheme of things" Thomas worried about, for here was the mammy monument conceived explicitly as a site of instruction in, and the generational transmission of, white supremacy.

Although the black press led and in fact dominated the campaign against the mammy memorial, resistance to the monument was varied and complex, and never broke down easily along racial lines. Some white individuals, organizations, and mainstream publications challenged the proposal. The Women's Relief Corps (WRC) of the Grand Army of the Republic, the closest corollary to the UDC on the opposite side, denounced the monument plan in language reminiscent of the Marjorie Delbridge custody struggle: "Agitation for a monument in the District to the colored mammy of the South is a 'sickly sentimental proposition' and the [WRC] 'forever protests' against it, it was declared in a resolution adopted by the corps at annual convention last night." The resolution went on to say that "the 'vast amount' the monument would cost would be better expended in bettering the conditions of the mammy's children."[65]

A less direct and more equivocal assessment was made editorially by the *New York World*. Using an argument similar to the one that Johnson had counseled for the NAACP, the paper wrote that a monument was fine but that what black Americans most needed was the protection of their rights: "Such a tribute would be well deserved . . . The colored

A DISGRACEFUL STATUE

"A Disgraceful Statue."   (*Chicago Defender*, July 14, 1923.)

mammies of the South have indeed brought up generations of white children with a devotion worthy of all praise. Southern writers alike of fact and fiction have eloquently described their faithful service." While embracing the fiction of the mammy, however, the *World* continued:

> More than such a memorial to certain of its class, the Negro race as a whole might value the ordinary rights of American citizens for all of its members. Negroes might well prefer to be free, in cities, from exploitation by rack-rent landlords in filthy "quarters," and, in the country, from sharp practice in the disposition of their crops against which it is often death to protest . . . All very well, the statue; but the race that it would compliment could get along quite contentedly if it could be assured of a fair chance in the republic its heavy toil enriches.[66]

While the white editors' challenge to the monument is weak in their failure actually to denounce it, black activists and readers of the *World* seized upon the editorial in a paper with one of the widest circulations in the United States as a platform for making stronger arguments. Notably, a black Republican activist from New Jersey, George E. Cannon, responded with a letter to the editor praising the paper's position by focusing only on the latter portion of its argument.[67]

Support for the statue and its patrons was to be found in surprising places. Some editors of black newspapers, particularly those tied closely to the old Tuskegee Machine of Booker T. Washington and his successor, Robert R. Moton, praised the campaign, drawing ire from many of their journalistic colleagues. The most prominent of these was P. B. Young of the *Norfolk Journal and Guide*, who published two early editorials in support of the plan. While his first editorial noted that it was probably more appropriate to locate a mammy memorial "in the heart of the South" than in Washington, he concluded with characteristic reliance on the gradual pace of social change: "To those who are irritated at the thought of such a memorial may we suggest that it is possible, and even probable, that the New South will do more as the years go by to insure civic justice and industrial opportunity for the lineal descendants of the black 'Mammy.'"[68] Young followed this editorial with another two weeks later that responded more to black criticisms of the monument, dropping his argument that it might be best constructed in the South of the old Confederacy:

> A great deal of opposition has developed against the erection of the proposed monument, but we do not think the arguments advanced are convincing. If the Daughters of the Confederacy want to memorialize the grand old "Colored Mammies" whom they loved and respected and who loved and respected them, and between whom ties of lasting affection and gratitude existed, we think it a gracious thing for the Daughters of the Confederacy to do. They cannot hate the descendants of those "Colored mammies" as much as some would make it appear or they would not wish to build the monument, and the presence of the monument in Washington might serve to shame those Southern Congressional politicians who insist upon keeping alive the race and color question to serve their selfish interests.[69]

Young's assertion relied on a vision of faithful slavery and gradual change through shame and cooperation that closely resembled Booker T. Washington's "Atlanta Compromise" of 1895.

Other editors of black newspapers who had challenged the monument campaign could not let this pass without comment. The *Washington Tribune* responded with an editorial charging Young with expressing an "'Uncle Tom' spirit," continuing facetiously but with a serious point: "We are perfectly willing to have the Daughters of the Confederacy erect that monument in Norfolk on the corner of Church and

Queen streets or Church and Princess Anne, but we do not want any such stigma here in the Capital of the Nation."[70] The *Journal and Guide* responded the following week: "We don't know what the Editor of the *Tribune* means by the 'Uncle Tom Spirit,' but we do know that 'Uncle Tom' was a gentleman. He was civil, polite, considerate, generous and genteel, and did not lose his good manners every time someone differed with him."[71]

Despite limited instances of black support for the monument, like Young's, African American responses were overwhelmingly negative. In stark contrast to Young's position, one paper resolved, "Let the Daughters of the Confederacy erect a monument to the 'Black Mammies of the South' in defiance of our wishes and we will put a bomb under it."[72] Along with other black papers, the *Journal and Guide* chose to reprint this editorial, giving voice to the explosive call while simultaneously distancing itself from it editorially. The complexities of one southern paper's coverage is illustrative of black responses to the campaign generally. They were remarkably varied and revealed the contested and always complicated ways in which faithful slave narratives shaped the black rhetorics of freedom and progress. This criticism was also extensive, prompting another black-owned paper, the *St. Louis Argus*, to remark, "No subject has brought forth a more unanimous protest, except lynching, since the Civil War, than has the proposed Black Mammy statue."[73]

5 THE VIOLENCE OF AFFECTION

It gives [white people] such a "superior" feeling to eat at a table in a dining room a few feet removed from a table occupied by Colored people; to sit in one coach of a train while they sit in another; to sit on the main floor of a theater while they [black people] have to sit in the balcony; to nurse at the breast of a "black mammy" and then lynch the "black mammy's" son or ruin her daughter.

—**Chicago Defender, 1923**

IN THE AFTERMATH of the Senate's passage of the mammy monument bill, black critics of the commemoration trained their protests directly on the vision of affectionate segregation embedded within it. They considered the "mammy" to be not merely an icon of white supremacy but a tool for its reproduction, arguing that faithful slave narratives were particularly insidious mechanisms of exclusion, coercion, and terror. African American activists and journalists charged that honeyed testaments of love for mammy swelled from the same bloodlust and white supremacist sentiment that fueled race riots, lynchings, rapes, and other abuses of black people. The figure did not stand in opposition to this violence, as the UDC claimed, but was very much a part of it. Rather than challenge the idea that commemoration represented actual affection, then, they charged that this love for the mammy was a form of violence and that the memorialization campaign itself was deeply vicious.

Narratives of African Americans' physical and sexual endangerment and the theft of black motherhood formed the centerpiece of these popular genealogies that equated paternalistic affection with violence. Critics of the monument drew potent political links between lynching and the mammy commemoration. They spoke of black families robbed of their members by white desires and the sexual threats to black women posed by white men, all of which were denied or cloaked by the mammy figure and its ever present shadow the black "jezebel." As the *Chicago Defender* argued, the figure of the mammy stood at the place where affection for her and sexual violence met and became indistinguishable from each other. White self-conceptions of superiority were nurtured, literally and imaginatively, in the everyday experiences of segregation, in the warm, affective folds where whites turned from the mammy's embrace to lynch her son or rape her daughter.[1] W. E. B. Du Bois made a similar argument in reference to the mammy memorial campaign in *The Gift of Black Folk* (1924): "Whatever [the mammy] had of slovenliness or neatness, of degradation or of education she surrendered it to those who lived to lynch her sons and ravish her daughters."[2]

Conceptions of faithful slavery, sexual and racial violence, and black citizenship clearly coalesced in the discussions of lynching that circulated throughout the monument controversy. While the number of recorded lynchings had begun a slow decline each year in the early twentieth century, the ability of this violence to intimidate black communities and embolden white ones escalated in the modern era. The violence itself grew more sadistic as victims suffered torture and mutilation before they were murdered, often in front of large crowds of white men, women, and children who actively participated or watched excitedly. Many more were able to view these lynchings in souvenir postcards that circulated frequently, made possible by the same cheap print technologies that facilitated the proliferation of faithful slave iconography. Victims of lynching remained overwhelmingly black, southern, and usually male, their supposed "crimes" commonly alleged to have been sexually threatening a white woman or girl.[3]

Black newspapers referred often to anti-lynching activism in their outraged coverage of the commemoration proposal, particularly with the defeat of the Dyer anti-lynching law in the Senate just weeks before the monument bill's success there. Harrowing reports of murder by lynching and federal indifference to it highlighted one way in which black citizenship was violently contested; some cast the erection of a statue in honor of a servile mammy as a similarly brutal attempt at domination. Discussions of lynching were explicitly joined in the black press to recognitions of widespread sexual assault against African American women historically and contemporaneously.[4] Presumed by many whites to be lascivious and predatory and thus supposedly not capable of being raped, black women were commonly threatened by the same white men who claimed to defend southern womanhood and civilization. The mammy figure's overdrawn maternalism and asexuality stood in opposition to this and represented a denial of sex, forced and otherwise, between white men and black women. But as the intimacy and sensuality of mammy stories showed, the faithful slave narrative emerged from the desires of white supremacy, not in spite of them.

So what may have appeared an uneven comparison at first glance—the torture, murder, and soul murder of lynching and rape likened to the representational power of the mammy monument—was in fact a pointed and critical connection forged by those who challenged the memorial. The comparison urged an understanding of the commemoration attempt as an act of violation, an assault on black bodies, identities, and communities. In this way, black activists and journalists sought to jar the casual, mundane associations of the mammy with affection in order to expose that love and pleasure for what it represented: violence.[5]

This included challenges to that which was most revered in the mammy icon, namely, the depth and power of a black woman's mother love for whites. A new female figure, the "slave mother," emerged in the black press to contradict the maternal characteristics celebrated in white-authored mammy narratives. Loosed from the constraints of white domesticity and faithfulness, the enslaved mother was heralded as a nurturing maternal force within black families in spite of the conditions of slavery. James Weldon Johnson echoed many when he said that "it would be more worthy to erect a monument to the black mother, who, through sacrifice, hard work and heroism, battled to raise her own children and has thus far so well succeeded."[6]

The act of bringing to light all that was concealed in the faithful slave narrative supported a range of black political claims. Responding to the declension of the African American from "faithful slave" to modern "Negro problem" promoted by the United Daughters of the Confederacy and their supporters, black elite critics of the monument put forth contrasting histories of emancipation and racial progress. From club women, editors, and journalists to members of the NAACP and the Republican Party, black activists asserted the arrival of the New Negro. The term itself was not so new. Beginning with the publication of Booker T. Washington's edited collection *A New Negro for a New Century*

(1900), a range of early-twentieth-century black politics from strategies of continued bourgeois uplift to radical socialism was driven by the imperative to define black modernity and civic legitimacy—to articulate the nature and worth of the New Negro—culminating in the cultural politics of the Harlem Renaissance.[7]

As diverse factions within African American communities debated the character of black activism and civic claims, employing the common language of the New as they disagreed over what it actually meant, they shared a fundamental concern with the idea of racial progress. As a concept, progress was highly variable. It could mean the development of working-class consciousness just as easily as it could describe the "uplift" of black bourgeois class and gender differentiation. But whatever social, economic, political, or cultural configuration the idea of racial progress was harnessed to, there was an overriding sense among black people in the 1920s that a New Negro had arrived, just as many whites believed that a new "Negro problem" was upon them. Embedded within these competing visions of the New was the necessary, defining corollary of the Old Negro. Because the measure of progress was difference, the Old was always articulated with the New even if not explicitly.[8] In the early months of 1923 the most common representation of the Old was the mammy. Locating protests against the monument campaign within the larger politics of the New Negro highlights the central place of gender as the productive mechanism of narratives of racial progress.[9]

The Senate's southern Democrats were flush with success from their recent victory over the Dyer anti-lynching bill when John Sharp Williams of Mississippi first introduced his mammy memorial legislation a few days later. It had taken almost four years of public and private lobbying, multiple versions of the legislation, and an enormous Republican majority after the sweeping electoral victories of 1920 for Representative Leonidas C. Dyer, a Missouri Republican, and the NAACP to marshal a federal anti-lynching bill through the House and on to the Senate. In the end, after the Democrats managed to keep the bill bottled up in committee for months, it would take only four days of filibustering to kill it, prompting NAACP assistant secretary Walter White to charge the senators with having "committed mob violence on the floor of the United States Senate."[10] With canny timing, Williams and his House counterpart, Charles M. Stedman of North Carolina, offered their mammy monument bills in the context of months of paeans to faithful slaves, "good Negroes," and white benevolence that had percolated throughout southern defenses of regional race relations.

The long journey of the anti-lynching bill had begun in 1918 in the aftermath of the horrific East St. Louis riot and the Houston Mutiny which followed a month later in the summer of 1917. The dramatically different federal and legal responses to each sent many—the NAACP, congressmen, and War Department officials—to the U.S. Congress with bills that would not only clarify federal jurisdiction over crimes of racial violence in the states but also ensure that the federal government did in fact intervene to protect the rights of black Americans.

The riot in East St. Louis, Illinois, started on the night of July 1, when a carful of armed white men was seen cruising through a black neighborhood full of migrants recently arrived from the South, shooting at their homes indiscriminately from the car. Black and white city residents had been on edge for months after labor strikes were broken in the meatpacking and aluminum ore industries, partly through the use of newly arrived black workers. Labor antagonism,

racism, housing shortages, anxiety, and local corruption mingled in a volatile stew that threatened constantly to boil over.
For many black East St. Louisans, those gunshots were an
offense that could not go unanswered. Assembling to protect their neighborhood and avenge the earlier attack, black
residents fired on a squad car driving slowly through the
same area, killing the two police officers inside. By the next
morning the police had parked the bullet-pierced and blood-
stained automobile in front of City Hall, which served as a
rallying point for white rioters. For the next twelve hours,
groups of white people fanned out across the black sections
of East St. Louis, attacking, beating, shooting, burning, and
killing black men, women, and children. They set fire to
black homes and then shot at the inhabitants as they fled.
For every rioter, many more white residents stood by and
cheered the violence. Among these spectators were several
local police officers who had helped to incite the riot and
now either did nothing to stop it or actively participated in
the terror. They were joined by five companies of the Illinois National Guard deployed to the city to restore order.
Witnesses later reported that far from quelling violence, the
guardsmen exacerbated it either by actually joining in the
mayhem or by expressing their sympathy with white rioters.
Guard troops were seen simply standing around and joking
with policemen as the riot raged about them. When it was
finally over, at least thirty-nine black and eight white people
were dead, hundreds more were injured, and 312 buildings
and 44 freight cars had been destroyed by fire.[11]

In the riot cases actually taken to trial by the state attorney
general's office, which had been consumed just months before by the Marjorie Delbridge custody case, more black
people went to prison for the murder of the two police officers alone than the entire number of whites who received
significant jail sentences. Those white rioters who were not

released during the night by sympathetic police were usually given little more than a few days in the city jail or a small fine. The first trials to consider riot crimes took place swiftly in October; all of the defendants at these earliest trials were black. While some were punished for their active participation in the violence, no police officer or national guardsman was held legally responsible for his inaction or failure to protect black lives and property. The troops' commanding officer was exonerated in a military inquiry that ultimately produced only seven courts-martial. Despite local requests from industrial interests in East St. Louis and briefs from Justice Department lawyers outlining federal jurisdiction, President Wilson and his attorney general, Thomas W. Gregory, refused to empanel a federal grand jury. At the instigation of Representative Dyer, the House did mount an investigation, sending a five-member subcommittee from its Judiciary Committee to East St. Louis to gather information. Dyer had served in the House since 1911 from Missouri's Twelfth Congressional District, which included much of St. Louis's south side. He felt keenly, along with his largely black constituency, the plight of terrorized black East St. Louisans, many of whom had crossed the river into St. Louis to flee the riots that hot summer night.[12]

While the subcommittee was conducting hearings in East St. Louis, court-martial proceedings began in Texas for African American soldiers from the Third Battalion, Twenty-fourth Infantry, who had mutinied in Houston a month after the riot in Illinois. Responding to police brutality, harassment, and the city's strict Jim Crow laws, around one hundred black soldiers defied the orders of their commanding officers and marched from Camp Logan, where they were stationed, into downtown Houston on the night of August 23, 1917. Earlier that afternoon a fellow soldier had been badly beaten and arrested when he stepped in to stop a police officer from hitting a black woman in the street. When another soldier inquired about his friend's arrest, he was also hit and shot at as he fled, before he, too, was caught and arrested. Word of the two arrests and a rumor that the second soldier had died from his gunshot wound made it back to Camp Logan, where it sparked the mutiny. The soldiers marched into Houston armed to take revenge against the police and conductors of segregated streetcars. In two hours of gunfire and commotion, the soldiers killed sixteen white people, including four policemen, two deputized civilians, and two soldiers, and seriously injured eleven more. The speed with which federal military officials made arrests and conducted trials for the Houston Mutiny mocked the struggles in Illinois to hold soldiers and police accountable for their actions there. In the first round of military tribunals, thirteen soldiers were sentenced to death, forty-two to life in prison, and four to shorter terms; four were acquitted. Many Americans were stunned to discover that in the early morning hours of December 11, 1917, the first thirteen soldiers were executed by hanging only days after their final sentencing. Many called it a "legal lynching" by the military intended to appease whites in Texas and throughout the country who were screaming for blood.[13]

The terrible counterpoint of these two violent racial struggles that summer, and the disproportionate responses by federal and local officials, drove many to demand federal anti–mob violence or anti-lynching measures. The following year, 1918, witnessed the introduction of a number of these, including the first version of Leonidas Dyer's anti-lynching bill. Dyer's proposal stated that the murder of a U.S. citizen by a mob or a "riotous assemblage" of three or more people constituted denial of the equal protection of the laws guaranteed by the Fourteenth Amendment. It held any participant in such an assemblage guilty of murder and subject to trial in a United States District Court. Particularly resonant in the aftermath of East St. Louis, the Dyer bill further held any state or local officer found to have failed to make a "reasonable effort" to protect a prisoner or prevent a lynching guilty of a federal crime, punishable by up to five years in prison and/or fines of up to $5,000. Additionally, any county in which a lynching occurred was responsible for paying reparations to the victim's dependents of no less than $5,000 and no more than $10,000. If no dependents existed, the money was to be paid to the federal treasury. Finally, any individual convicted under the Dyer law was to be barred from jury service for life. Some in the NAACP hesitated to support Dyer's proposal at the time, particularly members of the leadership who, like many in Congress, questioned the law's constitutionality or believed it too punitive to garner wide support. The organization considered a variety of measures that year, including a proposed constitutional amendment and a war powers bill, in addition to the Fourteenth Amendment legislation submitted by Dyer. None of these proposals made it out of committee in 1918–19, nor did Dyer's second or third version of his anti-lynching bill find success a year later.[14]

By late 1920, a presidential election year, the political climate and the subsequent fate of the Dyer bill had changed considerably. With the Great Migration and the ratification of the Nineteenth Amendment, the electorate was now much larger and more diverse than ever before. New constituencies seemed up for grabs, as urban Democratic machines in the North sought to wrest recent black migrants away from their traditional Republican allegiances, and everyone sought the women's vote. At the same time, "lily-white" Republicanism made some inroads in the Solid South in an attempt to draw disgruntled white Democrats to the party by ousting black members and claiming a shared belief in white supremacy. Although none of the anti-lynching measures introduced in the years before the 1920 elections had been successful, the NAACP had orchestrated enormous publicity campaigns for each, making lynching one of the central political issues of the postwar period. During his campaign for the presidency, Warren G. Harding stumped on the issue before northern and midwestern, often racially mixed, audiences, and the national Republican platform included an item urging "Congress to consider the most effective means to end lynching."[15] Notably, however, neither Harding nor the party ever explicitly supported the Dyer bill or anything like it. The Republicans remained vague and noncommittal, prompting many to accuse them of attempting merely to manipulate black voters. After Harding's landslide victory and the huge gains made by Republicans in the House and Senate as they took massive majorities in both, black voters and organizations that had supported the party and the new president had high expectations of rewards for their assistance.[16]

Where a federal anti-lynching bill was concerned, many had reason to be optimistic, at least initially. A day after the Sixty-seventh Congress convened on April 11, 1921, Harding gave a special address outlining his hopes for the upcoming legislative agenda and possible collaborations between the legislative and executive branches. He urged that "Congress ought to rid the stain of barbaric lynching from the banner of a free and orderly representative democracy."[17] Once again, however, the president failed to make reference to the Dyer bill or the equal protection clause explicitly. Leonidas Dyer nonetheless saw this as an opportunity to introduce a fourth version of his anti-lynching law the following day. Over time, the bill had been amended to increase the number constituting a mob to five or more, to define more explicitly as a conspiracy such a mob's deprivation of an individual's right to equal protection, and to remove the jury duty exclusion. On October 20 the bill was favorably reported out of the Judiciary Committee.

Dyer realized that he had to get his bill to the floor swiftly, lest it be allowed to languish at the bottom of the calendar; this had been the fate of the third version of his bill, which had gone unheard before the conclusion of the Sixty-sixth Congress. He sought to persuade the Rules Committee to pass a special measure to have the bill read as soon as possible. Meanwhile, its best and most persistent lobbyist, James Weldon Johnson, urged Harding to make clear to the House his desire for the passage of an anti-lynching law and to reiterate this support in his December message to Congress. Less than a week after the bill was referred to the House, Harding made one of the few speeches of his presidency that directly addressed race relations and black civil rights. Speaking before a segregated audience in the South's largest industrial city, Birmingham, Alabama, he stressed the need for ensuring black southerners' access to education, economic opportunity, and the ballot, but he endorsed segregation, saying that "both sides" must recognize "absolute divergence in things social and racial."[18] Harding did not take the opportunity to mention either directly or indirectly the Dyer bill or lynching. He continued his silence in December, saying nothing of the anti-lynching law or any other issue of express concern to African Americans in his address. Nevertheless, Republican support for the measure was widespread, and though the special ruling for an immediate hearing of the bill was debated fiercely, it passed easily in mid-December.

Mightily outnumbered, southern Democrats in the House lined up quickly against the Dyer bill, vying with one another for time on the floor and often later reading lengthy additions to their comments into the *Congressional Record*.[19] The protests of Democrats and the few Republicans who did not support the bill drew on popular beliefs that Reconstruction had been a criminal mistake and was a time of terrible corruption inflicted on the South by the federal government. The representatives challenged the post–World War I expansion of the federal state with familiar arguments for states' rights and, in the face of staggering evidence to the contrary, hailed the contemporary South as a paternalist racial utopia made possible by segregation. This idyll was threatened, they warned, by "outside agitators" like Dyer and the NAACP. They urged northern Republicans to consider their own states' growing black populations and argued that segregation was the most reasonable solution to the national "Negro problem." Many claimed further that while lynching was deplorable, it was the only effective means for dealing with the "black rapist." This white supremacist vision of paternalism and home rule was animated in the congressmen's speeches by the figure of the historically faithful mammy and contemporary "good southern Negroes."

The theme of *assault*—against the Constitution, against the South, against white women—organized the southern Democrats' opposition as they constructed the idea of domestic defense against federal intervention. Starting with the white home, in which women and girls were said to cower in fear of having to choose between rape or death, *Birth of a Nation*-style, in order to protect their racial and sexual purity, the congressmen described concentric spheres of domesticated public spaces radiating outward to encompass not just southern regionalism but ultimately the need for the southern brand of patriarchal "protection" nationwide. When the special ruling on the bill was called to the floor on December 19, southern Democrats attempted to stall it with parliamentary tactics. In arguing the rules, however, a number began to dispute the Dyer law itself, setting the outlines of the formal debate which was to come the following day. While each was quick to denounce the lynch mob, most also argued that it was an unfortunate regional necessity. "We who have been raised in the South," proclaimed Edward Pou of North Carolina, as he described the supposed "black rapist" threat, "know how hard a problem we have to deal with."[20] Pou was speaking in support of his colleague Finis Garrett of Tennessee, who had taken the floor and declared, to great applause, "Mr. Speaker, this bill ought to be amended in its title so as to read: 'a bill to encourage rape.'"[21] He claimed that without the threat of lynching, black rapists would go undeterred as those who had feared the lynch mob would now act on their wicked and barely controlled desires. James Aswell of Louisiana had prompted some of this rhetoric with his own similar call, arguing that the black rapist "is deterred, if at all, only by knowing in advance that when captured he will meet certain and immediate death."[22]

Not all black people were to be feared or killed, the southern legislators were quick to argue as they mobilized the "black rapist's" imaginative counterpoint, the "good Negro." They asserted that legal segregation shot through with old-time paternalism—their own version of affectionate segregation—provided the most workable solution to the "problem" of a multiracial society. In doing so, the congressmen claimed that segregation benefited black and white southerners alike, binding them with ties of mutual care and assistance while maintaining comfortable hierarchies. Nothing proved this better, some said, than the legacy of affection between white southerners and their black "mammies." Pou elicited loud applause from his colleagues when, in a moment of apparent spontaneity, he disrupted his own argument to claim, "There is one other thing that you men from the North cannot comprehend, that ineffable, indescribable, unspeakable love that every southern man feels for the old black nurse who took care of him in childhood." As the applause died down, Pou continued mistily: "The sweetest memories of my life go back to my old 'mammy' who faithfully and tenderly took care of my brother and myself . . . You gentlemen cannot comprehend the love and the tenderness that we feel for those black people who cared for us."[23]

Indeed, Pou and other southerners asserted, it was this

failure to understand the benefits of entrenched paternalism in their region that motivated misguided Republican support for the Dyer bill. This failure would prove the North's undoing, the southern Democrats charged, as the region confronted increasing numbers of black migrants. William C. Lankford of Georgia summed up many of these assertions late in the debate on the bill when he claimed that the majority of African Americans in the South were "courteous and true to the white man and his family" because they were "under the influence of the good old Negro daddies and mammies of the old days." This was in contrast to black populations in the North: "The time is fast approaching when the North will bitterly detest the whole Negro race. The worst Negroes of the South, if they miss the penitentiary, the gallows, and the occasional lynchings, are coming north to add to your already haughty, contemptible northern Negro population. This mixture of our worst with the northern bad Negro race will go on making themselves as obnoxious as possible to the white race."[24] These sentiments would resound throughout arguments in support of the national mammy memorial, intended as it was to provide this "influence" of the "mammies of the old days" to all African Americans, North and South.

Despite these intense and persistent arguments against the measure, the Dyer anti-lynching law was finally passed by the House on January 26, 1922. The gallery was crowded with black and white supporters of the bill, who cheered and clasped one another in victorious hugs, including James Weldon Johnson and many other NAACP activists. The voting had fallen mostly along partisan lines, meaning that the bill won by the significant margin of 231 to 119. The next day's NAACP press release celebrated House passage of the Dyer bill as "one of the most significant steps ever taken in the history of America."[25] The elation was tempered, however, by the knowledge that the bill would now move on to the Senate, and to a far more difficult fight for passage.

For the next five months the Dyer bill lay bottled up in the Senate Judiciary Committee as its constitutionality was debated fiercely. As Johnson lobbied individual committee members, the NAACP staged public rallies, held poignant silent protest marches, and gathered statements of support from church groups and politically influential organizations such as the American Bar Association. On June 30, 1922, the bill was reported out of committee favorably, but by a narrow margin. Once again, however, actually getting the bill to the floor for a vote proved difficult. On September 21 Republicans tried, but were thwarted by the parliamentary maneuverings of Mississippi's Pat Harrison. The second session of the Sixty-seventh Congress adjourned. The Dyer bill would have to wait until after the midterm elections in November. Those elections spelled the end of the Republicans' short-lived supermajority as state after state fell to the Democrats and Progressives. By late November the Republicans' Senate majority had fallen from over 20 seats to only 10, while the House's dropped staggeringly to 15 from more than 160.[26]

On November 27 Republicans tried again to bring the bill to the floor but were met with a barrage of quorum calls, objections, and other tactics by the southern Democrats. The final filibuster was on. The following day, after much of the morning had been similarly wasted, Minority Leader Oscar Underwood of Alabama rose to state explicitly what was already obvious: the Democrats were not going to allow consideration of the Dyer bill. "I want to say right now to the Senate," he announced, "that if the majority party insists on this procedure they are not going to pass the bill, and they are not going to do any other business."[27] After caucusing that evening, Republicans agreed to continue the fight for the time being, but fissures were already evident in their resolve. After three more days of filibuster, with a break for the Thanksgiving holiday, the Republicans capitulated formally. The Dyer anti-lynching law was dead. Throughout these crucial last days, not a peep had been heard from President Harding.

Supporters of the bill were devastated, and quickly charged Senate Republicans with never having intended to fight for the law. In the first days of the filibuster, the *New York Times* had reported that the Republicans seemed "not 'very angry'" at this turn of events, and later, after its defeat, noted editorially that it was "doubtless true that the Republicans in the Senate were not sincerely and whole-heartedly in favor of the anti-lynching bill."[28] James Weldon Johnson would later recall that the Republicans had seemed delighted to allow the southern Democrats to take responsibility for the bill's defeat. "Disgust was [my] dominant emotion," he wrote. "What I had for a week been sensing would happen—the betrayal of the bill by Republican leaders—had happened . . . My thoughts were made more bitter by a fact which I knew and which every senator admitted, the fact that the bill would have passed had it been brought to a vote."[29]

With the mammy monument bill's passage a few months later, many journalists and political cartoonists for the black press noted immediately the terrible confluence of the Senate's defeat of the Dyer bill and its prompt authorization of the UDC's memorialization scheme. The weekly *Philadelphia Tribune* editorialized: "There can be no sincerity in the action of the Congress for the same men refused to pass the Dyer Anti-Lynching Bill. Everyone with an ounce of brain realizes that the passage of a law to protect the descendants of those women would be more beneficial and a greater tribute than any monument erected with stone and mortar."[30] The issue of sincerity, whether on the part of the Senate or the UDC, was not the main one for most black critics of the monument, however. Rather, what they found particularly troubling was the fact that the wish to valorize the faithful slave stood side by side with lynching among the white supremacist tactics of racial control. This had been abundantly clear to those who had watched from the gallery or read about the debates surrounding the Dyer bill a year earlier. This language of incongruity remained useful, however, as an effective vehicle for making claims about broken Republican promises and for assessing the fraught relationships between black Americans and the federal state in this period.

Editorials, poems, and letters to the editor responding to the monument bill's success in the Senate were filled with references to the Dyer bill, both explicit and subtle. The most striking of these comparisons appeared in political cartoons, which tapped into the growing prevalence of mammy iconography in advertising and on film as well as widely circulated images of lynched black bodies. The cartoons subverted popular representations of black men and women and deployed them to different ends. An editorial cartoon from the *Chicago Defender* made visual the theme of ironic legislative counterpoint to harrowing effect. Run under the caption "Mockery" it depicts a baffled-looking colonel type labeled "The South" presenting the "Plans for Black Mammy Statue" to the dangling, lifeless body of a lynched man. Though not referred to specifically, the Dyer bill's defeat is figuratively represented by the lynching it has failed to prevent, invoking both the tragic imbalance of the Senate's response to racial violence and the continuation of that violence that would be ensured by the monument's glorification of slavery. "Mockery" thus carries a double meaning here, referring to the travesty of the Senate's priorities as it simultaneously exposes the ultimate outcome of all that affection for mammy: violence, torture, and death.[31]

The *Baltimore Afro-American* linked the two bills in a car-

"Mockery." (*Chicago Defender,* April 7, 1923.)

"Use that monument fund to pass a law that will *stop* lynching of my children." (*Baltimore Afro-American*, March 2, 1923.)

toon that similarly substituted for explicit mention of the Dyer bill's defeat its visual trope, the lynched black male body. In the foreground of the image stands a mammy figure, coded as such by her headscarf, apron, advanced age, and ample size. Reflecting the commodified iconography of the mammy narrative, the spotted pattern of her scarf and shawl is nearly identical to that worn by the Aunt Jemima trademark. With a stiff posture suggesting monumentality, the figure holds a scroll that bears an inscription asking Congress to "use that monument fund to pass a law that will *stop* lynching of my children." In the distance, behind this figure of a pained and pleading black mother, is the silhouette of a lynched man hanging from a tree. The scene of this lynching, Washington, D.C., is clearly indicated by its other monumental architecture, the Capitol dome and the Washington Monument.[32] Visually echoing White's assertion that senators had mobbed the Dyer bill, killing it in a subversion of the legal process on the Senate floor, the image represents the legislative defeat as a lynching in the capital city.

While both of these cartoons carried messages about the denial of equal citizenship through violence and federal complicity, another image from the *Defender* explicitly engaged the complex relationship between African American citizens and elected officials who, like the Senate Republicans, appealed to them for votes yet did little for them once elected. Embedded within this civic narrative was a subtle regional framing. While images of lynching evoked the violence of segregation and the disfranchisement of southern black populations, here we have a representation of northern black people granted a place at the table, literally, but continually disappointed in their civic aspirations. Run under the heading "Rotten Service!" the front-page editorial cartoon depicts an African American man, identified as "All of Us," recoiling from the rotten egg of the "Proposed 'Black Mammy' Statue" served to him by a grotesque figure of the "Senate" resembling Uncle Sam. Disgusted, the black man remarks witheringly, "I didn't order that mess!!!—I ordered the Dyer Bill!!"[33] In its representation of an Uncle Sam–like Senate serving a black man, the image provocatively inverts the

"Rotten Service!" (*Chicago Defender*, March 17, 1923.)

common depiction of black servitude. The *Defender* cartoon is also striking in its iconographic similarity to, but narrative difference from, an image run in the *New York Age* in the months following the United States' formal entry into the First World War. The hopeful, elated editorial cartoon hailed the dawn of a new chapter in American race relations grounded in the changing political and economic status of black citizens generated by wartime mobilization. In this earlier cartoon, Uncle Sam smiles with approval as he prepares to serve up a hot dish labeled "Real Democracy" to a well-heeled black man holding the "Wine of Prosperity" and sitting at a table piled high with cash, his "Fruits of Perseverance," and the cigars representing his success. The table's bounty includes references to a number of war measures and related events, such as the promotion of black officers to lead black regiments.[34]

Much had changed—and, more to the point, not changed—in the six years separating the two cartoons. Employing the same metaphor of government service and the dining table, the images offer very different assessments of the relationship between the federal state and its black citizens. What the cartoons do share, however, is the use of a black man dressed in evening clothes to represent all African Americans. Despite the importance of black women voters to northern Republican coalitions during and after 1920 and the mass movement north of working-class African Americans, the *Defender* artist persists in depicting the relationship of black citizens to the state as one of elite men, black and white, contending over the figuratively absent mammy. Countering the desire of the UDC and the Senate to see all ("of us") African Americans as faithful, enslaved mammies, the cartoon substitutes a very different icon to represent the whole: the successful, "uplifted" man.

Under the facetious heading "Since Statues Seem to be

All the Rage, Suppose We Erect One," the *Defender* proposed a counter-monument to the mammy memorial that would honor the "White Daddy." Alluding to the power of monuments to confer authority and universality on what were in actuality distinct historical narratives, the caption suggests that black people had quite a different story of "affectionate" interracial contact and parenting to tell. The cartoon monument presents a leering white man assaulting a young black woman who struggles to fend him off but appears to be overpowered. Inscribed simply "A White Daddy," the moonlit tableau is a richly layered critique not only of the dangerous nostalgia inherent in the mammy figure but also of the dominant racial narrative of rape in the early twentieth century, foregrounding the violent interconnectedness of both. Although the woman does not conform in age or physical appearance to mammy iconography, she is coded as a maternal figure by the sobbing child behind her, a witness to the abuse. The toddler's presence suggests that this white man may well be his or her father.[35] With its reference to the white rapist who fathers a black woman's child, the image explodes the myth of surrogate family ties between black and white people embodied by the maternal mammy and forms a powerful counterpoint to the grouping of the Confederate soldier, enslaved woman, and children on the Confederate Monument at Arlington. In addition, by setting the scene at night, the illustration suggests the silencing and secrecy surrounding black women's experiences of sexual assault. In his column "The Onlooker," which ran alongside the cartoon, A. L. Jackson suggests that "if these white folks just must have a statue that they make it a group affair and place alongside of that mammy of sacred memory her daughter and a statue of her lord, owner and master, the slave driver, with his whip in hand." In drawing together these three figures, Jackson collapses the boundaries between af-

"Since Statues Seem to be All the Rage, Suppose We Erect One."
(*Chicago Defender*, April 21, 1923.)

fection and violence and ties cultural memories of enslavement to the contemporary racial landscape. He continues: "If mammy must be honored for nursing white babies let her also be honored for what she had to take in dishonor from the white fathers. If these white folks want to perpetuate something let them make some effort to present the whole picture."[36] The duality of the term "white fathers" or "white daddy" here is crucial, as it is employed to mark southern patriarchy and paternalism as well as white men's fatherhood, through coercion, of black women's children. Under enslavement, these children belonged, as property, to their white fathers because they belonged racially to their mothers.

Many black activists and journalists argued that the UDC's mammy commemoration was an explicit attempt to deny the prevalence of interracial sex, forced and otherwise, both in the South and beyond its regional boundaries. "Maybe the Daughters of the Confederacy wish to get their closets cleaned out by erecting a 'black mammy' statue in Washington," an anonymous editorialist for the *Defender* had suggested a month earlier. "Pale-faced sheiks will tell them that one 'yaller gal' is worth a dozen 'mammy' statues."[37] While the mammy monument was intended to expel the skeleton of miscegenation from southern closets with its focus on maternal contact between the races, the desire of menacing white "sheiks" would continue to blur the carefully drawn racial boundaries and endanger black women. The reference to eroticized "yaller gals" compounds the argument, locating the children produced by these sexual relations as most desirable to those who hypocritically decried racial mixing. The cleaning-the-closet metaphor is made even more ironic by the fact that the mammy figure was, of course, a domestic slave who literally as well as figuratively cleaned the closets.

These counternarratives of violent "affection" in the *Defender*, like those in many black weeklies, reveal the ways in which dominant notions of beauty and sexuality continued to shape their protests. Recall the image of the "white daddy" and the absence of a recognizable mammy figure within the pictorial narrative of sexual danger. While attempting to topple the very mammy iconography designed to cloak the fact of sex between white men and black women, the image reveals a similar investment in the notion that the mammy's age, size, and demeanor made her undesirable or suggested asexuality. Likewise, the use of the term "sheik," common in this period to describe womanizers and philanderers as it also marked a particular kind of Orientalist male eroticism, introduces another layer to the process of sexual racialization. A clear reference to the wildly popular 1921 Rudolph Valentino film *The Sheik*, the word acted as a useful and alluring referent in advertisements and headlines in black newspapers.[38] Adding the modifier "pale-faced" to "sheik" starkly highlights the icon's dominant remove from the category of whiteness as it simultaneously defies this racial exclusion. Once again, in this case the counternarrative cannot be detached fully from dominant racial narratives of uncivilized, unbridled male sexuality.[39]

By focusing on sex across the color line and placing the onus directly on white male predators, black critics spotlighted the nexus of racial crossings that most confounded the Daughters' vision of affectionate segregation as they simultaneously turned the lynching narrative on its head. Countering the supposed asexuality of the mammy, they figured sex as the violent core of race relations. At the same time, this assertion was a denial of the black vixen iconography that formed the other side of the white supremacist construction of black women's sexuality. Just as the mammy was utterly nonsexual, in popular white representation the uncontrollable and predatory "jezebel" figure explained the sexual relationships between black women and white men that were made unavoidably apparent by their children.

For many who stressed the damage threatened by the proposed monument, the fate of these children was a central concern. W. J. Wheaton, a columnist for the black weekly *California Eagle*, employed the tropes of both white-authored mammy iconography and black counternarrative to present a picture of the sexual assaults experienced by enslaved "mammies" and the subsequent humiliations endured by their children. "One of the most subtle means of perpetuating the humiliation of the Negro is the bill in the Senate sponsored by Sharp Williams to commemorate in marble the loyalty of the 'Black Mammies' of antebellum days," he argued.

> After debauching our womanhood who suffered the sensual attacks of their masters under duress, and creating a race which struggles for a place in the sun, they would now perpetuate their beastiality [*sic*] by erecting a marble shaft to the women who through instinct of feminine loyalty kept a vigil over the safety of the wives and children of the men who were striving to keep them in bondage. It was not enough to create a mongrel race by debauching the womanhood of the helpless peoples whom they held as chattel, but now they propose to tell the world by the erection of a marble statue that they have pride in their beastial accomplishment.[40]

References to "their beastiality" and "pride in their beastial accomplishment" identify the senators who voted for the monument bill as themselves rapists and monsters, as "white daddies." Wheaton collapses support for memorializing mammy with the act of "debauching" her, so that affection and assault become one. It should be noted that his overriding concern was clearly the biracial children produced by rape, whom he called a "mongrel race," rather than black women's constrained choices and experiences of sexual violence. Wheaton's sentiments were echoed in the *Philadelphia Tribune*, which editorialized a few weeks later: "A monument to 'black mammies' is a mockery, a farce, and a disgrace . . .

[I]t is an affront to every American citizen that descends from those saintly women who were sacrificed to the avaricious beastly nature of Southern gentlemen."[41] By naming the "white daddy" and casting "Southern gentlemen" and senators as the beasts, critics of the monument overturned the narratives of paternalism, race, and sexual danger that had shaped opposition to the Dyer anti-lynching bill.

Much like narratives of sexual coercion, activists' focus on the pain of black mothers and their love for their enslaved children tore away the myth of interracial affection promoted in the UDC's mammy memorial drive. The monument controversy provided black critics an opportunity to challenge the erasure of black motherhood that was manifest in mammy iconography, as well as to make claims about contemporary black families and communities. This was particularly true of challenges to the monument by African American clubwomen for whom the valorization of the mammy represented not just the denial of black womanhood and domesticity but a direct challenge to their own respectability, elite persona, and activism. Organized black women in Washington staged protests against the monument through direct petitions to Congress and Vice President Calvin Coolidge's office, letter-writing campaigns to white- and black-owned newspapers, and efforts within their organizations on a national scale.[42] In a letter to the editor of the *Washington Evening Star* that was reprinted in a number of black weeklies, the first president the National Association of Colored Women (NACW), Mary Church Terrell, challenged the warm sentiment conjured by the Daughters with tragic details of the family lives of enslaved women: "The black mammy had no home life. In the very nature of the case she could have none. Legal marriage was impossible for her. If she went through a farce ceremony with a slave man, he could be sold from her at any time, or she might be sold from him, or she might be taken as a concubine by her master, his son, the overseer, or any other white man on the place who might desire her."[43] Here the white household is the scene of forced work and treachery, not sentimentality, let alone civilization. "Home life," defined by Terrell as domesticity founded on marriage and motherhood, is impossible for enslaved black women, and the families they forge are "farcical" in their solubility and transience.

Just as slave marriages were constantly threatened by the domestic slave trade, estate settlements, and white debt, black motherhood was always shadowed by loss or impending loss. Terrell argued that for black women, the mammy memorial would embody a very different memory of slavery from that described by the UDC and its supporters: "No colored woman could look upon a statue of a black mammy with a dry eye when she remembered how often the slave woman's heart was torn with anguish, because the children, either of her master or their slave father, were ruthlessly torn from her in infancy or in youth to be sold 'down the country,' where, in all human probability she would never see them again."[44] Terrell's subjective transition from the "mammy" represented in the UDC's monument to the "slave mother" of the black historical counternarrative is notable. Hallie Quinn Brown, who was at the time president of the NACW as well as involved in education, made a similar argument in her protest to the monument published in the association's newspaper, *National Notes*.[45]

Loss and absence were multifaceted and did not always entail physical distance. Terrell noted that those children not sold away from their mothers were robbed of their attention. Mammies, those paragons of maternal affection and skill within white racial mythology, were unable to care for their own children or support their own families because their labors were co-opted into the white family economy: "The black mammy was often faithful in the service of her mistress's children while her heart bled over her own babies, who were thus deprived of their mother's ministrations and tender care, which the white children received."[46] In foregrounding the mammy figure's enslavement, and describing the pain and coercion this entailed, critics like Terrell emancipated the icon from white sentimentality, which refused to understand the mammy as a mother within her own black family.

Terrell's letter captured the imagination of many readers, white and black, as it was reprinted in a number of newspapers and periodicals. Originally published in a white-owned paper, it appeared widely in the black press. One such paper was the *St. Louis Argus*, where it caught the eye of *Literary Digest*, which included it among other reprints in an article titled "For and Against the 'Black Mammy's' Monument." This expanded Terrell's readership to a larger national audience. Although the substance of the letter remained unchanged, the argument shifted as it was presented for different readers. Published from 1890 to 1937, *Literary Digest* reached the peak of its readership and influence in the years following the First World War, commanding a national circulation of 900,000.[47] The *Digest's* main selling point was its claim to be a journal of national opinion that was itself without one. Each article contained excerpts and images from other papers and magazines that *Digest* editors wove into a narrative with an introduction, conclusion, and transitional sentences. The *Digest* was far from impartial, however, a fact made clear in its coverage of the monument controversy. "For and Against the 'Black Mammy's' Monument'" was weighted heavily against the memorial. But while Terrell's ideas now reached an enormous audience, she as an individual black woman did not: her authorship of the piece was not identified by the *Digest*.

The large readership provided by the reprinting of Terrell's letter nevertheless offered a prominent platform for the criticisms of white women contained in it. Terrell concluded with a severe indictment of the Daughters and all who supported their memorial. She wrote, "One cannot help but marvel at the desire to perpetuate in bronze or marble a figure which represents so much that really is and should be abhorrent to the womanhood of the whole civilized world."[48] The desire to commemorate the coercion and family ruin central to black women's enslavement was not only racist, said Terrell, but barbaric by the very standards of civilization and paternalist refinement the UDC claimed to uphold. Inverting the eugenic equation of barbarism with blackness, Terrell pushed the white women of the UDC outside the bounds of the "civilized world" and put herself, and black women generally, within it.[49]

Another prominent black clubwoman, Charlotte Hawkins Brown, was similarly direct in her challenge to the UDC, although she relied on different tactics. Employing a complex strategy of appeals to regionalism, interracial cooperation, and shame, Brown seized upon popular white concerns about the "Negro problem," charging that the UDC and its backers were actually contributing to it in their failure to support the advance of black southerners. Turning the white rhetoric of paternalistic care against them, she accused the women of shirking the very responsibilities they congratulated themselves for undertaking in the monument drive. Brown initiated a letter-writing campaign to prominent white southerners and politicians requesting that the focus of the UDC's memorial drive be turned toward funding the education of black youth. From the vantage of her position as principal of the Palmer Memorial Institute, a normal and industrial school for African Americans, and president of the North Carolina Association of Colored Women's Clubs, Brown first made her case to the director of the Woman's Department of the Southern Interracial Committee, an organization she worked with often. She urged the director to throw her own influence as a white southern woman behind efforts to encourage the UDC to redirect its energy into funding "a foundation for the education of the 'Beloved Mammies'" children," which, she claimed, would "mean more to the Negro race and spell gratitude in our hearts. Intelligent Negro women everywhere deplore such a memorial and think of it as 'hollow mockery.'"[50]

Brown found a considerably less receptive audience in Representative Charles Stedman, champion of the monument bill in the House. Brown wrote to him suggesting that it was unfortunate that such a worthy sentiment "should take the form of a 'Mammy Monument.'" With skepticism creeping into her otherwise ingratiating tone Brown continued, "If the fine spirited women, the Daughters of the Confederacy, are desirous of perpetuating their gratitude, we implore them to make the memorial in the form of a foundation for the education and advancement of the Negro children descendants of those faithful souls they seem anxious to honor."[51] Adept at reading her white audiences after years of fundraising for the Palmer Institute, Brown softened her critique of the monument significantly here and, while apparently biting her tongue, praised the spirit of the UDC's and Stedman's plan. This was not the first time Brown had sought to manipulate popular affection for the mammy figure to mobilize white southern commitments to black advancement. In 1919 she published a sentimental novella, *Mammy: An Appeal to the Heart of the South*, in an effort to shift the base of her school's financial support from northern philanthropists to white North Carolinians.[52] In *Mammy*, she crafted a distinctly regional plea suggesting that commitments to black education and interracial association in the manner of the Committee for Interracial Cooperation (CIC) were the true legacies of Old Southern paternalism. In doing so she appealed, in both senses, to the racial fantasies and status aspirations that whites expressed in their paeans to faithful slaves.

While narratives of motherhood denied were prevalent in black descriptions of the mammy figure, more common were stories of heroic black mothers working to care for their children within a range of possibilities constricted by enslavement. These stories detailed black women's motherly affections, care, and hopes for their children, despite a system that both denied those feelings and profited from that denial. Above all, these were narratives of sacrifice. The coercion of black women's maternal labor within white households carried high emotional and material costs. A critical element in the black press's deconstruction of the mammy figure was a public reckoning of that debt and the reclamation of black motherhood for black children and communities. This focus on mothering meshed with popular political narratives of black progress from slavery to freedom. Late in the monument controversy, the *Baltimore Afro-American* ran a small obituary under the headline "Her Living Monument," which identified what was most important about "mammy's" life and legacy as her black descendants:

> Dying at the age of 82, Mrs. Jane Bennett, Tenn., leaves 1,600 direct descendants, the survivors including 13 children, 142 grandchildren, 565 great grandchildren, 775 great-great grandchildren, and 100 great-great-great grandchildren. There is no better monument than excellent descendants, quality counting more than numbers, and the memory of Mrs. Jane Bennett is likely to outlast that of many other persons who rely on a towering shaft of granite.[53]

In most of these maternal progress narratives, mammies, individually or in general, were always dead. Their stories and contributions were relayed by their children and grandchildren. This served a variety of rhetorical and political purposes. In arguing that mammies were a thing of the past, dead and gone, black activists situated their supposed faithfulness, diffidence, and potential complicities in the past as well. These were characteristics that could not describe the New Negro.

A central theme in the struggles over the mammy monument was the contest over who could speak for the enslaved. When black activists and authors sought the ear of white audiences by writing letters to wide-circulation white-owned newspapers and periodicals, they often identified themselves as relatives of black mammies, thus positioning themselves as authentic spokespeople to counter the prevalence of white-produced mammy narratives. This was a direct challenge to the UDC, southern politicians, and Plantation School writers and professional historians who claimed that southern whites were the "best friends of the Negro" and knew the mammy best. In its coverage of the monument controversy, *Literary Digest* printed portions of two such letters to its editors. Introducing a submission from George Cannon as an "intimate and personal explanation" of his concerns about the monument plan, *Digest* editors noted that Cannon felt "that many Negroes of to-day are blamed for protesting against the monument idea, because their point of view is not understood." To shed light on this position, Cannon explained:

> We are not ashamed of the old black mammy, for I am the grandson of one of them. If we are not "superior grandchildren" to the old black mammy, then sixty years of training in the white man's civilization proves that his civilization is a failure. Neither are we "putting on airs" because we fail to see any virtue in our ruthless oppressors pretending to revere our grandmothers. Yes the old black mammy was "loyal, faithful and loving" to her foster white child, but I will tell you what

was in her soul! My old grandmother (one of those black mammies) used to tell me that, when the white baby was nursing her breast and her own child the other, that she sent up a prayer to God that some day her black child might be free like the white child. That is what she would say if she "could speak" to-day.[54]

While granting enslaved women's possible sincerity in their affections for their white charges, Cannon argued that whites who understood mammy only within the coercive environment of white domesticity could never *really know* her. They might have owned black women's labor and commanded their maternal care, but they could not own their emotions and their souls.

Focusing on the suffering caused by white people, black protesters heralded the sacrifices made by black women who worked for a better future for their children. Cannon's letter to the *Digest* was followed by another from an African American woman, Adella C. Williams, who identified herself as "the granddaughter of a slave mammy who went to her grave with the marks upon her body from a 'master's whip.'" Williams wrote that if she could describe the UDC's monument campaign to her grandmother, the old woman would reply:

No, child, they don't need to do no such thing as that for me. Had they helped me find my brothers and sisters sold from my mother's bosom, and my own children sold from mine, that would have been all the monument I cared for. Or if even now they would vote to give you and your children protection from mob violence and give you and yours a chance to hold a civil service position, in any department for which you were capable, instead of barring you because of your . . . skin.[55]

In a letter to the editors of the *Washington Evening Star*, Neval Thomas constructed a similar narrative of heroic black motherhood:

We are glad that the white race appreciates the divine virtues of truth and loyalty which the "black mammy" had, and has in abundance, but it overlooks the other divine virtue that is hers, a divine love for her offspring. She bore her sufferings in patience because she believed that through them America's conscience would quicken and give her children and her children's children the justice they so richly deserve. My own beloved mother was one of those unfortunates who had the flower of her youth spent in a slave cabin, and I know the heart of a slave mother, its intense longing for better things for her children.[56]

Like Cannon, Thomas concedes—or allows his white readers to believe—that the "mammy's" affections and loyalty to those who enslaved her may have been significant but challenges whites to recognize that the family she most loved was her own. Pointedly, he casts this "loyalty" to whites as fundamentally strategic, a way to better the condition of other black people, particularly black children who might one day know freedom.[57]

Common to all three of these letters intended for white readers is each writer's authenticating claim to be the child or grandchild of a mammy. This was crucial to staging the reclamation narrative within a white public sphere of newspapers and periodicals in which the fictional stories and personal reminiscences by whites "raised" by black mammies circulated more widely.[58] Within these stories of abuse, theft, and recovery, there is a slippage between representations of the mammy as a stereotypic figure—one to be replaced with the "slave mother" or "slave woman"—and potentially strategic recognitions of the figure as an actual person with a very different history from the one promoted by the UDC and other white proponents of the faithful slave narrative.

Eulogizing the enslaved mother was a way not only to reassert her affection and sacrifice but also to retrieve slavery's history and cultural memory from the grip of plantation romance. In doing this, however, black critics of the monument feminized that history, equating the Old Negro and the old days with black women. They anchored a narrative of progress within an account of enslaved mothers' contributions that gained its very momentum from the death of the feminine. This left little room for recognizing the contemporary experiences and strategies of black women in their quest for full citizenship. This was clear in the *Boston Chronicle*'s outrage over the monument scheme: "Mammy's sons and grandsons are peonized on Southern plantations; are disfranchised; are Jim Crowed on public carriers; are maltreated and lynched and—all because they are the offspring of 'Black Mammy.'"[59] This list of public humiliations, civic denials, and violence enacted against black men defines political struggle as masculine and consigns women to serving primarily as the source of the physical marker of race, a variation on the slave power rule that status followed the mother. The monument became an important vehicle for publicizing the exploitation of black women in freedom and slavery, yet there remained a surprising level of silence concerning the mammy's daughters and granddaughters. Activists like Charlotte Hawkins Brown, Mary Church Terrell, and Hallie Quinn Brown did address these issues, but they had to contend with limited access to publicity as well as negotiate the tight gender confines of the dominant culture and the fight for black freedom.

As critics of the memorial campaign came to focus on the descendants of enslaved mothers, the fate of one "son" in particular, Walter L. Cohen, took center stage in the black press. In the same week the Senate passed the monument bill, the *Washington Tribune* drew an explicit comparison between the treatment of "'Mammy's' Monument vs. 'Mammy's Son.'" On "Tuesday of this week," the *Tribune* reported, "the Senate turned down the President's nomination of Walter Cohen . . .

for Collector of Customs for the Port of New Orleans. That was the Senate's tribute to Mammy's son."[60] In the weeks that followed a number of black newspapers and periodicals would similarly report these actions of the Senate in tandem. As the southern Democrats' filibuster of the Dyer antilynching bill had continued day after day in late 1922, other legislation and business awaited the attention of the Senate, which was due to recess for the holidays. Foremost among these was the confirmation of nearly one thousand presidential nominees, including Harding's nomination of Walter L. Cohen for the customs post of comptroller of the Port of New Orleans. A longtime black Republican operative in Louisiana and federal appointee during the McKinley and Roosevelt administrations, Cohen was a familiar figure to many in the South and was known to African American readers of black-owned newspapers across the country. His nomination, and the Senate battles it sparked over the next two years, thrust him into the national spotlight as never before, however.

Regardless of their individual political affiliations, most in the black press cheered the president's nomination because it was the first federal appointment for an African American since the Theodore Roosevelt administration. Cohen, a confidant and political ally of Booker T. Washington, was an attorney and a successful businessman in New Orleans as well as a powerful figure among Louisiana Republicans. His work for the party dated back to Reconstruction, when he had been a page in the Louisiana state legislature, and more recently had included service as secretary of the Louisiana State Republican Committee and as a delegate to the Republican national conventions of 1912, 1916, and 1920. He had held federal appointments under two earlier presidents, acting as register of the Land Office in Louisiana during the McKinley and Roosevelt administrations.[61]

When the possibility of Cohen's nomination for the customs position was first reported in the summer of 1922, many expected an easy confirmation. They were surprised when just weeks after the announcement the governor of Louisiana, John Parker, went to Washington to ask Harding to withdraw Cohen's name. When the president refused, Parker went to the Senate and made a public plea to the body at large that it deny confirmation. Some chalked the performance up to Parker's desire to challenge Senator Joseph Ransdell for his seat in the approaching Louisiana Democratic primary.[62] Wondering if Harding would "stick to Cohen" in the aftermath of the midterm elections, in which Republicans had lost so many seats, the *Baltimore Afro-American* noted that Parker freely admitted that his "only objection is that Mr. Cohen happens to be a Negro."[63] Not to be outdone by the governor, Ransdell and his fellow Louisiana Democratic senator, Edwin Broussard, also voiced their objections to the appointment.

When the Senate adjourned in December without confirming Cohen, Harding made a formal nomination for consideration after the holidays. In the meantime, Ransdell and Broussard filed their objections with the Commerce Committee, and Walter Cohen traveled to Washington to meet with Republican senators and make his own case. Finding the Louisiana senators' objections to be based only on the nominee's race and thus insufficient, the committee reported the nomination favorably. At that point Ransdell and Broussard made it known that they would rely on the tradition of senatorial courtesy to defeat Cohen. Customarily, the Senate would deny an appointment if senators from the nominee's state claimed that he was "personally obnoxious" to them. In presenting such a claim the senators were not required to make explicit their objections. The strategy had been employed before to defeat the nominations of African Americans and would be used again after the Cohen debacle. In March, Cohen's nomination was defeated by a vote of 35 to 27. Ten Republicans, dubbed the "Traitor 10" by the *Chicago Defender*, were among those voting against. The roll call had been sealed, but black journalists quickly set out to discover and publish the identities of the "traitors." This did not spell the end of Cohen's appointment struggle, however. Harding waited for the Senate to adjourn and then gave Cohen the position in a recess appointment. When Harding died in office, Calvin Coolidge carried on his predecessor's drive to get Cohen formally appointed to the post. It would eventually take two presidents, two years, constitutional debates, and political threats, but Walter L. Cohen was finally confirmed as comptroller of the Port of New Orleans in March 1924 by a vote of 39 to 38. He had been serving in the position for over a year with no salary, and would go on to hold the post until his death in 1929.[64]

As the Sixty-seventh Congress became history in March 1923, the mammy monument bill and the initial failure of Cohen's confirmation came together in the black press in a larger narrative of the Senate's overriding racism and refusal to respect the rights of African Americans. This was driven by other legislative failures, most notably the defeat of the Dyer bill. Throughout March and April a number of black newspapers and periodicals reflecting diverse regional and political stances reported the passage of the monument bill and the defeat of Cohen's confirmation together, either in the same story or positioned side by side on the page.[65] They drew cognitive and political links between the faithful mammy held in such high esteem by the senators and the party faithful Republican "son" denied a federal job by southern Democrats as well as members of his own party. The *Chicago Defender* connected the two in a single, infuriated headline that highlighted the gender underpinnings of this protest: "Monument to 'Mammy' Wins Senate—Pays Respect to Uncle Tom's Wife; Refuses to Give a Man's Job to W. L. Cohen."[66]

The troubled Cohen appointment brought into focus arguments within black communities concerning the efficacy of unwavering support for the Republican Party and the ability of traditional party politics to achieve black aims. The decline of Booker T. Washington's political machine and the rise of the NAACP signaled a shift in the character of interracial political collaborations and the historical investments of black elites in Republican Party activism and the federal government. Although the Wilson presidency had reenergized black commitments to the Republican Party, contributing to the wide support of African Americans for Harding in 1920, many no longer automatically associated their best interests with the "party of Lincoln." Masses of black working people who had long been alienated from formal politics continued to move to southern cities or migrated out of the region in ever-increasing numbers, pushing black leaders to follow in their more radical footsteps. Some looked to the labor activism and socialist philosophy espoused in the pages of A. Philip Randolph and Chandler Owen's magazine *The Messenger*. Many more joined Marcus Garvey's United Negro Improvement Association.

The concept of the New Negro took on fresh meaning in the context of these political struggles. Where the label had once been employed by Booker T. Washington and those of similar social and political ilk, activist-journalists like Randolph and Owen now aggressively appropriated the term to call for a widespread revolution of black workers.[67] They shifted the axis of Old and New, positioning the gradualism of Washington and the liberal reform agenda of the NAACP, along with the capitalist individualism that defined them both, as passé, inefficient, and complicit with white supremacy. Rather than displace the association of the Old Negro with slavery, however, this articulation of the New Negro melded servility with accommodation and called it "Uncle Tomism." Several editors and writers who disagreed with *The Messenger*'s economic critique but believed in the need for new strategies similarly examined the failure of Cohen's confirmation and the passage of the monument bill through the lens of New Negro politics.

Where others in the black press employed this pairing to decry the injustice of Cohen's defeat, *The Messenger* argued that he was just as detrimental to black struggles for political and economic justice as the mammy figure. The journal celebrated the failure of Cohen's confirmation because it exposed the contempt of both political parties for black people and struck a blow against liberal reform efforts:

> Another slap in the face for the colored Republican brethren! Still, for the rank and file it is a blessing, for we are relieved of the encumbrance of one more reactionary, hat-in-hand, me-to-boss job holder, who can be of no earthly service to the race. On the contrary, such appointments are a positive menace, for they tend to make Negroes think they have got *something* when in reality they have got *nothing*. It lulls them into a false sense of security. FIFTEEN MILLION TOILING NEGROES CAN RECEIVE NO BENEFIT FROM ONE OR TWO BIG NEGROES RECEIVING FAT JOBS. A rational political policy will concern itself with the economic and social life of the LITTLE NEGROES, those who sweat from sunrise to sunset for a bare existence.[68]

On the preceding page, adjacent to the article on Cohen as readers held the magazine in their hands, was an editorial by Chandler Owen about the mammy monument. This time, however, the juxtaposition was not between the Old mammy and a New politician; rather the two were linked as complimentary parts of the same Old problem. Titled simply "Black Mammies," the article was bordered at the bottom with the subhead, "This Is the New Negro's View of the Black Mammies' Monument."[69]

Owen devoted his article to a discussion of the power of monuments to shape political culture and to delineating the characteristics of the new working-class black militant—to outlining everything that Cohen was not. He opened with a long discourse on the potential of memorial art to shape the political future. Like others, Owen argued that equating the history of slavery with the mammy figure would be detrimental to the civic and civil aspirations of the new generation of African Americans. "We want the children of this generation to abhor and forget those days" of enslavement and white domination, he urged. "We want to orient ourselves—turn our faces from the dark and discouraging past, and direct it toward a bright and hopeful future." If anyone was to be honored in the capital, let it be the black Union soldiers of the Civil War, he suggested. Erect a statue to those "who fought to wipe out slavery and to unfurl the flag of freedom and let it float like a cloud over this land. We favor a salute to these men who helped save the Union, who indeed were a great factor in crushing out the iniquitous viper—slavery—which had vitiated the entire American atmosphere with its venomous and poisonous breath."[70] By turning from the figure of the mammy to the black Union soldier, Owen countered the nostalgic white supremacist figure of the faithful slave with its historical antithesis, the enslaved man who freed himself to fight for the freedom of others. He heralded black men as the agents of democracy who had earned their citizenship because they were its best expression.

Chandler Owen was not alone in calling for a memorial to honor the sacrifice and valor of these men. In 1916 a National Memorial Association was organized for the purpose of erecting in Washington a monument to "commemorate the heroic deeds of the Negro soldiers and sailors in all the wars of our country." The expansive language was intended to include those who had fought in the American Revolution, the Civil War, the Spanish-American War, and World War I. Three years later, while working for passage of his anti-lynching legislation, Leonidas Dyer introduced a bill to empanel a commission for choosing a site and a design for the structure, but it was blocked because of economic concerns. The passage of the mammy monument bill brought new urgency to the campaign for a soldiers' and sailors' memorial. Listing the National Memorial Association's officers and board, which included Robert R. Moton and Adam Clayton Powell, the *Chicago Defender* reported that they were "doing work in sharp contrast to the humiliating and insulting 'Mammy Monument.'" The association's plan would never be realized, however. A monument to black veterans of the Civil War, called *The Spirit of Freedom*, would have to wait until the summer of 1998 to be erected in Washington, D.C..[71]

Meanwhile, another monument was needed, Owen argued, to commemorate the men fighting in the streets and on shop floors under the banner of "the New Negro, who [are] carving a new monument in the hearts of our people." Build a memorial, he urged, for "the Negroes of Washington, Chicago, Longview, Texas, Knoxville, Tenn., Tulsa, Okla., and Philadelphia, who rose in their might and said to the authorities: 'If you cannot protect us, we will protect ourselves—if you cannot uphold the law, we will maintain constituted authority.'"[72] This list of cities would have been recognized at once by readers as among those torn by bloody race riots during Red Summer. The New Negro was a soldier for justice, in Owen's estimation, who defended democratic institutions and protected "constituted authority" because the agencies and individuals entrusted with that task would not.

The subjects Owen proposed to be most worthy of monumental honors reveal the contours of his vision of the New Negro and the black freedom struggle. Owen concluded his critique of the mammy memorial by suggesting a very different monument to the black mother—not the enslaved woman of historical sacrifice but a "New Negro Mother": "Let this 'mammy' statue go. Let it fade away. Let it be buried in that blissful oblivion to which the brave sons of this nation have consigned it; and when it rises again, let its white shaft point like a lofty mountain peak to a *New Negro Mother*, no longer a *'white man's woman,'* no longer the sex-enslaved *'black Mammy'* of Dixie—but the apotheosis of triumphant Negro womanhood."[73] While this would ostensibly be a monument to motherhood, Owen's primary focus was still to honor the "brave sons" who would consign the mammy and her memorial to the bin of historical "oblivion" in order to claim black women, meaning their sexuality and their motherly affections, as their own.

In one of the few essays in Alain Locke's edited collection *The New Negro* (1925) to address directly the experiences of black women, Elise Johnson McDougald could not "resist the temptation to pause for a moment and pay tribute to these Negro mothers," working women who "face the problem of leaving home each day and at the same time trying to raise children in their spare time." Although it was published almost two years after the conclusion of the mammy commemoration controversy, McDougald's contribution, "The Task of Negro Womanhood," showed that the UDC's campaign was still fresh in her mind as she sought to counter both the mammy narrative and the overwhelming focus of New Negro politics on the future prospects and abilities of black men. "If the mothers of the race should ever be honored by state or federal legislation," she wrote, "the artist's imagination will find a more inspiring subject in the modern Negro mother—self-directed but as loyal and tender as the

much extolled, yet pitiable black mammy of slavery days."
Devoted to explicating African American working women's
lives and toil, in its very title the essay suggested poignantly
that being a black woman in America was in itself hard work.
And lurking all around that labor was the figure of the faithful slave mammy.[74]

6 CONFRONTING THE MAMMY PROBLEM

*In the first place, you do not love me; you may be fond
of me, but that is all . . . In the second place, I am not
just like one of the family . . . You think it is a compli-
ment when you say, "We don't think of her as a servant . . .[,]" but after I have worked myself into a
sweat cleaning the bathroom and the kitchen . . .
making beds . . . cooking the lunch . . . washing the
dishes and ironing . . . I do not feel like no weekend
house guest. I feel like a servant, and in the face of
that I have been meaning to ask you for a slight raise
which will make me feel much better toward everyone
here and make me know my work is appreciated.*

—Alice Childress, *Like One of the Family:
Conversations from a Domestic's Life*, 1956

THE FAITHFUL SLAVE NARRATIVE presented particular dilemmas
for black women as workers, activists, mothers, and citizens
in the twentieth century—a "mammy problem." They struggled with dominant white supremacist conceptions of black
women's servitude, maternity, and sexuality, as well as black
activist understandings of African American civic identity
and racial progress as fundamentally masculine. This was

particularly true for black domestic workers, the largest segment of black women's paid labor in the early twentieth century, who faced a white popular culture that persistently conflated or compared their work and their lives with the fictitious mammy figure.[1]

The United Daughters of the Confederacy had proposed its national mammy memorial in the midst of that era's dramatic transformation of domestic service. By the 1910s, hired household labor in the United States was increasingly defined as the sole purview of non-white women, predominantly African Americans. At the same time, the conditions under which this work was performed were also shifting. For the first time, a majority of domestic laborers no longer lived in their employers' homes; instead they demanded set hours and wages rather than the nebulous workday of the live-in servant, on the job all the time. The faithful mammies whom the UDC saw as a generation quickly passing away represented a domestic service relationship that was passing away as well. This fact was widely lamented by whites as the "servant problem" of the early twentieth century, which was easily conflated with that period's supposed "Negro problem."

Persistent attempts by employers to cast the domestic workers they employed in the mold of the faithful mammy came at great cost to black women. A woman identified only as "A Negro Nurse" described to a journalist oppressively long days and terrible wages as a live-in servant in an unnamed southern city in 1912. She was allowed only one Sunday afternoon every two weeks with her children, who in turn were prohibited from visiting her at the home she worked and lived in. Except for those afternoons, she was on duty twenty-four hours a day. "It's 'Mammy, do this,' or 'Mammy, do that,' or 'Mammy, do the other,' from my mistress all the time. So it is not strange to see 'Mammy' watering the lawn in front with the garden hose, sweeping the sidewalk, mopping the porch and halls, dusting around the house, helping the cook, or darning stockings . . . You might as well say that I'm on duty all the time—from sunrise to sunrise, every day in the week. I am the slave, body and soul, of this family."[2] This woman's story reveals how the continuing effects of both racial slavery and popular historical memory shaped twentieth-century domestic work. The demands of this domestic worker's job felt like a reconstitution of enslavement, while her employer's insistence on calling her "Mammy" was an expression of the white woman's fantasy of having a slave.

Black women who performed domestic labor were not alone in grappling with the mammy problem, but their struggles were specific to them. All black women confronted, and continue to face, the faithful slave narrative in the figure of the mammy. The challenge of black clubwomen to the mammy memorial was emblematic of their responses to the mammy problem, both of them framed in terms of "uplift" and the "politics of respectability."[3] Analyzing their activism, which is revealed through dense archives of national newsletters, the black press, and the collected papers of many of the movement's leaders, makes clear the difficulty of finding the historical voices of domestic workers. These women left few documents deemed worthy of the archives, and they were written *about* much more than they were allowed to speak for themselves. Reading these kinds of documents alongside first-person narratives of white and black women's experiences of hiring and doing paid domestic work nevertheless makes it possible to piece together black women's struggles not only for justice in the workplace, emotional and physical safety, and civic self-determination, but also in contending with the figure of the faithful slave. In published oral interviews collected in the 1980s, women recall experiences dating as far back as the 1920s.[4] They do so from a position of significant historical distance, however, across intervening years marked by the civil rights movement and feminism and the radicalization of both in the late 1960s and 1970s. The fact that the faithful slave narrative, and the notions of family, hierarchy, tradition, and segregation embedded in it, remained so powerful in the minds and actions of these informants is a testament to its lasting hold on American culture.

At the same time, however, the oral histories reveal how tenuous the grip of the idea of faithful slavery became in the aftermath of the Montgomery bus boycott. In the year of its success, which would not have been possible without the perseverance of the city's domestic workers, Alice Childress published *Like One of the Family: Conversations from a Domestic's Life* (1956).[5] Written in the voice of Mildred, a funny, angry, politically astute domestic worker originally from the South but living and working in New York City, the novel challenged the faithful slave narrative while exploring what it meant to confront it on a daily basis. Mildred gives her employers no room to assume that she loves them, to imagine that she is their mammy, or that they actually love her. Thousands of domestic workers walking the streets of Montgomery, Alabama, in protest had been telling their employers the same thing.

The much decried "servant problem" of the post–World War I period referred not to a lack of workers to perform domestic labor but rather to the dearth of women willing to do that work under the conditions that had characterized it at the turn of the century. "Servants," most of them now black women, became a "problem" when they refused to live in, began working for multiple families, demanded fixed hours and set wages, and simply walked away from homes where these demands were not met. The figure of the enslaved black mammy stood at the center of this "problem" for both employers and black domestic workers. The white women who continued to be largely responsible for hiring and managing household labor longed to see their employees as faithful black caretakers but were commonly discouraged in their efforts to do so. Confounding these desires, and their concomitant effects on one's personal dignity, wages, and work conditions, was a daily struggle for black women who resisted the "mammy" label and the behaviors it demanded.

By 1920, domestic work in the United States was performed primarily by black women, who had available to them few other options for employment. The census for that year shows that 46 percent of all employed black women were in "domestic and personal service," which largely included work as household servants or launderers. This figure continued to grow with the entrenched racialization of domestic labor, increasing to 53 percent in 1930 and 60 percent in 1940.[6] Many factors contributed to these numbers, including the increasing options and needs for white women's employment, the explicit funneling of black women into domestic service by the educational system and employment offices, and the intertwined political economies of racism and gender discrimination.

Not indicated in these figures, but equally significant, was the fact that by the 1920s, few domestic workers in the United States still lived in the homes in which they were employed. This mass movement from "living in" to "living out," while never absolute, was the result of black women's broad refusal to sustain the fantasies of ownership and limitless service entertained by many of their employers. Refusing to live in was a concrete denial of the domestic arrangements that had allowed employers to describe these black women as "like one of the (white) family." This shift from "servitude to service work" denoted, in part, domestic workers' attempts to define themselves, and to be defined, as people who performed a certain job rather than being identified inherently and categorically as servants.[7] The experiences of many black women who migrated north were shaped by a "determination to transform a master-servant relationship into an employer-employee relationship."[8] Migrants were not alone in their determination, however, and although the old pattern was often more difficult to disrupt in the South, changes to it were still significant there.

This dramatic transformation made greater self-determination possible for black women and increased their opportunities for influencing the conditions of their own labor. Most notably, day work made it easier to quit a job where wages were especially low, or unpaid, where conditions were especially bad, or where a woman was physically, emotionally, or sexually endangered. The qualification "especially" here is crucial, however, because throughout the period, hours remained very long, wages depressed, and conditions often terrible. State-level protective legislation rarely included domestic and agricultural workers among those covered by minimum wage and maximum hour provisions—the two categories in which black women were most highly concentrated. In her 1923 study of domestic work in the United States, Elizabeth Ross Haynes, who had served as domestic service employment secretary in the U.S. Employment Service from 1920 to 1922, noted that of the twelve states with such laws covering women and children, none explicitly included domestic workers in private homes. Three states explicitly excluded these women, and seven failed to include domestic service at all in the categories of "occupations and industries" covered under the acts.[9] Haynes called for greater state and federal regulation of domestic service, as well as increased training in public schools. The latter suggestion emerged from her contradictory logic that wages would rise if the field were professionalized and the work more highly valued, while at the same time absenteeism and turnover, the crux of the "servant problem," would decrease if black women were trained to think of themselves as professionals with responsibilities to their employers. This reasoning was based on her specious assumption that this "problem" stemmed from the personal failings of black domestics rather than resistance to unfair labor practices.

Despite the long hours and the isolating nature of private domestic labor, some domestic workers in the 1920s and 1930s managed to form cooperatives or unions to petition for inclusion in protective legislation, government regulation, and the right to negotiate contracts collectively. Organized domestic workers had a legacy dating back at least to the famed Atlanta washerwomen's strike of 1881. It is notable that while their numbers were limited, many of these domestic workers' unions formed in other southern cities.[10] More effective and far more common than unions were the cooperative associations or "penny-saver" clubs many workers organized, participated in, and socialized through. These cooperatives served a variety of social and economic purposes, not the least of which was enabling members to make individual savings from tight wages and providing emergency funds when their expenses could not be met.[11] These kinds of clubs, designed to ameliorate labor exploitation, legal neglect, and isolation, continued to be a significant source of financial and emotional support for domestic workers throughout the early twentieth century. At the same time, the fact of their existence denotes the workers' continued lack of access to federal, state, and local labor protections. A Department of Labor Women's Bureau report published fifteen years after Haynes's study revealed that very little had changed in this respect by the late 1930s: "Rough estimates made in the Women's Bureau indicate that only about 1 in 10 of all Negro women workers are covered potentially by minimum-wage legislation . . . It is evident that minimum-wage laws thus far have not been an important factor in raising the wages of the bulk of Negro women workers."[12] This was true largely because southern political pressure resulted in New Deal legislation that recapitulated state exclusions of domestic and agricultural workers at the federal level.[13]

Less easily quantified than issues of wages and hours were the unique conditions of domestic labor. The spatial proximity to employers gave black workers intimate knowledge of white families' "private" lives, and these arrangements were shot through with suspicion, desire, and emotional demands on the part of white employers.[14] This emotionally larded spatial intimacy was pervasive in the contexts of southern domestic labor, but the long-standing national romance with the plantation idyll and its narrative of the faithful slave also shaped the desires and expectations of white employers outside the South who hired recently migrated black women. They searched the women's accents and colloquialisms, listening for the mammy's soft, loving croon described so often in plantation fiction.[15]

A domestic worker's failure to return to a job, perceived "insolence," or refusal to muster visible affection for employers were all seen as breaches of contract. But in denying the intimacy whites craved or flouting the mutual obligations of paternalism, workers made it terribly clear that these were not commonly shared investments. This rendered employers' desire for faithful mammies all the stronger, as they looked wistfully back at a time when, they believed, domestics had not behaved so defiantly.[16] Herein lay the crux of the "mammy problem," in which racial inequality and unrealistic expectations combined with low wages, long hours, and the punitive resentment of employers. Surely some domestic workers found it easier to perform the role, discovering that there were some gains to be had from sustaining the fantasy of an emotional relationship in their jobs. The costs of such strategies of dissemblance are difficult to measure but were no doubt profound.[17]

Two articles published within months of each other in the *New York Times* in 1919 and 1920 are widely emblematic of white perceptions of what exactly constituted the "servant problem," and the resulting nostalgia for the supposed faithful servitude of southern slavery and pliant antebellum black labor. In "House with No Servant Problem," Hortense McDonald marveled at a farm in Tennessee "where for fifty-four years the man of all work has always been on the job, where for forty-five years the mistress hasn't worried about a cook, where for thirty years the laundress has never gone on a strike, and where for twenty-five years the gardener has faithfully tended his garden." Astounded, she continued: "This is a true story. It concerns the loyalty and devotion of a group of antebellum negroes who in these days of servant problems, strikes for higher wages and clashes of temperament over 'conditions' have stuck to their posts, giving years of faithful endeavor as their measure of service." Leaving no doubt that underlying this estimation of "loyalty" was the fantasy of benevolent slavery, McDonald spelled out the association explicitly for her readers: "All of them are 'befo' de wah' types. Like the veterans of that day, they are rapidly passing away. While they last, however, they know no other creed than that of duty to the family that 'raised' them and 'de chillun' they in turn 'raised.'" Casting slavery as a civilizing institution that also made possible the "raising" of faithful workers, McDonald devotes much of the article to the epitome of this service, the "black mammy . . . who has mothered the five grown men of the family and presided in the kitchen for forty-seven years."[18]

While readers of the *Times* puzzled over where they might

find this kind of domestic help in New York City, the paper offered a suggestion a few months later: "Why Not Import Your Servant?" Referring to the massive dislocations of European workers generated by World War I, the article opens provocatively: "Thousands of young women would like to become domestic servants in New York homes. Moreover, as a class they have been brought up in conditions that have inculcated economy, neatness, and respect for the desires of the mistress of the house." The article urged potential employers frenzied over New York's "servant problem" to cast their eyes across the Atlantic, where relief, faithful service, and the grateful appreciation of a live-in domestic was only a "quickly crossed" ocean away.[19] Built largely around interviews with the U.S. Bureau of Immigration and one of New York State's congressional representatives in Washington, D.C., the article assured readers that the importation of private household help would not run afoul of recent immigration restrictions and was exempted from the contract labor exclusion. The article made clear that it was also legal to pay the ocean passage of a contracted private domestic worker in advance within the complex web of immigration legislation passed after the war and prior to the mass exclusions of the 1924 Immigration Act.

The framework of indenture was legal, the article claimed, but risky, given the literacy test immigrants were required to pass upon their arrival. This lent great significance to New York congressman Isaac Siegel's fight to amend the literacy requirement with an exemption for domestic workers. Educated Europeans proficient in English were unlikely to seek jobs as domestics, he argued, "and to keep the bar of illiteracy as respects servants will have the effect of preventing the relief needed. The ability to read twenty words is not so important as that. What fine cooks the old 'black mammies' were, and they could not read a word."[20] Within the logic of the article, and in Siegel's estimation, the best example of the good servant was the enslaved black mammy, whose presumed illiteracy—the product of her enslavement—was not a hindrance to her performance but a benefit. Siegel's nostalgic reference to slavery in what is essentially a call to replace free black workers by exploiting a devastated European population amplifies the implications of "importing" labor from across the Atlantic.

Reliance on immigrant domestic workers was nothing new. It had long characterized household service in the Southwest and West, particularly the employment of Latinas and Asian women and men. As racial definitions of this work hardened after the First World War, the trend continued in these regions, encompassing recent immigrants as well as Native Americans and U.S.-born Asians and Latinas. The structural inequalities, labor laws, and educational practices that confined so many African American women to domestic labor similarly affected these populations.[21] Segregated public education was a primary engine of this tracking, both in its emphasis on industrial training for nonwhite students and in the consequent neglect of the humanities, arts, and sciences. Despite this, many of those who decried the "servant problem" and, in the case of black workers, found it to be part and parcel of the "Negro problem," pointed to failures in education as a significant causal factor. Lurking heavily about these claims was the implied assertion that the absence of slavery, the "plantation school," was the true culprit.

This was never clearer than in the founding of the Black Mammy Memorial Institute in Athens, Georgia, in 1910. According to a local white-owned newspaper, the *Banner*, the idea for the institute came to its founders in response to publicity surrounding various campaigns in southern communities to commemorate the enslaved mammy, a trend deemed significant enough by the *Banner* to be termed "The Black

Mammy Memorial Movement."[22] Rather than mourn the passing of the "old-time Negroes," the founders insisted that contemporary southern black workers could be trained in their fashion, and that the institute could graduate new generations of mammies:

> There is a movement well under way to erect a monument to the memory of the "Old Black Mammies of the South" in the form of a memorial industrial building in Athens, Ga. You will notice that it will not be a shaft of stone—cold and speechless—but a living monument where the sons and daughters of these distinctively Southern characters may be trained in the arts and industries that made the "old Black Mammy" valuable and worthy of the tender memory of the South. It will be a memorial where men and women learn to work, how to work and love their work; where the mantle of the "Old Black Mammy" may fall on those who go forth to serve, where the stories of these women will be told to the generations that come and go.[23]

Underscored in this assertion are the mingled "Negro problem" and the "servant problem," which in the South included black migration out of the region and away from exploitation in the homes, fields, and shops of the school's founders. The notion that black southerners must be taught "how to work and love their work" makes clear the ideologies of racial inferiority that assumed African Americans' flight from these labor conditions to be the product of their laziness, irresponsibility, and lack of respect for white employers.

The institute was started with a land grant and $2,000 from the city of Athens, then turned to private investments from southerners across the region to raise funds for classroom buildings, shops, dormitories, and teachers' salaries. Its promotional material appealed to popular longings for the black mammy figure, much as the UDC would in its national memorial campaign a decade later. Yet while the national memorial was intended to be widely instructive to both black and white Americans, the institute's founders believed that a "cold and speechless" monument was simply not equal to the task at hand. The failures of contemporary black workers to conform to the mammy model were too great and the need for training too dire:

> The MONUMENTAL INDUSTRIAL INSTITUTE to the "OLD BLACK MAMMY" of the South will be devoted to the industrial and moral training of young negro men and women. The work that is to receive special emphasis is the training of young women in DOMESTIC ART . . . The young men will be taught the trades, INDUSTRIAL STABILITY and SKILL in the trades and domestic arts, and especially the proper regard for the SACREDNESS of CONTRACT are among the GREATEST, if not the greatest, NEED of the WORKERS of the race. The MORAL EFFORT of this institution is to train students to a deeper sense of the merits of a reliable, intelligent and concentrated life to service for which they are best fitted.[24]

"Moral" education would inculcate within individual workers a commitment to racially defined capitalist labor relations in which the measure of faithfulness was the "sacredness of contract" and the unquestioned, grateful acceptance of conditions defined by employers, of hierarchies set and dominated by whites, and of a belief in one's "place."[25] The institution of slavery had provided this training in the past, the founders claimed, and had sustained an organic paternalism. Black freedom had ripped these relationships apart, unsettling the very foundations of southern society and economies, and necessitating, they argued, the artificial replacement of the Mammy Institute:

> The Black Mammy was trained in a school that passed with the institutions of her day. Where shall those who receive her mantle be fitted for the places that were dignified by the industry, purity and fidelity of those distinctively Southern

characters whom the South loved and will ever hold in tender memory. Shall not her MEMORIAL, the MONUMENTAL INDUSTRIAL INSTITUTE, perpetuate not only her memory but her SPIRIT of SERVICE in the lives of her children and grandchildren?[26]

Romantic notions of paternalist race and labor relations embodied in the mammy figure were defined in this vision of New Southern capitalism and industrial growth. Here one set of presumed historical obligations was made to stand in for another—the contractual relationship.

While the school was intended to fit contemporary black workers to the frameworks of racial hierarchy, industrial and domestic labor, and the modern paternalism of "affectionate" segregation, it was also heralded as signaling a new epoch in interracial cooperation among southern elites. Credited with the idea for the school and its name, University of Georgia chancellor D. C. Barrow would later say this honor belonged to an African American, Samuel F. Harris, the institute's principal, who, along with four other black residents of the city, constituted the school's "Board of Colored Directors." Harris was a prominent black educator in the mold of Booker T. Washington who had at one time been the principal of the public Athens Colored High School. Frustrated by "classical high school" education and what he perceived to be a shortage of effective industrial courses, resulting in the overeducation and undertraining of black youth, Harris left the public system to found an independent evening school for industrial training in 1909.[27] The all-white board of trustees was a veritable Who's Who of the political and industrial elite of Athens and the state broadly, including the presidents of the Athens Electric Railway Company, the Moss Cotton Company, and the Georgia Northeastern Bank of Commerce, as well as a former mayor of Atlanta, a former governor of the state, and the aforementioned chancellor of the university. Among the original incorporating trustees were also the presidents of the Southern Mutual Insurance Company and the Empire State Chemical Company.[28] This collection of individuals starkly highlighted the investment of the New South in the sentiments and activism of the Lost Cause.

The Black Mammy Memorial Institute was one of many attempts to establish private schools of domestic training for African Americans designed to assuage the "servant problem." While others were not so explicit in their desire to create modern mammies, visions of faithful service girded by modern economic relationships fashioned in the fantastic image of Old Southern paternalism remained a central goal. In 1921 and 1922, for example, the Domestic Efficiency Association of Baltimore, Maryland, operated a training school for black domestics that offered a complete one-month course and optional shorter-term lessons. The tuition and board was $5 a week, or $20 for the full course, the equivalent of about three weeks' wages. If a student were unable to pay the tuition up front, she could still attend by agreeing to secure work only through the association and repaying the debt at a rate of at least $2.50 a week.[29] Given the likelihood that few women could afford the tuition in advance, the program was designed to keep workers tied closely to association members through their debt. As a response to the living-out trend, this training method afforded increased levels of employer surveillance and control over black women's mobility.

Black clubwomen such as those in the National Association of Colored Women similarly urged training and the professionalization of domestic service, although to very different political ends. Like Samuel F. Harris and Booker T. Washington, they believed that professional behavior, evident skills, and modern techniques would elevate the menial positions to which so many black women were relegated.

This elevation in status would in turn help to lift the race and facilitate the gradual accumulation of civil and political rights, in part by impressing white employers disgruntled with the "servant problem." NACW members founded the National Training School for Women and Girls in 1909 to meet this goal, among others.[30]

Despite the increased independence provided by the move to day work, domestic workers still faced long hours on the job, extended commutes to their places of work in segregated neighborhoods, additional long hours at home attending to their own housework and families, and consequent exhaustion. "Leisure time" was often without much leisure. But relaxation, socializing, entertainment, club activities, and, for many, involvement with churches, in addition to an improved quality of family life, were all made possible in the transition to living out. The prevalence of day work as the dominant mode of domestic labor, however, worried employers since it did not allow them to know what workers did with their free time and where they spent it. A statement from the president of the Baltimore Domestic Efficiency Association in 1924 reveals the intense suspicion many white employers had concerning workers' time away from the homes they toiled in:

> The desire to live out so prevalent today among the negro workers should be discouraged for many reasons principally on the serious question of health. Negroes are notoriously prey to disease, particularly to tuberculosis, a veritable scourge among them. Most negro women who demand to go home at night do so for two reasons. Either they really go to their homes to do the work they must neglect during the day, or particularly the younger ones, want to amuse themselves and spend much too large a portion of the nights at dances, movies, festivals, etc. In either case, they are trying to burn their candles at both ends, and their health suffers, while the employer suffers from a tired servant utterly unequal to the requirements of her day's work.[31]

The association president assumed that once the women were released from the discipline and careful watch of the white household, their feckless pursuits would make them ineffective as workers, whether they spent their time watching a movie or doing their own housework. The fear that living out put the domestic at risk of contracting tuberculosis and then, more to the point, exposed her employers to infection reveals the deep discomfort engendered by household workers' easy passage across segregated communities and into white domestic spaces.[32]

While workers who refused to play mammy were perceived as potential sources of contagion, poisoning white society, the lack of twenty-four-hour surveillance troubled many whites with the nagging fear that the women they *did* consider faithful, loving caretakers might not be. In his 1941 memoir and thick declaration of his own elite, paternalist racial knowledge, *Lanterns on the Levee: Recollections of a Planter's Son*, William Alexander Percy warned, "The gentle, devoted creature who is your baby's nurse can carve her boy-friend from ear to ear at midnight and by seven A.M. will be changing the baby's diaper while she sings 'Hear the Lambs a-calling.'"[33]

Recalling her years of hiring black domestic workers and a childhood populated with similar women employed by her mother, Mary Patricia Foley told researcher Susan Tucker about a former maid, Delores: "Delores had worked for my mother. Everybody's dream, I know, to have a maid who used to work for your mother."[34] Foley's assumption that Tucker, also a white southerner, would quickly recognize this as a "dream" common to all white women like themselves is telling. She describes the passage of racial and gendered domestic authority from one generation to another, a continuity figured through the working and (presumed) affectionate body of a single black woman. This triangulation makes possible a belief in the historic continuities of hierarchy, as

Delores, whose last name Foley never recalls, came to work for her in the midst of the civil rights activism of the late 1950s and early 1960s.[35] The "dream" displaced, but deeply present here, is the fantasy of ownership, mutual affection, and faithful black service; it is the dream of having a mammy. For Foley's generation, this fantasy was reinvigorated by the popularity of the film version of *Gone With the Wind* and Hattie McDaniel's portrayal in it of the character identified only as "Mammy."[36]

White women employed a variety of tactics to convince themselves and the black women they hired that theirs was a unique, emotionally potent relationship. This was no simple matter of "cold" employer-employee interactions, they would insist, but the expression of the mutual obligations and affections of paternalism draped in popular white recollections of the plantation South.[37] Scholars of domestic labor have noted the powerful historic hold of slavery on the organization of household labor post-emancipation.[38] This mix of memory, history and commodified fantasy animated these relationships above as well as below the Mason-Dixon line. The faithful slave narrative was sunk deep in the framework of postbellum domestic service. This was not the inevitable outcome of the history of race and slavery in the United States, however. It required a great deal of effort on the part of white employers to reify and continually assert faithful servitude, a task made all the more arduous by the persistent refusals of the mammy mantle by black women.

The element of post–Civil War domestic service that most confounded the faithful slave construct was the act of paying wages to a domestic worker. Giving money to the black women who toiled in white homes clearly connoted that they were not there because they felt a special responsibility to or love for the families they worked for; they were there because they were being paid. A statement from one of Tucker's white interviewees is broadly indicative of the ways in which this unsettled white employers: "Nowadays . . . it's gotten too businesslike. Like in the old days, if they [domestic workers] stayed thirty minutes longer, that didn't mean anything. Nowadays, they're all on the clock and they've—they've got to be paid to the minute, and it's become a more businesslike relationship rather than a friendly, personal relationship."[39]

In the years before the First World War, when most domestic workers still lived in their employers' homes, coercion and deceit cloaked in paternalist rhetoric about the "friendly, personal relationship" allowed many white families to continue the practice of not paying wages directly to workers or, at times, not pay them at all. Instead, they "offered" a place to sleep, food, visits to doctors, and promises of money in the bank. Practices such as these highlight some of the ways in which the broad shift to living out presented new hardships even as it constituted a significant advance in the lives of these workers, as domestic labor continued to be mired in exploitation, racism, and gender discrimination. Some workers were denied wages well into the twentieth century. For example, as late as 1937 a study of domestic workers in Lynchburg, Virginia, noted that two women were paid no wages at all, as "there was one report of payment in the form of a house 'on the lot' rent-free, and one of payment made only in clothing."[40]

While paying wages for domestic service became nearly unavoidable as a result of the change to day work, white employers persisted in their attempts to keep the cash nexus of their relationships with black domestic workers as distant from their minds and actions as possible. They clung to and daily enacted their fantasies of paternalism and mutual affection, to the significant cost and frustration of those they hired. Domestic workers' narratives are filled with examples of their employers' attempts to avoid the moment of actually handing them money or "supplementing" their wages with offers of food, shelter, or old clothing. Recalling her days as a domestic in Atlanta in the early twentieth century, Willie Mae Cartwright described one employer's practice of giving her castoff items and deducting their "value" from her wages: "One woman I worked for, I'd work all week and then she'd say: 'Here's a nice dress I'd like to sell for fifty cents.' It be so big I could have flung a fit inside it and never popped a seam . . . Regular, every week, she'd palm off things on me that way."[41] Cartwright felt unable to refuse the items for fear of losing the job altogether. Another woman from Atlanta, Alice Adams, called the family she worked for "lovely peoples" but qualified the statement by adding, "She [her employer] was willing to do anything to help me but the money—no money." When she needed money promptly to pay rent or buy necessities, her employer would pay her landlord or buy the needed items for her but would never just give her cash directly.[42] This allowed the white woman to enact her own paternalism before other whites, the landlords and shopkeepers, while asserting her control over Adams's life and insinuating that Adams herself was incompetent and untrustworthy with money.

The desire to resist white employers' attempts to sustain paternalistic relationships with their domestic employees underlay some black women's expressed disdain for "pan-toting." The phrase described household workers' common practice of carrying home leftover food to make up for their low wages and the fact that their long workdays left little time for doing their own cooking. While some white employers cited the practice as evidence of black people's propensity for thievery, many recognized it as a mutually expected component of employing domestic labor. Recent scholarship on black working-class life has urged the recognition of pan-toting, along with slow-downs, absenteeism,

destruction of property, and ruining food, as a form of resistance to labor exploitation and racism.[43] A number of domestic workers refused to "tote," however, believing that
the practice helped justify low wages and whites' claims that
they were paternalistically supporting the extended families
of black domestics.[44]

These acts of substituting goods for wages were also explicit attempts to reduce the cost of domestic service. Lottie
Cooksey, who worked in Washington, D.C., in the 1920s, related a story of one woman who gave her old clothes at the
end of her day's work instead of the wages they had previously agreed on. The work was done, but the woman would
not—or could not—pay her. This was the last time such a
thing happened to Cooksey, who said that after this experience she always asked for her wages to be paid up front.[45]
Still, attempts to replace wages with other goods were common among the many women who could barely afford the
domestic workers they felt compelled to hire, whether to offset their own absence from the home owing to outside employment or to the less easily quantifiable but no less powerful pressure to maintain the standards of white domesticity
that demanded the presence of black household laborers.

While it dramatically changed the lives of workers, the
transformation in domestic service to day work for wages significantly affected the population of women able to hire help
as well. The increased employment among white women, leading to the demand for child-care services and assistance with housework, coupled with the depressed wages of
domestic workers, meant that domestic help was no longer
uniquely the privilege of elite and middle-class families. In
ever-growing numbers after World War I, working-class white
women hired black women as domestics.[46] Underlying this
change was the continued devaluation of housework generally and persistent definitions of the work as the responsibil-

ity of women alone. Most black women did not and could not similarly employ others to do this work. They had no recourse to hired labor to offset their own child-care and housework needs.[47]

In spite of the multilayered inequalities it signaled, the mystique of social advance and paternalism still clung tightly to the presence of a black woman working in a white household. This was particularly true in the South, where the ability to claim the status of empowered whiteness was tied directly to enacting one's authority over black labor. For working-class women especially, this provided a measure of status otherwise limited by their class, their work, and their social contexts. Melissa Howe, a domestic worker, noted, "See, these white people, soon as they get able, they used to get a colored person to do for them."[48] Another, Juliana Lincoln, observed that the woman who hired her "didn't have half as many clothes as I did! So some of those whites had maids, and they didn't have anything else."[49]

The ability to hire help was often a matter of what people were willing to sacrifice. Leila Parkerson noted of her own employment with a poor family after World War II: "It was a struggle for them to pay me that little twenty dollars a week! All of them [the mother and her older daughters] had to make it up together to pay that twenty dollars a week." This struggle on the part of her white employers did not limit their desire to perform paternalistic benevolence, and probably enhanced it. As Parkerson observed: "It's so funny, though. Every white person, poor or rich, always thought they could give me something. This family even—they give me an old blouse with stains under the arms, perspiration stains. I took it and dumped it in the nearest trash can on the way home."[50] In light of their expectation that Parkerson would be pleased with this "gift," and surely self-satisfied with their gesture of giving her something, the stained castoff is an apt symbol for the white women's assertion of the racial and social distinction between themselves and Parkerson despite their similar class backgrounds.

Some black women working for poor whites felt certain affinities for them, witnessing struggles in their lives not wholly dissimilar from their own. Essie Favrot spoke of the thirteen years she spent working in the 1940s and early 1950s for a family of eight, the Elliots, in which both parents worked. "My neighbors used to laugh because those Elliots were such poor people," Favrot recalled. "Everyone knew they were. I mean not poor white trash—no. Just working people like myself."[51] Unlike in her relationships with other employers, Favrot remained in contact with the Elliots after she no longer worked for them, and thought of them with an affection tempered by sympathy: "I was fond of those kids. I still am. I worked for them until my son was born. We still keep in touch. One of the girls just died. She had cancer; that was very sad. And their mother, I worry about her. She's had a hard time. Working for them—since they had all those kids, it was more like a family for me there. I feel still sort of protective and maternal towards them."[52] Keenly aware of the ramifications of a black woman expressing affection for the whites she worked for, Favrot was quick to add, "Not like I do my own family, no, but like I would any children I'd cared for that much."[53]

In the post–World War I years employers adopted a variety of practices both overt and subtle to fit their employer-employee relationships into the romanticized master-slave dyad. The most obvious of these was the routine custom of calling black domestic workers "Mammy" or "Aunt," acts of naming that persisted throughout the twentieth century. In her discussion of the prevalence of these names in white women's accounts, Susan Tucker notes that by using them, the women sought to locate black domestic workers "within the paternalistic, segregationist order."[54] One of her black informants put it succinctly, noting that "whites 'wanted to see an old mammy' in every black woman" they employed.[55] More than this, the act of calling any black woman who worked in a white home "Mammy" suggested these women's interchangeability as it was simultaneously intended to denote a unique intimacy. "Mammy" could be any black woman; she was special in the eyes of whites only because she cared for *them*. It was actually *whites'* specialness, *their* status, which was coded through the use of the name.

One white woman's narrative suggests that employers not only wanted to see a mammy but also wanted to see slavery as the explicit context of the relationship. Leigh Campbell, born in 1914 and telling her story in the early 1980s, recalled one domestic worker in her family in these terms: "Then, there, we had Geneva, and her mother was our slave. She [the mother] was Mammy."[56] It is possible that Geneva's mother was born into slavery and continued to work her entire life as a domestic for Campbell's family—long enough for her to have been the "mammy" who "was our slave" to an infant Leigh Campbell in the 1910s. Still, the elision suggesting that Geneva was the family's "slave" at this time denotes a deep historical incongruity and misrepresentation of the relationship. The "dream" of employing one's mother's maid is recapitulated as a kind of perpetual slavery in this narrative, as Campbell recalls employing "Mammy's" daughter, Geneva.

Black women's resistance to the practice of naming them "Mammy" and the romance of faithful slavery it sustained is revealed inadvertently in another narrative from one of Tucker's white informants. Corinne Cooke, born in Florida in 1897, recalled the following story from her childhood:

> And Uncle Phillips, his children had Mammy. Mammy would fix us to go to bed at night and bathe us in the morning when I stayed there. And I wanted so badly for Becky to be called Mammy, but Becky said no, she was not Mammy—she was

Becky. I don't know why. She said she had a hard enough time being Becky. She didn't want to be Mammy! Mammy was buried with our cousins. She's the only one besides the Davises in their lot. And Becky said she didn't care a speck about being buried with us! We thought she was just one of those new types, but we were very fond of her.[57]

Becky's refusal to be called "Mammy" by a white child is illustrative of black women's resistance to the label and the fictive familial ties it described. This denial is made powerfully clear in a story told by a domestic worker, Aletha Vaughn, about her next-door neighbor: "White people came out there and ask her, call her Aunt Alice. She said, 'I ain't none of your damn auntie. I ain't no kin to you. My name is Alice Caldwell Smith, and nothing that white is in my family. You see how black I am. I am not your aunt. Don't call me aunt.'"[58]

Not all black women performing domestic labor cleaned homes and cared for children. The second-largest category of "domestic and personal service" for black women in the 1920s, according to the census, was laundering clothes.[59] Contemporaries referred to these women as "laundresses" or "washerwomen." Cleaning, bleaching, drying, starching, and ironing clothing and linens was done either in white homes or, much more often, within their own homes when they "took laundry in." Punishing labor in the early twentieth century, laundering involved scrubbing clothes over washtubs, wringing them, hanging them to dry, and pressing them with heavy irons. For some household workers, doing the wash was a chore in addition to their cleaning and child-care work.

The common slippage between domestic labor and laundering is apparent in a political cartoon protesting the UDC's national mammy memorial campaign that appeared in 1923 in the *Baltimore Afro-American*. Distinct from many of the other cartoons produced by the black press throughout the monument controversy, this image stands out in its representation of an angry, militant "black mammy." Run under the heading "Another Suggestion for the 'Mammy' Monument," the image blends the predominant mammy iconography with that of the washerwoman to make broad claims about the legacies of slavery and black women's experiences at the time as low-wage laborers. The figure's polka-dotted headscarf recalls Aunt Jemima, yet this woman's frown stands in stark contrast to the trademark's toothy smile. There is no warmth for her white employers here. Her face reveals no deep affection for her so-called "white family," and the precariously dangling white child in her left hand challenges the notion that mammies felt particular love for their small white charges. Rather than a steaming stack of pancakes, this mammy extends an empty, upturned right hand, asking for payment of the wages she never received. The proposed statue stands on a washtub pedestal with a washboard plaque reading, "In grateful memory to one we never paid a cent of wages during a lifetime of service." Slavery and contemporary wage labor are collapsed in this single image and presented as essentially the same. Far from being content with her servitude, this mammy is angry, demanding compensation for past and present injustice.[60] This was a mammy's monument worthy of the nation's capital, declared the *Afro-American*. The caption beneath the image suggests that the statue be "cast in bronze 30 feet high and stand upon a marble shaft 20 feet square and 100 feet high." Such enormity of size and sentiment deserved pride of place: "It should also be erected on the Mall midway between the Lincoln Memorial and Washington's Monument."[61] While the *Afro-American's* powerful, militant mammy proposal is unique among the many images of devastated enslaved and free black women, lynched men, and claims of masculine heroism and citizenship that fueled the black press's critique of the UDC's

From the "Afro-American," Baltimore.

A COLORED ARTIST'S SUGGESTION.

"Since the Daughters of the Confederacy have obtained Senatorial sanction for the erection of a monument to the 'Black
Mammies' of the South," runs the commentary, "we offer the
above suggestion. It should be cast in bronze 30 feet high and
stand upon a marble shaft 20 feet square and 100 feet high. It
should also be erected on the Mall midway between the Lincoln
Memorial and Washington's Monument. The right hand of the
statue is extended for the back pay due."

"A Colored Artist's Suggestion." (*Literary Digest*, April 28, 1923.)

monument scheme, it ultimately found a much wider circulation than these other protests. In its coverage of the monument controversy, the *Literary Digest* reprinted this cartoon
as the only illustration accompanying "For and Against the
'Black Mammy's' Monument," broadcasting the demand to
the magazine's wide national readership.[62]

Carter G. Woodson linked the mammy figure to the washerwoman in a damning critique of the former and a call
to honor the latter, arguing: "The Negroes of this country
keenly resent any such thing as the mention of the Plantation
Black Mammy, so dear to the hearts of those who believe in
the traditions of the Old South. Such a reminder of that low
status of the race in the social order of the slave regime is
considered a gross insult." But if the mammy figure was a
grave insult to African Americans, there was a representative
of black women's work often shielded behind her that was
worthy of grand memorialization and gratitude. "There is in
the life of the Negro, however, a vanishing figure whose
name every one should mention with veneration," Woodson
continued, playing on the white supremacist rhetoric of the
vanishing mammy. "She was all but the beast of burden of the
aristocratic slaveholder, and in freedom she continued at this
hard labor as a bread winner of the family. This is the Negro
washerwoman."[63]

The washerwoman was "vanishing," according to Woodson,
owing to the growth of the steam laundry industry since
World War I. A woman with only a washtub and an iron
found it increasingly difficult by 1930 to compete with the
speed of mechanization, and her only option was often to
lower rates drastically. Beyond the lure of modernization,
at least one commercial laundry in Richmond, Virginia, attempted to mobilize fears of interracial contact, status slippage, and bodily intimacy to pull business away from these
women. Its advertisement read: "When the washerwoman

takes your clothes home, you don't know what she does with them. She may be so careful of them that she will keep some of them next to her. To have clothes washed and not worn, send them to T & E Laundry, Inc."[64] The suspicion that domestic workers' breaching of segregated spaces was going too far could have a serious financial impact on the livelihoods of such women.

The trend Woodson identified was reversed for a short time with the deepening of the Great Depression, a fact that signals much about the disproportionate, racialized effects of economic dislocation. A federal Women's Bureau study of the mid-1930s noted that the southern laundry industry's leading complaint was about competition from black women willing to take in clothes and linens at much lower rates. Industry informants also complained about the common expansion of day workers' domestic duties to include laundry. Families that had taken their laundry to commercial facilities found they could get the same work done for little to no increase in the wages they already paid to household workers. The bureau's report noted: "If there was anything else to employ the colored women or even the colored men at a living wage these women would not be such a factor . . . When times were good the colored women's husbands had jobs and there was not so much home washing." In other words, the labor exploitation made possible by the depression, segregation, and the chronic underemployment of African American men was now being cited by white laundry owners as the source of black women's "unfair" labor practices. Bemoaning the inability to compete in this environment, one laundry manager reported that he "knew of a number of wash-women who were glad to get a day's work for carfare, lunch, and an old dress."[65]

Few black observers denied the importance of black women's labors to their communities and families, and often held up the washerwoman in particular as a model of sacrifice and savings. Within strategies of "uplift" and community betterment, accounts of washerwomen's thrift despite low wages and backbreaking labor were proffered as lessons to impoverished and better-off black people alike. In many ways, Carter Woodson's call to honor these women operated within this vein. More explicit in its didactic references was a news item from the *Savannah Tribune* which recounted the passing of an aged black "washer woman" in Middleton, New York, who died leaving an estate of more than $12,000: "Times were just as hard for her, surely, as they are for the average person—yet she saved. There is a great lesson that all of us can learn from this woman of humble station." And what could the *Tribune*'s readers learn from this story? "We can have a bank account if we are willing to forego [*sic*] some of the needless pleasures of life—those things we call a good time . . . Let us gain heart from the example of the washer-woman who by practicing the greatest of all virtues, self-sacrifice, proved that we can all save if we want to."[66]

The reference to shunning "needless pleasures" and "a good time" suggests that the "us" of the editorial's address was actually quite specifically directed toward Savannah's black working-class population. Black workers' public pursuits of leisure and entertainment—dancing, drinking, and carousing—might be seen as forms of resistance to labor exploitation, coercion, and racism in southern cities.[67] Exhausting one's body on the dance floor, feeling it differently, more loose, even inoperable with drink, and laughing and shouting in the streets were all acts of reclaiming one's time and self-ownership. The body required to labor on the job, disciplined and constantly under surveillance by employers, became a source of pleasure in one's off hours. But this pleasure-seeking also came under concerned surveillance by whites who considered it not merely irresponsible and detrimental but the inevitable result of black inferiority and lack of self-control. For this reason, members of the black elite and middle class, like the editors of the *Savannah Tribune*, also looked on it with horror and disapproval.

During the summer immediately following the monument controversy, the *Baltimore Afro-American* ran an editorial outlining some inappropriate behavior and dress in the community, titled "They Need Your Help." Those needing the help of the neighborhood, "rather than your criticism," were the "thotless" [*sic*] neighbors who undercut the advancement of the entire community or race. The editorial counseled a little friendly persuasion to bring these neighbors into line. While the paper asserted that there were many kinds of thoughtlessness, it focused on four types, and illustrated them in an accompanying editorial cartoon drawn by the same artist, Jim Watson, who had depicted the militant mammy monument suggestion of a few months earlier. The paper urged that the caricature could itself be a tool of "friendly" prodding: "Cut out Mr. Watson's cartoon and send it to somebody you think needs it."[68]

Among the public embarrassments the cartoon illustrates is a quartet of men, identified as drunk by the caption noting that they are "home from the cabaret." The editorial identifies them as "the quartette which comes home from a party after midnight and wakes everybody up with loud singing along the street. It looks 'smart' to come home way after the time when tired bodies should be in bed getting rest for the next day's work. Next day they will complain of the heat or of how hard their boss is on employees who are late."[69] The editorial suggests that diligence on the job is a public indicator of respectability that could put white suspicions to rest as well as challenge the racist ideologies that inform them. By extension this implies that working-class leisure activities that reduce productivity could tarnish the race as a whole.

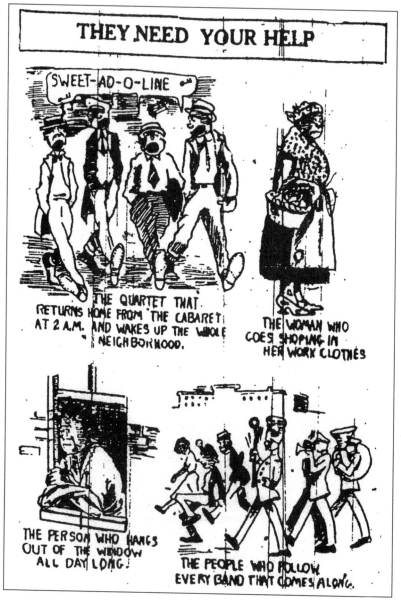

"They Need Your Help." (*Baltimore Afro-American*, July 20, 1923.)

If hard work was the mark of a respectable man, the working woman who dressed like one while out in public was also in need of a reprimand: "When she gets ready to go to market or into the downtown department stores, she puts a handkerchief over an uncombed head and a shawl over a soiled dress and is ready to mingle with people who are fresh and clean." The illustration, labeled "the woman who goes shopping in her work clothes," bears an uncanny resemblance to the mammy figure. Her polka-dotted headscarf and shawl instantly conjure up images of Aunt Jemima. Thus, in the editorialist's estimation, just as threatening to black advancement as public drunkenness, sloppy work habits, and the appearance of laziness is the black woman who looks like a mammy. The problem with the working woman here was not that she *worked*—her labor was a necessity—but that she *looked* like she worked. The performance of ease by means of a fresh appearance and neat, fashionable clothing was a gendered representation of respectability that countered the realities of labor. This recommended strategy of public presentation added yet another layer of effort, responsibility, and financial sacrifice to the black woman's burden.

In the immediate aftermath of World War II, *Ebony* magazine published an editorial that shared several of the assumptions and didactic aims of the *Baltimore Afro-American* while proposing a radically different role for black women. Cheering the prosperity of the postwar boom and framing the domestic containment that characterized it for its African American readership, the magazine proclaimed, "Goodbye Mammy, Hello Mom." The editorial described how the wartime employment of black men and women had allowed many to leave menial labor and domestic work for the higher wages of industrial jobs, not only raising family incomes but also taking "Negro mothers out of white kitchens" and putting "them in factories and shipyards." With the return of soldiers and the mass movement of black and white women out of those jobs, African American women "went back to the kitchens," reported *Ebony*, "but this time their own . . . And so today in thousands of Negro homes, the Negro mother has come home, come home perhaps for the first time since 1619 when the first Negro families landed at Jamestown, Virginia."[70] The magazine celebrated the freedom of black mothers to care for their own families while being supported by a male breadwinner. The end was in sight to centuries of white people's theft of black maternal labor. The widest-circulation black periodical of the day framed this ultimately as a rejection of the faithful slave: "Goodbye Mammy."

Just as critics of the mammy memorial had in the 1920s, *Ebony* concluded that the measure of advancement in black life was to be found in the children raised by African American mothers. Notably, the child the black woman now had time to nurture and support was a son—a New Negro for the nuclear age: "Just ask Junior, who's been getting his bread and peanut butter sandwiches regularly after school and finding that rip in his blue jeans mended when he goes out to play."[71] Junior's appearance proclaimed the respectability of his home, tended by a good, caring mother and supported solely by the income of a father. Where the *Afro-American* had worried about the clothes worn in public by black working women, in *Ebony's* scenario black women were safely distanced from public work, now "free" to nurture in private the public presentations of their children and husbands.

Ebony's was a conservative vision tempered by caution about the economic future and class-specific ideas concerning career possibilities for some black women. The editorial noted that a majority of black women continued to labor outside the home, mostly as domestic workers. Large numbers of those who had left domestic service for industrial jobs during the war years had now returned to it and were in no position to stop working for wages, as the category of domestic employment itself continued to become more racialized. And should the economy take a plunge and bring layoffs and lower wages for black men, the magazine acknowledged, many black mothers would need to return to the paid workforce: "But even if she is forced back into white kitchens, the Negro mother . . . will not stay. She is bound to escape the first chance she gets." The desire to see full-time homemaking become an option for all African American women was of course patriarchal and restrictive despite being grounded in claims of racial equality. As the nuclear family and normative models of domesticity were becoming the core of American national identity within cold war ideology, *Ebony* proclaimed the fundamental patriotism of black families and their right to conform. These economic and political demands for the right of black women not to work outside their own homes—or the right of black men to a breadwinner's wage, as was more often the point—could put women in a very tight bind, in which resistance to staying at home was resistance to the advancement of the race.[72]

Some women could join the workforce and still be celebrated for their contributions. *Ebony* concluded its editorial with the assurance that it did not intend to confine women to their own kitchens indefinitely: "Nobody wants to tie a woman to her hearthstone with hackneyed phrases and ideas about where her place is. But every family should be able to live on the income of one breadwinner. And every woman should be able to choose whether she wants to devote her days to her children and her home or to a career girl's job."[73] Cast as the less mature of the two options—a "girl's" choice—the decision to pursue a career was not likely to include domestic service. There were other possibilities for women, such as the black celebrities whose pictures filled

Ebony's pages. The "Goodbye Mammy, Hello Mom" editorial was immediately followed by a food article that included a coffee cake recipe attributed to Dorothy Dandridge, illustrated with photos of the glamorous actress baking. This quick recipe, the magazine observed, was "perfect for a busy career girl like Dorothy, who is also a perfect mother and a good housewife."[74]

Neither the average housewife's retreat to her own home and family nor the publicity-managed lives of celebrities bore much relation to the lived experiences of many of *Ebony's* readers. Rather than a record of common postwar experience, the magazine presented a standard to be valued and worked toward, not unlike the *Afro-American* cartoon of twenty years earlier. *Ebony* promised that at mid-century, black women would "find freedom and independence in their own home[s]."[75] This sentiment must have held enormous appeal for women who labored daily in white homes and grappled with the mammy problem, even if it failed to describe reality for most of them.

In 1955 domestic workers in Montgomery, Alabama, would say good-bye to mammy in a very different manner, arguing through their support of the bus boycott that independence and freedom were to be found in the streets and in collective political action. When Rosa Parks refused to yield her seat to a white man and was arrested for it, the longtime activist and seamstress at the Montgomery Fair department store ignited the protest and inspired thousands of other working people to resist segregation openly. Alabama's capital city was home to 50,000 black residents, about 37 percent of the overall population. Some 17,500 black people rode the buses twice a day, mostly to and from work. A majority of these riders were women who were domestic workers in white homes or cooks and cleaning people for white-owned businesses: 63 percent of all black women in Montgomery worked in domestic service in 1955. These figures are meaningful in a number of ways, not the least of which is the power of that many people to sustain an almost total boycott of Montgomery's bus system for 381 days until they were successful in gaining its desegregation. The significant rate of black bus ridership before the boycott resulted from residential segregation in the city and the limited work options of the black people who lived there, particularly the majority who were poor and had little education. Domestic workers had to travel long distances to get to the white homes in which they toiled. Many reported the daily humiliations and frustrations they faced while riding the buses, which included having to stand over empty seats designated for whites or, as Parks was, being told to vacate seats bordering the white section when white riders overflowed their allotted rows in the front of the bus. Harassment and verbal abuse from white drivers was common. They were known to drive away as black women walked from the front door, where fares were collected, to the back door, which African Americans were required to use for boarding the bus, leaving the women stranded at the curb and ten cents poorer.[76]

Black working people, especially women, saw themselves and their own experience in Rosa Parks's action, and it strengthened their commitment to the boycott despite the economic, emotional, and physical costs they disproportionately bore. Interviewed while on her way to work about six weeks into the boycott, an unnamed domestic worker reportedly told Willie M. Lee, a researcher from Fisk University in Nashville, Tennessee, that Montgomery blacks were "boycottin' the buses 'cause dey put one of our 'spectable ladies in jail and we didn't lack it. You know, child, you can jest take so much and soon you git full. Dat's what happen here. Dey just put us in jail and put us in jail, and Lord knows we tied of it."[77] Two days later another domestic worker who identified herself as Beatrice told Lee: "I had heard about Rosa Parks getting put in jail because she would not get up and stand so a white man could sit down. Well, I got a little mad, you know how it is when you hear how white folks treat us." She related that when her next door neighbor, a Mason, showed her the flier produced by Jo Ann Robinson and the Women's Political Council on Sunday evening, the night before the proposed boycott, "it felt good. I said this is what we should do. I got on the phone and called all my friends and told them, and they said they wouldn't ride."[78] Others reported similarly that hearing of the boycott and planning to participate made them "feel good." A middle-aged woman working as a cook for a white family told Lee: "I found a note on my porch and it said dey had put Mrs. Parks in jail and next time it may be me and it said fur us not to ride de buses. I felt good, I felt like shoutin' 'cause de time done come for dem to stop treating us like dogs."[79]

Deciding not to ride the bus meant that all 17,500 black people who relied on public transportation for their livelihoods would have to find other ways to get to work or to shop downtown and that children would need a different means of transportation to school. Initially, for many this meant walking significant distances each day. "During the rush hours the sidewalks were crowded with laborers and domestic workers, many of them well past middle age, trudging patiently to their jobs and home again, sometimes as much as twelve miles," observed Martin Luther King Jr. "They knew why they walked, and the knowledge was evident in the way they carried themselves. And as I watched them I knew there is nothing more majestic than the determined courage of individuals willing to suffer and sacrifice for their freedom and dignity." King, who first came to wide regional and national attention as a civil rights leader through his involvement in the boycott, noted: "So profoundly had the spirit of the protest become a part of people's lives that sometimes they even preferred to walk when a ride was available. The act of walking for many had become of symbolic importance."[80]

This symbolism was not lost on white employers of black domestic help as it unsettled their fantasies of faithful service and mutual affection. While many workers reported subtle or overt support from the whites they worked for, many more talked of lost jobs, suspicion, and of feeling empowered to stand up to white people in new, more direct ways. In her interview with Willie Lee, Beatrice described her employer's response to the boycott and to her participation in it:

> She said to me when I went to work that Wednesday [the third day of the boycott, December 7, 1955], "Beatrice, you ride the bus don't you?"
>
> I said, "I sure don't."
>
> She said, "Why Beatrice, they haven't done anything to you."
>
> I said, "Listen, Mrs. Prentiss, you don't ride the bus, you don't know how those ole nasty drivers treat us, and further when you do something to my people you do it to me too . . ."
>
> "Beatrice, don't feel that way. I've always been nice to you."[81]

Mrs. Prentiss's quick movement from the topic of systemic segregation to her own relationship with Beatrice, from "they haven't done anything to you" to "I've always been nice to you," reveals her desire to see her association with her domestic worker as something separate and disconnected from the coercive and degrading framework of segregation. In her account of the conversation, Beatrice agrees that Mrs. Prentiss has been nice in the past but questions the white woman's commitment to her, asking if she would care about her or continue to employ her if she were unable to work for two or three weeks: "'Course I would, Beatrice," the woman replies, "but I just can't see white and colored riding together on the buses. It just wouldn't come to a good end." With this Prentiss falls back on the sexual argument that was always present in defenses of segregation and represented the other side of all that white affection for the women who worked in their homes, arguing that segregation policed interracial sexual desire, protecting white women from black men and white girls from black boys, whether on buses or in classrooms. Again, Beatrice not only refuses to let the statement pass but directly challenges her employer's argument as well:

> "You people started it way back in slavery. If you hadn't wanted segregation, you shouldn't got us all mixed up in color."
> "Beatrice, you don't know anything about that, and it's not happening now."
> "That's what you say. I read about it and my aunt told me about it, and right now I can sit on my porch, and when it starts getting dark I can look down the street by those trees and see colored women get in the cars with policemen. And what about that colored boy who had to leave town 'cause that white woman out here was going crazy about him. So you can't tell me that it's over."[82]

Throughout the rest of the recounted conversation, Mrs. Prentiss continues her attempt to draw Beatrice into her confidence, to compel her to confirm a special closeness between them and end her participation in the boycott. In addition to smearing King's reputation and challenging other ministers' involvement, she says: "I'm going to tell you this, Beatrice, because I know you can keep your mouth shut. In the White Citizen Council meeting, they discussed starving the maids for a month. They asked me to lay our maid off for a month, that they'll be glad to ride the buses again. If they do, I still want you to come one day a week." With a sharp "thanks, but no thanks" for this "favor," Beatrice replies: "Well, Mrs., I just won't come at all and I sure won't starve . . . I was eating before I started working for you."[83] Like giving old clothes or extra food, Mrs. Prentiss's gift of her trust and her belief that Beatrice would be more faithful to her than to the boycott stem from her assumptions about her own benevolence and her paternalistic relationship with Beatrice. The domestic worker's response that she had been and would continue to be more than fine without her employer tears at the very heart of that assumption.

Irene, another domestic worker, argues that white expressions of love for domestic workers are always manipulative, coercive, and insincere. She recounts how one of the women she worked for, whose husband was a bus driver, had called Irene into her yard saying that she had some bacon grease to give her: "She told me don't let her husband see it 'cause he told her don't gimme nothin' else. I told 'er if her husband seyd don't gimme nothin' else, den don't gimme nothin' else." Then the woman asked her what had happened at the protest meeting the night before, accusing Irene of lying when she replied only that they had sung and prayed: "And girl, I seyd to myself, she must take me fur a fool—thank I'll come back here and puke everything my folks seys to her, and then for some little ole stinkin' bacon grease at dat." Irene goes on to say that this was not the first time her employer had taken her for a fool: "She thought all dat stuff she told me I b'lieved. But she didn't know every time she told me her chillen loved me, I put a pin dere; when she sey dey like de way I iron, I put a pin dere; and when dey talked 'bout how good I cooked, I put a pin dere, and all twee dem pins I reads. And I know dey don't mean a thang they seys. So Irene don't pay 'em no mind." In the past, Irene had paid this woman's fantasies of faithful servitude "no mind," had ignored but not disabused her of the notion. In the context of the boycott, however, Irene resists her openly, refusing to tell her about the protest meeting and finally saying that if she was so eager to know what was going on, then she should "go to de meetin' fur [her]self." The woman, now infuriated, replies, "Irene, I didn't know you wuz so damn stupid."[84]

Like Irene's employer, thousands of white women in Montgomery who managed black domestic workers and believed they loved and were loved by them were astounded by what they had not known before the boycott. Some responded with fury born of hurt and an abiding belief in white supremacy and their own benevolence toward the black women they employed. One such woman was Mrs. George L. Foster, who wrote a letter to the editor of the *Montgomery Advertiser* after the first month of the boycott calling for white women to counter-boycott black domestic service. Foster noted that she had heard of bus drivers' rudeness to black riders before, but "noticing since the boycott how most of the Negroes have become sullen and indolent I feel perhaps the bus drivers dealing with these people collectively have seen a side of them that we dealing with them singly have not seen and evidently the patience of the most tactful drivers has been tried." White people's goodwill had been taken advantage of and was now being spat upon, she said, and it was time to show black workers what their lives would be like without it:

> Most of us housewives have been patient through this past month, allowing our household servants to be late and to leave early when a ride is available (most of the servants taking advantage of us). The time has come when we housewives must quit being so lazy, get together and tell the help to either ride the buses and get to work on time or quit. We white people have tried to be understanding of our servants for years and I feel we were understanding until some outside influence put fear in them. We have been good to our Negroes but now is the time to make them understand a few things. We should quit paying taxi fare, quit going for them or taking them home, quit paying their social security tax, quit lending them money for debts contracted for unnecessary items, etc.[85]

With expanding regional and national news coverage of the boycott in Montgomery and federal legal challenges, more and more white people questioned their ideas about black domestic workers and faithfulness. As Foster's letter suggests, one might miss or willfully ignore the day-to-day resistance and self-preservation strategies of a black woman working in her home, but the collective resistance of thousands was unmistakable and profoundly unsettling. Despite her vitriol, Foster still clutched at the shreds of the faithful mammy narrative, finding some solace in the belief that she had not been wrong about her relationships with black women but that some "outside influence" had changed Montgomery's African Americans. The cry of outside agitation would be heard from many white southerners in response to the modern civil rights struggle, signaling a widely held desire to hold on to "their" faithful Negroes and the conviction of affectionate segregation. It marked not only a refusal to see moral corruption in segregation but also the belief that their mammies had been corrupted through no fault, or initiative, of local black people.

Far more ambiguous than the angry responses of women like Foster were the motivations of the many white women who chose to drive their maids to and from work. Several critics, including Foster, suggested that the boycott could be broken if domestic workers could not rely on white women to transport them. Why the women chose to drive was unclear, however, and remains so. Was it a reflection of complex and mutually caring relationships framed through common femininity? Or was it an enactment of paternalistic benevolence framed by fantasies of faithful slavery? Did it signal the commitment of some white women to challenging segregation? Finally, did much of it simply come down to the pragmatic desire to get the housework done and the white women's unwillingness or inability to do it themselves? Arguably all of these motivations played a factor in white women's decision making. King noted the ambiguity of the relationship from the perspectives of both white employers and black domestic workers: "Certainly, if selfishness was a part of the motive, in many cases affection for a faithful servant also played its part. There was some humor in the tacit understandings—and sometimes mutually accepted misunderstandings—between these white employers and their Negro servants." King goes on to tell of one old domestic worker's response to her white employer's query, "Isn't this bus boycott terrible?" The black woman replied: "Yes, ma'am, it sure is. And I just told all my young'uns that this kind of thing is white folks' business and we just stay off the buses till they get this whole thing settled."[86]

Writing *Stride toward Freedom: The Montgomery Story* (1958) less than two years after the boycott's successful conclusion and as his own reputation was expanding nationally and internationally, King was hopeful but clear that the struggle in Montgomery, as in the rest of the United States and throughout the world, was far from over. He worried, for instance, that even after the buses were integrated, older black residents and domestic workers still tended to sit at the back of the bus and that black and white riders rarely shared a double seat. While he believed that the protest had had "lasting and beneficial effects" on black communities in the city, creating bonds across lines of class, generation, and church affiliation as never before, King's own vision was still very much trained by class-based expectations and concerns about the public behavior of poor black people—the same people without whom the boycott could never have worked. Although King must have been acutely aware of the assumptions and biases of his readers as he crafted his story of the boycott, his own deep adherence to the politics of uplift and respectability at this time were clear in statements such as "The increased self-respect of even the least sophisticated Negroes in Montgomery is evident in the way they dress and walk, in new standards of cleanliness and deportment." He also linked participation in the boycott to decreases in crime, divorce, and alcohol consumption and increases in church attendance among working-class blacks.[87]

Without meaningful economic transformation, King concluded, the black freedom struggle would never be successful. Segregation on city buses was a major part of the problem, but so was the fact that so many black people were locked into low-wage jobs. Of great concern and detriment to black communities was that fact that large numbers of bus riders were black women working outside their own homes. A decade after *Ebony* declared "Goodbye Mammy, Hello Mom," King asserted:

> Economic insecurity strangles the physical and cultural growth of its victims. Not only are millions deprived of formal education and proper health facilities but our most fundamental social unit—the family—is tortured, corrupted, and weakened by economic insufficiency. When a Negro man is inadequately paid, his wife must work to provide the simple necessities for the children. When a mother has to work she does violence to motherhood by depriving her children of her loving guidance and protection.[88]

Higher wages for black and white working people would bring mothers of both races home, King went on to argue in an assertion of a shared commitment to manly independence and the right to be the sole breadwinner. Missing in King's argument is a recognition that many elite and middle-class white women in the South employed domestic servants and stayed home to manage those workers and their households. What drove this decision was an attachment to the romance of faithful slavery and the desire for a mammy that was so prevalent in normative white households. In this sense the domestic labor of black women was a necessity because white self-worth, gender, and class identities depended on it.

The Montgomery bus boycott made visible in new ways

the daily negotiations and struggles of domestic workers trying to shrug off the mantle of faithful slavery, to reject the burden of supporting white people's aspirations and soothing their status anxieties. When these women refused to ride segregated buses to their jobs in segregated white enclaves, they demanded recognition as citizens and as workers with expectations of respect, safety, fair compensation, equality, and freedom. Many were depicted in local and national news reports and photographs as they publicly protested by walking miles to work rather than ride segregated public transportation, shattering popular notions that the black women who worked in white homes were treated and felt like "one of the family." The bus boycott and the modern civil rights movement that flowed from it did not solve the "mammy problem" or spell an end to the tenacious hold of the faithful slave narrative on American culture. It did, however, change the terms of resistance considerably.

EPILOGUE:
RECASTING THE FAITHFUL SLAVE

*Together the three generations of Negro women who
have personified Aunt Jemima span the entire history
of processed foods and represent vividly the emancipation of the American housewife from the drudgery of
virtual slavery in her kitchen to the ease of food preparation in today's wonderland of easy-to-cooks, ready-
mixes, ready-to-serves, and frozen prepared foods at
prices every housewife can afford. This emancipation
begins with Aunt Jemima.*

—Arthur Marquette, *Brands, Trademarks, and Good Will*, 1967

IN THE MIDST of the Montgomery bus boycott, Disneyland
opened a popular restaurant in the Frontierland section of
the California theme park called Aunt Jemima's Pancake
House, where a black woman named Aylene Lewis appeared
as the trademark full-time. For the next several years, three
other black women toured the country making personal appearances as Aunt Jemima, and Quaker Oats hired blues
singer and actress Edith Wilson to portray her in new television spots. In 1962 Disneyland and Quaker Oats expanded
the restaurant to accommodate more customers and changed
its name to Aunt Jemima's Kitchen.[1] In addition to the obvi-

ous benefit of allowing for a more varied menu, the change in name also served to lock Aunt Jemima conceptually within the private sphere of the home. This fact was underscored five years later when company historian Arthur Marquette celebrated the notion that Aunt Jemima's presence there had emancipated the (white) American housewife from *her* slavery in the kitchen.

As activists with the Student Nonviolent Coordinating Committee and the Congress of Racial Equality staged sit-ins and freedom rides and were jailed and brutalized across the South, and the involvement of Martin Luther King Jr. and the Southern Christian Leadership Conference continued to bring national publicity to the Albany movement in Georgia, Disneyland and the Quaker Oats Company capitalized further on the continued popularity of Old Southern fantasy and the faithful slave myth. The restaurant reassured customers that this beloved black woman was not out on the streets demonstrating or in jail for her activism, that she was not radically changing or even dissatisfied, but remained happily in the kitchen and ready to serve. More than this, visitors to the park's eatery could see, touch, and talk to "Aunt Jemima," which they did by the hundreds of thousands. By 1963, 1.6 million customers had been served in the Aunt Jemima restaurant while untold numbers had had their picture taken with Aylene Lewis, including several celebrities and the prime minister of India, Jawaharlal Nehru.[2] It is striking that at a moment when the mainstream civil rights movement's nonviolent direct-action tactics, inspired by Mahatma Gandhi, were so visible nationally via televised news and the print media, Nehru's visit to Disneyland during his 1961 official trip to the United States would be marked by a photo of the statesman clasping the hand of a woman portraying a happy, faithful slave.

Like Nancy Green's first performance in Chicago at the

Columbian Exposition, the presence of Aunt Jemima "live" in Disneyland placed the popular mammy figure at the very heart of mainstream American culture, national identity, and consumerism. The restaurant's location at Disneyland, a place deemed so synonymous with the best cold war America had to offer that it was included on Nehru's official itinerary, lent a kind of commonsense credibility to the trademark's moonlight-and-magnolias version of history. In view of the fact that stories of faithful slavery have always been reactionary, it is perhaps not surprising that the 1950s and 1960s witnessed a surge in the popularity of the mammy figure in direct response to the emergence of the modern civil rights movement.

Conceived at the dawn of the Jim Crow era in the late 1880s, the trademark mammy continued to bedevil and undermine black struggles for political and civil rights and self-determination in the mid-twentieth century. Southern activists and their allies put their bodies on the line—both by taking direct action that defied the color line and by putting themselves at risk of insult, imprisonment, injury, and worse—in order to defeat segregation, organize others, ignite the nation's sense of moral urgency, and compel the federal government to act. Their strategies resulted in a steady stream of images that countered southern apartheid's assertions of unproblematic race relations built on traditional hierarchies, mutual understanding and affection, and a combination of black servility and white paternalism. Yet the popular image of the faithful slave held on, invested with new significance as an old retort to black activism.

As black women worked to disentangle themselves from the "mammy problem," a new narrative of African American mothering was gaining ground in the political discourse of President Lyndon Johnson's Great Society and the War on Poverty. In 1965 Daniel Patrick Moynihan, then an assistant secretary of labor and director of the Office of Policy Planning and Research, released his report, *The Negro Family: The Case for National Action.* In it Moynihan argued that the most enduring and destructive legacy of slavery for black Americans was the distortion of traditional gender roles that had resulted in contemporary family "disorganization" and black "matriarchy." This "tangle of pathology" was perpetuated, the report claimed, through women who headed their families alone or exceeded their male partners in economic power and parental authority. The situation was dire, Moynihan concluded, stating that most urban black youth, who were his primary concern, were already lost to these destructive patterns and inappropriate models of gender behavior.[3] Referred to popularly as the "Moynihan Report," the study appealed to many with its suggestion that racial inequality and economic dislocation persisted, despite the passage of federal civil rights legislation, because of deep-seated problems within black families rather than in the wider society. It also generated storms of criticism and scholarship designed to refute it and set off numerous debates about race, urbanization, and poverty, the threads of which still wind their way through contemporary policy and politics. Activists noted that despite the report's claim to be a "case for action," it seemed largely designed to provide a rationale for federal retreat from racial concerns by arguing instead that African Americans must literally attend to their own houses.[4]

A dramatic transformation in dominant representations of black women's mothering from the mammy in the white home to the matriarch running—and ruining—the black family was under way. Although black women and their allegedly deviant motherhood, rather than systemic factors and racism, were increasingly identified as the root causes of African American poverty, disfranchisement, and marginalization, the rise of the matriarch did not spell an end to the popularity of the mammy stereotype. Just as, according to Deborah Gray White, the mammy and the jezebel could be used to describe the same black woman, depending on the context and needs of whites doing the describing, so the beloved mammy could slip into the negative role of matriarch simply by leaving the white home and family to take care of her own.[5] Moynihan's report perpetuated elements of the same conversations about urbanization, differences in black and white domesticity, and black women's maternalism that had been current in the Marjorie Delbridge custody case of 1917. Not only was the report a testament to the persistence of these stories and stereotypes, but also it had a profound effect on popular conversations about black families, urban economies, and government responsibility that continue today.

Black women daily resisted this addition of the "matriarchy crisis" to the "mammy problem." Again, the voices that speak loudest in the archives belong to those who were involved in movement politics and black feminist organizations.[6] Arguing for the wide revolutionary potential of black women's liberation in 1969, Mary Ann Weathers urged women not to allow themselves to be "intimidated" by this "nonsense." "Black women are not matriarchs, but we have been forced to live in abandonment and been used and abused," she argued. "The myth of the matriarchy must stop, and we must not allow ourselves to be sledgehammered by it any longer."[7] The intimidation Weathers challenged was aimed at black activist women from several directions, including from within the movement itself. The Moynihan Report appeared at the moment when the civil rights movement was shifting from one based on liberal claims of rights and equality to the more radical political and economic critiques and the cultural nationalism of Black Power. Popular assertions about matriarchy meshed with the gender politics of this transition, which cast black mothers who seemed too independent or too strong as a threat to black men and, thus, a threat to black liberation. By the late 1960s, all claims for politicized black mothering ran headlong into the figure of the "matriarch." The mammy was not displaced in this narrative but incorporated as the matriarch's supposed historical forebear. The mammy figure was now argued by some to have been a race traitor all along and a collaborator with whites.[8] In *Soul on Ice* (1968), Eldridge Cleaver argued that "[the white man] turned the black woman into a strong self-reliant Amazon and deposited her in his kitchen—that's the secret of Aunt Jemima's bandana."[9]

The Aunt Jemima trademark was an index of these cultural and political changes as its longevity signaled the resilience of faithful slave myths and the tenacity with which many Americans continued to cling to them. While the decade opened with the expansion of the promotional campaign's reach, the 1960s closed with several changes in Aunt Jemima advertising as Quaker Oats was pushed into action by black protest and shifting social and political environments. Tellingly, the company did not choose to get rid of its lucrative trademarked mammy altogether. In 1967, the same year Arthur Marquette lauded Aunt Jemima for freeing American housewives from their virtual enslavement, Rosie Hall became the last woman to portray the character in person. When she died, Quaker Oats decided not to hire another actor to replace her. The following year the company unveiled a package that depicted a slightly slimmer woman who no longer wore the mammy's signature headscarf. Instead, her hair was pushed back by a wide headband made of the same yellow and red diamond-print material, visually linking the new image to the old one. Then, in 1970, Disneyland quietly removed the name "Aunt Jemima" from its Frontierland restaurant.[10] In their continued resistance to the icon, black activists also sought to "update" the trademark for a new era.

Shaped by the philosophies of Black Power and the Black Arts movement, several African American visual artists, including Murry N. DiPillars, Jon Onye Lockard, and Betye Saar, explicitly challenged the power of the faithful mammy image and the trademark by depicting Aunt Jemima's liberation in their work. Their Aunt Jemimas burst through the packaging that contained them with defiant fists and exploded off boxes of pancake mix with severe expressions, guns, and grenades.[11]

In 1989, on the one-hundredth anniversary of the trademark, the Quaker Oats Company made the most significant change in the image of Aunt Jemima yet. The new box carried the same woman's face and smile, but she was now much thinner and wore carefully coiffed, exposed hair, small earrings, and a crisp white collar. This is the version of the trademark that continues to smile from store shelves and freezer sections across the United States and around the world today. Company spokespeople argued that the figure had been updated for contemporary tastes and was intended to look like a "working mother." Not just a mother, notably, but a *working* mother. As if Aunt Jemima had not always represented a working woman. This qualification was indicative of the ways in which the faithful slave narrative continued to pervade the deep currents of popular understandings of race, urban poverty, welfare, and affirmative action. In the racist discourse of the 1980s, the black "matriarch" had become the "welfare queen," and in 1989 Quaker Oats was careful to suggest that Aunt Jemima did not fit this category.[12] Just as notable as the changes to the trademark, however, were those things that remained very much the same—namely, a black woman's warm smile beside the same anachronistic name printed in the same font that had been used for most of the twentieth century, serving as a reminder not just of slavery but specifically of the mammy image that had once been on the box. The juxtaposition of the new figure with the old name testified more starkly than ever to the fundamental appeal of the Aunt Jemima trademark, asserting that *any* black woman could be Aunt Jemima.

The 1990s witnessed a sudden swell in the popularity of "black collectibles," a market euphemism for the racist material culture of the late nineteenth and early twentieth centuries. Vintage Aunt Jemima premiums—the dolls, pitchers, signs, sheet music, and other ephemera that had carried the trademark name and image—were prized by collectors and fueled a lucrative secondary market that sparked the production of numerous reproductions. The trade in these collectibles, now additionally valued as "antiques," a categorization that simultaneously and erroneously suggested that the racism they depicted was also antique and locked away in the past, was encouraged by the consumption boom made possible by the Internet.[13] The faithful slave narrative has made a full, terrible circle. Just as popular memories of slavery and the plantation South infused American modernity, so now they animate and illuminate the social, political, and economic transformations of the twenty-first century. We are still clinging to Mammy.

NOTES

INTRODUCTION

1. Marilyn Kern-Foxworth, *Aunt Jemima, Uncle Ben, and Rastus: Blacks in Advertising Yesterday, Today, and Tomorrow* (Westport, Conn.: Greenwood Press, 1994), 61–113; M. M. Manring, *Slave in a Box: The Strange Career of Aunt Jemima* (Charlottesville: University Press of Virginia, 1998), 60–78; Arthur Marquette, *Brands, Trademarks, and Good Will: The Story of the Quaker Oats Company* (New York: McGraw-Hill, 1967), 137–158. *Missouri Farmer* is quoted in Manring, *Slave in a Box*, 77.

2. The persistent historical inaccuracy surrounding the trademark is detailed in Manring, *Slave in a Box*; and Doris Witt, *Black Hunger: Food and the Politics of U.S. Identity* (New York: Oxford University Press, 1999), 21–53.

3. Jill Watts, *Hattie McDaniel: Black Ambition, White Hollywood* (New York: Amistad, 2005).

4. On narrative and history, see Sarah Maza, "Stories in History: Cultural Narratives in Recent Works in European History," *American Historical Review* 101 (1992): 1493–1515.

5. V., "Diary of an Invalid: The Portrait," *Southern Literary Messenger* (July 1836): 491.

6. Ibid., 494.

7. Steven Deyle, *Carry Me Back: The Domestic Slave Trade in American Life* (New York: Oxford University Press, 2005), 289; Walter Johnson, *Soul by Soul: Life inside the Antebellum Slave Market* (Cambridge: Harvard University Press, 1999); Jonathan D. Martin, *Divided Mastery: Slave Hiring in the Antebellum South* (Cambridge: Harvard University Press, 2004). For the 875,000 figure, see Deyle, *Carry Me Back*, 289.

8. "A Couple of Loveletters," *Southern Literary Messenger* (March 1838): 160.

9. On the mammy as an invention of antebellum whites, see Catherine Clinton, *The Plantation Mistress: Woman's World in the Old South* (New York: Pantheon Books, 1982), 201–203; Elizabeth Fox-Genovese, *Within the Plantation Household: Black and White Women of the Old South* (Chapel Hill: University of North Carolina Press, 1988), 137; Deborah Gray White, *Ar'n't I a Woman? Female Slaves in the Plantation South* (New York: W. W. Norton & Company, 1985), 46–66.

10. Patricia A. Turner, *Ceramic Uncles and Celluloid Mammies: Black Images and Their Influences on Culture* (New York: Doubleday, 1994), 46.

11. Harriet Beecher Stowe, *Uncle Tom's Cabin, or Life Among the Lowly* (1852; reprint, New York: Penguin Classics, 1986), 66–67.

12. Eric Lott, *Love and Theft: Blackface Minstrelsy and the American Working Class* (New York: Oxford University Press, 1995), 211–233; Linda Williams, *Playing the Race Card: Melodramas of Black and White from Uncle Tom to O. J. Simpson* (Princeton: Princeton University Press, 2001), 45–95.

13. Willie Lee Rose, "The Domestication of Domestic Slavery," in William H. Freehling, ed., *Slavery and Freedom* (New York: Oxford University Press, 1982), 18–36.

14. On non–slave owners' stake in the system, see Johnson, *Soul by Soul;* Stephanie McCurry, *Masters of Small Worlds: Yeoman Households, Gender Relations, and the Political Culture of the Antebellum South Carolina Low Country* (New York: Oxford University Press, 1995).

15. Nell Irvin Painter, *Exodusters: Black Migration to Kansas after Reconstruction* (New York: Norton, 1992).

16. David Blight, *Race and Reunion: The Civil War in American Memory* (Cambridge: Belknap Press of Harvard University Press, 2001). On the Gilded Age mammy narrative in particular, see Jo-Ann Morgan, "Mammy the Huckster: Selling the Old South for a New Century," *American Art* 9, no. 1 (Spring 1995): 87–109.

17. On the Plantation School, see Blight, *Race and Reunion;* Sterling A. Brown, "Negro Character as Seen by White Authors," *Journal of Negro Education* 2, no. 2 (April 1933): 179–203; Thomas L. Connelly and Barbara L. Bellows, *God and General Longstreet: The Lost Cause and the Southern Mind* (Baton Rouge: Louisiana State University Press, 1982); and Lawrence J. Friedman, *The White Savage: Racial Fantasies in the Postbellum South* (Englewood Cliffs, N.J.: Prentice-Hall, 1970).

18. Frederick Douglass quoted in David Blight, "'For Something beyond the Battlefield': Frederick Douglass and the Struggle for the Memory of the Civil War," *Journal of American History* 75, no. 4 (March 1989): 1169.

19. For studies of the mammy figure in the twentieth century, see Kenneth W. Goings, *Mammy and Uncle Mose: Black Collectibles and American Stereotyping* (Bloomington: Indiana University Press, 1994); Michael D. Harris, *Colored Pictures: Race and Visual Representation* (Chapel Hill: University of North Carolina Press, 2003), 83–124; Kate Haug, "Myth and Matriarchy: An Analysis of the Mammy Stereotype," in *Dirt and Domesticity: Constructions of the Feminine* (New York: Whitney Museum of American Art, 1992), 38–56; K. Sue Jewell, *From Mammy to Miss America: Cultural Images and the Shaping of U.S. Social Policy* (New York: Routledge, 1993); Kern-Foxworth, *Aunt Jemima, Uncle Ben, and Rastus*; Patricia Morton, *Disfigured Images: The Historical Assault on Afro-American Women* (Westport, Conn.: Greenwood Press, 1991); Cheryl Thurber, "The Development of the Mammy Image and Mythology," in Virginia Bernhard, Betty Brandon, Elizabeth Fox-Genovese, and Theda Purdue, eds., *Southern Women: Histories and Identities* (Columbia: University of Missouri Press, 1992), 87–108; Turner, *Ceramic Uncles and Celluloid Mammies.*

20. W. E. B. Du Bois, *The Souls of Black Folk* (1903; reprint, Greenwich, Conn.: Fawcett Publications, 1961), vi.

1. THE LIFE OF "AUNT JEMIMA"

1. Nell Irvin Painter, *Creating Black Americans: African-American History and Its Meanings, 1619 to the Present* (New York: Oxford University Press, 2007), 180.

2. Patricia Turner argues: "In her homespun calico garb with a turban around her head, Aunt Jemima comforted the public; in her business-like attire with a fashionable hat on her head, Ida B. Wells vexed the public. Aunt Jemima's was the kind of face people wanted to remember; Ida B. Wells's was the kind they wanted to forget." Turner, *Ceramic Uncles and Celluloid Mammies: Black Images and Their Influence on Culture* (New York: Anchor Books, 1994), 50. Ida B. Wells-Barnett, *Southern Horrors: Lynch Law in All Its Phases* (New York: New York Age, 1892).

3. For general histories of the trademark, see Michael D. Harris, *Colored*

Pictures: Race and Visual Representation (Chapel Hill: University of North Carolina Press, 2003), 84–124; Marilyn Kern-Foxworth, *Aunt Jemima, Uncle Ben, and Rastus: Blacks in Advertising, Yesterday, Today, and Tomorrow* (Westport, Conn.: Praeger, 1994), 61–113; M. M. Manring, *Slave in a Box: The Strange Career of Aunt Jemima* (Charlottesville: University Press of Virginia, 1998); Arthur F. Marquette, *Brands, Trademarks, and Good Will: The History of the Quaker Oats Company* (New York: McGraw-Hill, 1967), 137–158; Jo-Ann Morgan, "Mammy the Huckster: Selling the Old South for a New Century," *American Art* 9, no. 1 (Spring 1995): 87–109; and Doris Witt, *Black Hunger: Food and the Politics of U.S. Identity* (New York: Oxford University Press, 1999), 26–30. On Rutt's decision to use the name, see Kenneth Goings, *Mammy and Uncle Mose: Black Collectibles and American Stereotyping* (Bloomington: University of Indiana Press, 1994), 40; Kern-Foxworth, *Aunt Jemima, Uncle Ben, and Rastus*, 63–66; and Manring, *Slave in a Box*, 60–72. On Billy Kersands and "Old Aunt Jemima," see Harris, *Colored Pictures*, 84–86; and Robert C. Toll, *Blacking Up: The Minstrel Show in Nineteenth-Century America* (New York: Oxford University Press, 1974), 254–261.

4. Witt, *Black Hunger*, 29–30.

5. The works of M. M. Manring and Doris Witt are important exceptions to this rule. I inadvertently repeated some of this erroneous information in my doctoral dissertation, Micki McElya, "Monumental Citizenship: Reading the Mammy Commemoration Controversy of the Early Twentieth Century" (New York University, 2003), 23–24.

6. Manring, *Slave in a Box*, 86–115.

7. This is the title and organizing concept of Manring's book, cited in note 3.

8. Manring, *Slave in a Box*, 72–74.

9. Jeanne Madeline Weimann, *The Fair Women* (Chicago: Academy Chicago, 1981), 121.

10. Ibid., 152.

11. Quoted ibid., 123.

12. Robert W. Rydell notes that only one thousand black visitors participated in "Colored People's Day." Rydell, *All the World's a Fair: Visions of Empire at American International Expositions, 1876–1916* (Chicago: University of Chicago Press, 1984), 53.

13. On this struggle for inclusion, see Gail Bederman, *Manliness and Civilization: A Cultural History of Gender and Race in the United States, 1880–1917* (Chicago: University of Chicago Press, 1995), 31–41;

Rydell, *All the World's a Fair*, 52–53; Turner, *Ceramic Uncles and Celluloid Mammies*, 49–50; and Kimberly Wallace-Sanders, "Dishing Up Dixie: Recycling the Old South in the Early-Twentieth-Century Domestic Ideal," in Rosemary Marangoly George, ed., *Burning Down the House: Recycling Domesticity* (Boulder: Westview Press, 1998), 215–231. On Wells's boycott of "Colored People's Day," see Patricia A. Schechter, *Ida B. Wells-Barnett and American Reform, 1880–1930* (Chapel Hill: University of North Carolina Press, 2001), 95–97. On the World Congress of Representative Women, see Wallace-Sanders, "Dishing Up Dixie," 219–224. Booker T. Washington's participation in the Labor Congress is detailed in Rydell, *All the World's a Fair*, 83. On Douglass's participation, see Bederman, *Manliness and Civilization*, 40.

14. Jo-Ann Morgan mistakenly places the R. T. Davis Milling Company booth and Nancy Green on the Midway Plaisance. Morgan, "Mammy the Huckster," 88.

15. Marquette, *Brands, Trademarks, and Good Will*, 145–146.

16. Hubert Howe Bancroft, *The Book of the Fair: An Historical and Descriptive Presentation of the World's Science, Art, and Industry, as Viewed through the Columbian Exposition at Chicago in 1893*, vol. 1 (1894; reprint, New York: Bounty Books, 1973), 396.

17. Elizabeth Lloyd, "Letters from the World's Fair, III," *Friends' Intelligencer*, July 29, 1893; *The Chicago Record's History of the World's Fair, Copiously Illustrated* (Chicago: Chicago Daily News Co., 1893), 65; Marian Shaw, "Chicago Letter: A Spicy Letter from Our Special Correspondent at the White City," *The Argus* (Fargo, N.D.), August 30, 1893, in Ann Feldman and Leo J. Harris, eds., *World's Fair Notes: A Woman Journalist Views Chicago's 1893 Columbian Exposition* (St. Paul: Pogo Press, 1992), 33. In a report reproduced in several newspapers, the author refers to free food and the Aunt Jemima product by name. It is accompanied by two illustrations, one of "Aunt Jemima" in a headscarf and shawl serving two well-dressed white women in large hats, and the other of a young white woman serving free hot chocolate to a similarly well-dressed crowd. "Chicago Is Level," *Lincoln (Neb.) Evening News*, August 14, 1893, 2; *Middletown (N.Y.) Daily Times*, August 12, 1893; *Newark (Ohio) Daily Advocate*, August 12, 1893, 7; and *Fitchburg (Mass.) Sentinel*, August 14, 1893.

18. *Ladies' Home Journal* 14, no. 2 (January 1897): 27. "Aunt Jemima's Lullaby" (1896), words by George Cooper, music by Samuel H. Speck.

19. Goings, *Aunt Jemima and Uncle Mose*. Grace Elizabeth Hale traces the

racialization of modern consumption, including the Aunt Jemima image, in *Making Whiteness: The Culture of Segregation in the South, 1890–1940* (New York: Pantheon, 1998), 151–168. Thomas C. Holt argues that racial identity and racism were (or are) produced and reproduced in the everyday quality of objects such as these. Holt, "Marking: Race, Race-Making, and the Writing of History," *American Historical Review* 100 (February 1995): 1–20. In her discussion of the late-nineteenth-century shift from scientific to cultural discourses of imperialist racialization in a British context, Anne McClintock refers to the explosion of this sort of kitsch as "commodity racism." McClintock, *Imperial Leather: Race, Gender, and Sexuality in the Colonial Contest* (New York: Routledge, 1995), 207–231.

20. Witt, *Black Hunger,* 28.

21. "'Aunt Jemima' of Pancake Fame Is Killed by Auto," *Chicago Tribune* (hereafter *CT*), September 4, 1923, 13. The *Missouri Farmer* is quoted in Manring, *Slave in a Box,* 77–78.

22. "'Aunt Jemima' of Pancake Fame Is Killed by Auto," 13.

23. Everything but the title is a verbatim reprint of the *Chicago Tribune* obituary. "'Aunt Jemima' Victim of Auto—Colored Mammy of Pancake Fame Crushed to Death in Chicago; Born in Kentucky," *Cook County Herald* (Arlington Heights, Ill.), October 12, 1923, 7. Census records related to the Walker family show that they moved to Chicago from Covington, Kentucky, sometime between 1870 and 1880, when Charles and Samuel Walker were both young. (They were twenty and fourteen years old, respectively, in 1880.) Nancy Green was never listed as a domestic worker in their household, although other black and white women were. This does not mean that Green did not move from Kentucky at the same time or follow them purposefully, but it also does nothing to prove that she did. U.S. Bureau of the Census, *Ninth Census of the United States, 1870,* Covington Ward 1, Kenton, Ky., Roll M593–478, 335; U.S. Bureau of the Census, *Tenth Census of the United States, 1880,* Lake View, Cook, Ill., Roll T9–201, 253.

24. Burke Adams and Harry S. Seymore were driving separate vehicles that collided, pushing Seymore's car onto the sidewalk, where it hit Green. Both were charged with manslaughter and held over for the grand jury. See "2 Drivers Held for Killing of 'Aunt Jemima,'" *CT,* September 8, 1923, 8.

25. "Aged Woman Killed When Autos Crash," *Chicago Defender* (hereafter *CD*), September 8, 1923, 1.

26. A. L. Jackson, "The Onlooker," *CD*, September 29, 1923, 12.

27. U.S. Bureau of the Census, *Twelfth Census of the United States, 1900*, Chicago Ward 30, Cook, Ill., Roll T623–281, 7A; U.S. Bureau of the Census, *Thirteenth Census of the United States, 1910*, Chicago Ward 30, Cook, Ill., Roll T624–276, 4A; U.S. Bureau of the Census, *Fourteenth Census of the United States, 1920*, Chicago Ward 30, Cook, Ill., Roll T625–313, 5A.

28. For other examples of the struggle to recover a black woman's life history from the mammy narratives that consumed it, see Lynn M. Hudson's analysis of popular representations and the creative self-presentation of Mary Ellen Pleasant in *The Making of "Mammy Pleasant": A Black Entrepreneur in Nineteenth-Century San Francisco* (Chicago: University of Illinois Press, 2003); and Benjamin Reiss, *The Showman and the Slave: Race, Death, and Memory in Barnum's America* (Cambridge: Harvard University Press, 2001), a study of Joice Heth, the woman P. T. Barnum exhibited as George Washington's "nurse."

29. Rydell, *All the World's a Fair*, 74–80.

30. *Harper's Weekly*, November 23, 1895, 1109.

31. Edward Ayers, *The Promise of the New South: Life after Reconstruction* (New York: Oxford University Press, 1992), 322; David Blight, *Race and Reunion: The Civil War in American Memory* (Cambridge: Belknap Press of Harvard University Press, 2001), 328–29; Hale, *Making Whiteness*, 148–150.

32. Rydell, *All the World's a Fair*, 80.

33. *Hosford's Handy Guide to the Cotton States and International Exposition, Atlanta, 1895*, scanned and made available by the Piedmont Park Conservancy, Atlanta, www.piedmontpark.org/history.

34. Hale, *Making Whiteness*, 150; Rydell, *All the World's a Fair*, 87.

35. For a discussion of the irony of the pairing, see Ayers, *Promise of the New South*, 324. The entrance is framed as a progress narrative in "Is He a New Negro?" *Chicago Inter Ocean*, September 28, 1895, reprinted in *The Booker T. Washington Papers*, vol. 4, ed. Louis R. Harlan (Chicago: University of Illinois Press, 1975), 34; and Blight, *Race and Reunion*, 329.

36. Ruth M. Winton, "Negro Participation in Southern Expositions, 1881–1915," *Journal of Negro Education* 16, no. 1 (Winter 1947): 37–38.

37. Ayers, *Promise of the New South*, 324.

38. Booker T. Washington, *Up from Slavery* (1901; reprint, New York:

Doubleday, 1998), 161–162. On turn-of-the century racial categories and the processes by which eastern and southern European immigrants were becoming "white" in the American contexts of segregation and imperialism, see Matthew Frye Jacobson, *Whiteness of a Different Color: European Immigrants and the Alchemy of Race* (Cambridge: Harvard University Press, 1998).

39. William J. Cansler to Booker T. Washington, September 26, 1895, in *Booker T. Washington Papers*, 4:30.

40. Houston A. Baker Jr., *Modernism and the Harlem Renaissance* (Chicago: University of Chicago Press, 1987), 15–41; Houston A. Baker Jr., *Turning South Again: Re-thinking Modernism/Re-reading Booker T.* (Durham: Duke University Press, 2001); Kevin K. Gaines, *Uplifting the Race: Black Leadership, Politics, and Culture in the Twentieth Century* (Chapel Hill: University of North Carolina Press, 1996), 19–46; Leon F. Litwack, *Trouble in Mind: Black Southerners in the Age of Jim Crow* (New York: Alfred A. Knopf, 1998), 354–355.

2. ANXIOUS PERFORMANCES

1. "Arche Club Members Have Rag-Time Afternoon Way Down South," *CT*, November 30, 1901, 5.

2. On dialect, see Shane White and Graham White, *The Sounds of Slavery: Discovering African American History through Songs, Sermons, and Speech* (Boston: Beacon Press, 2005), 81–84.

3. Grace Elizabeth Hale, *Making Whiteness: The Culture of Segregation in the South, 1890–1940* (New York: Pantheon Books, 1998), 85–119. A scene similar to the one at the Arche Club meeting in Chicago was reported at a charity function in Tacoma, Washington, in 1894. As forty young women performed a revue in blackface, the "original Aunt Jemima" served samples of pancakes and advertised a local grocery store. "Lady Minstrels—They Had a Crowded House and Looked Well in Black," *Tacoma Daily News*, March 29, 1894, 3; "Aunt Jemima," ibid.

4. The Arche Club was originally organized as an art appreciation group. "For the Love of Art," *CT*, March 30, 1885, 8.

5. It is likely that this woman was Agnes Moody, also of Chicago. "Did You Know That," *CD*, April 9, 1921, 16.

6. Thomas C. Holt, "Marking: Race, Race-Making, and the Writing of History," *American Historical Review* 100 (February 1995): 7.

7. Gertrude Langhorne, *Mammy's Letters* (Macon, Ga.: J. W. Burke Company, 1922), 7.

8. Ibid., 5.

9. On the post–World War I surge in popular interest in the Civil War, see Sarah E. Gardner, *Blood and Irony: Southern White Women's Narratives of the Civil War, 1861–1937* (Chapel Hill: University of North Carolina Press, 2004), 211.

10. Thomas Nelson Page, *The Negro: The Southerner's Problem* (New York: Scribners, 1904), 176.

11. Ibid., 177. Lawrence J. Friedman notes that "Page's choice of words suggested more than a close personal relationship with Ma' Lyddy; it pointed to a profoundly satisfying sensual relationship." Friedman, *The White Savage: Racial Fantasies in the Postbellum South* (Englewood Cliffs, N.J.: Prentice-Hall, 1970), 71. For an illuminating discussion of the mammy figure, white spanking fantasies, and the trope of the "beaten biscuit," see Doris Witt, *Black Hunger: Food and the Politics of U.S. Identity* (New York: Oxford University Press, 1999), 54–76.

12. Page, *The Negro*, 27.

13. The use of slavery and of enslaved people to represent white aspirations has a long history that dates back to the heyday of the antebellum domestic slave trade. Walter Johnson, *Soul by Soul: Life inside the Antebellum Slave Market* (Cambridge: Harvard University Press, 1999), 13.

14. *Congressional Record*, 67th Cong., 2d sess., December 19, 1921, vol. 62, pt. 1, 549. Studies that apply the psychoanalytic notion of "abjection" to the mammy figure facilitate this kind of analysis. See Diane Roberts, *The Myth of Aunt Jemima: Representations of Race and Region* (New York: Routledge, 1994); Witt, *Black Hunger*, 15–16; Patricia Yaeger, *Dirt and Desire: Reconstructing Southern Women's Literature, 1930–1990* (Chicago: University of Chicago Press, 2000), 113–149. Peter Stallybrass, Allon White, and Anne McClintock historicize abjection in the hidden role of the domestic servant in Freud's family romance. See Stallybrass and White, *The Politics and Poetics of Transgression* (Ithaca: Cornell University Press, 1986), 149–170; McClintock, *Imperial Leather: Race, Gender, and Sexuality in the Colonial Contest* (New York: Routledge, 1995), 84–91.

15. Deborah Gray White, *Ar'n't I a Woman? Female Slaves in the Plantation South* (New York: W. W. Norton & Company, 1985), 46.

16. This gets played out to provocative ends in Alice Randall's *Gone With*

the Wind parody, *The Wind Done Gone* (New York: Houghton Mifflin Company, 2001), in which Mammy is not only the enslaved surrogate mother of the household but also "Planter's" (Gerald O'Hara's) lover—making her mammy and jezebel simultaneously.

17. Langhorne, *Mammy's Letters*, 32–33.

18. Ibid., 37.

19. Ibid., 38.

20. United Daughters of the Confederacy, *Minutes of the Twenty-fifth Annual Convention, Louisville, Kentucky, April 1–5, 1918*, 324. Courtesy of the Caroline Meriwether Goodlett Library, UDC National Headquarters, Richmond, Va.

21. W. Fitzhugh Brundage, "White Women and the Politics of Historical Memory in the New South, 1880–1920," in Jane Dailey, Glenda Elizabeth Gilmore, and Bryant Simon, eds., *Jumpin' Jim Crow: Southern Politics from Civil War to Civil Rights* (Princeton: Princeton University Press, 2000), 115–139; and W. Fitzhugh Brundage, *The Southern Past: A Clash of Race and Memory* (Cambridge: Harvard University Press, 2005), chap. 1.

22. Scholars have explored the inconsistencies of the UDC's devotion to tradition and the Old South and its simultaneous promotion of public political roles for women. See, for example, Karen L. Cox, *Dixie's Daughters: The United Daughters of the Confederacy and the Preservation of Confederate Culture* (Gainesville: University Press of Florida, 2003); Anastasia Sims, *The Power of Femininity in the New South: Women's Organizations in North Carolina, 1883–1930* (Columbia: University of South Carolina Press, 1997); Angie Parrott, "'Love Makes Memory Eternal': The United Daughters of the Confederacy in Richmond, Virginia, 1897–1920," in Edward Ayers and John Willis, eds., *The Edge of the South: Life in Nineteenth-Century Virginia* (Charlottesville: University Press of Virginia, 1991), 219–238; LeeAnn Whites, *The Civil War as a Crisis in Gender: Augusta, Georgia, 1860–1890* (Athens: University of Georgia Press, 1995). Drew Gilpin Faust addresses this matter in the final chapter of her *Mothers of Invention: Women of the Slaveholding South in the American Civil War* (Chapel Hill: University of North Carolina Press, 1996).

23. Tara McPherson analyzes white womanhood and ways of "feeling southern" in a present-day context in her *Reconstructing Dixie: Race, Gender, and Nostalgia in the Imagined South* (Durham: Duke University Press, 2004), 205–256.

24. Sims, *Power of Femininity*, 130.

25. Shawn Michelle Smith, *American Archives: Gender, Race, and Class in Visual Culture* (Princeton: Princeton University Press, 1999), 136–156.

26. Nessa Johnson of Richmond, Virginia, became a member of a local chapter there. "In Brief: Virginia," *Washington Post* (hereafter *WP*), March 7, 2002, B3. Essie Mae Washington-Williams, Strom Thurmond's posthumously acknowledged biracial daughter, concluded her 2005 memoir with the note that she had applied for membership to the UDC and DAR through her father's side of the family. Washington-Williams and William Stadiem, *Dear Senator: A Memoir by the Daughter of Strom Thurmond* (New York: Regan Books, 2005), 221–223. In 1894 the DAR officially excluded black women from its membership. Smith, *American Archives*, 138.

27. On this shifting class structure, see Grace Elizabeth Hale, "'Some Women Have Never Been Reconstructed': Mildred Lewis Rutherford, Lucy M. Stanton, and the Racial Politics of White Southern Womanhood, 1900–1930," in John C. Inscoe, ed., *Georgia in Black and White: Explorations in the Race Relations of a Southern State, 1865–1950* (Athens: University of Georgia Press, 1994), 177.

28. Rutherford biographical information taken from a brief sketch that was run alongside her directive to UDC historians in *Confederate Veteran* (hereafter *CV*) 20 (February 1912): 54. See also Hale, "Some Women Have Never Been Reconstructed."

29. It is impossible to consider the life and work of Rutherford without commenting on her determination and success in her endeavors. David Blight, for example, argues that "Rutherford gave new meaning to the term 'diehard'" (*Race and Reunion*, 279). Karen L. Cox states that Rutherford "set a standard that was extremely difficult for her successors to meet" (*Dixie's Daughters*, 103).

30. "Requests by the UDC Historian General," *CV* 20 (February 1912): 54–55. The published version was edited slightly for length.

31. Mildred Lewis Rutherford, "An Open Letter to All State Historians, Chairmen of Historical Committees and Chapter Historians of the United Daughters of the Confederacy," UDC Collection, Box 2, Rutherford Papers, 1912, Museum of the Confederacy, Richmond, Va. (hereafter MOC). All citations in this discussion refer to this source.

32. Mary Poppenheim et al., *The History of the United Daughters of the*

Confederacy, vol. 1 (1938; reprint, Richmond: United Daughters of the Confederacy, 1994), 139.

33. Rutherford, "Open Letter."

34. Mildred Lewis Rutherford, "Extract from 'Wrongs of History Righted," *CV* 23 (October 1915): 443–444. Ulrich Bonnell Phillips, *American Negro Slavery* (1918; reprint, Gloucester, Mass.: Peter Smith, 1959).

35. Elizabeth Coffee Sheldon, "Black Mammy and Her White Baby," in *Tributes to Faithful Slaves*, vol. 47, Rutherford Scrapbook Collection, 1911–1916, MOC.

36. "The Old Slave's Lament," ibid. Sally McMillen argues that very few enslaved women actually served as wet nurses; see her "Mothers' Sacred Duty: Breast-feeding Patterns among Middle- and Upper-Class Women in the Antebellum South," *Journal of Southern History* 51 (August 1985): 333–356.

37. Mrs. James K. Gibson, Wheeler Chapter no. 1077, "Our Faithful Slaves," unpublished, date unknown. Rutherford Collection—Tennessee Manuscripts, Box 2, MOC.

38. M. Alison Kibler, *Rank Ladies: Gender and Cultural Hierarchy in American Vaudville* (Chapel Hill: University of North Carolina Press, 1999); Michael Rogin, *Black Face, White Noise: Jewish Immigrants in the Hollywood Melting Pot* (Berkeley: University of California Press, 1998).

39. Because of its links to education and status, this popular oratorical culture provided key avenues for black activism as well. See, for example, on Hallie Quinn Brown's contributions to elocution, rhetoric, composition education, and racial uplift, Keith Gilyard, "African American Contributions to Composition Studies," *College Composition and Communication* 50, no. 4 (June 1999): 628–629; Susan Kates, "The Embodied Rhetoric of Hallie Q. Brown," *College English* 59, no. 1 (January 1997): 59–71.

40. Mary Bell pamphlet, File: "Unsorted Correspondence," Randolph Papers, Box 17, undated, MOC. The pamphlet was produced sometime after 1910, as it refers to "Ex-Senator Gordon of Mississippi," who retired in that year.

41. Ibid.

42. Ibid. On Polk Miller, see Tim Brooks, *Lost Sounds: Blacks and the Birth of the Recording Industry, 1890–1919* (Urbana: University of Illinois Press, 2004), 215–233.

43. Eric Lott, *Love and Theft: Blackface Minstrelsy and the American*

Working Class (New York: Oxford University Press, 1993), 64; David R. Roediger, *The Wages of Whiteness: Race and the Making of the American Working Class* (New York: Verso, 1991).

44. In her study of the early-twentieth-century American circus, Janet M. Davis argues that promotional media stressed the elite or middle-class status of female performers to forestall any questioning of their respectability and virtue. Their motivation for working was not identified as need; instead they were said to perform for adventure and "pin money." Davis, *The Circus Age: Culture and Society under the American Big Top* (Chapel Hill: University of North Carolina Press, 2002), 95.

45. "Negro Dialect and Slave Songs," *CV* 6 (July 1898): 344.

46. "Preserving Amiability of Black Mammy," *CV* 17 (August 1909): 427.

47. On the early-twentieth-century Chautauqua, see Frederick J. Antczak and Edith Siemers, "The Divergence of Purpose and Practice on the Chautauqua: Keith Vawter's Self-Defense," in Gregory Clark and S. Michael Halloran, eds., *Oratorical Culture in Nineteenth-Century America: Transformations in the Theory and Practice of Rhetoric* (Carbondale: Southern Illinois University Press, 1993), 208–225; John E. Tapia, *Circuit Chautauqua: From Rural Education to Popular Entertainment in Early-Twentieth-Century America* (Jefferson, N.C.: McFarland & Company, 1997); and Andrew Chamberlin Reiser, "Secularization Reconsidered: Chautauqua and the De-Christianization of Middle-Class Authority, 1880–1920," in Burton J. Bledstein and Robert D. Johnston, eds., *The Middling Sorts: Explorations in the History of the American Middle Class* (New York: Routledge, 2001), 136–150.

48. On Chautauqua attendance, see Tapia, *Circuit Chautauqua*, 7. Robert Rydell puts attendance at the Chicago World's Columbian Exposition at 27,529,400. Rydell, *All the World's a Fair: Visions of Empire at American International Expositions, 1876–1916* (Chicago: University of Chicago Press, 1984), 40. He notes that attendance at the Atlanta Cotton States and International Exposition was 1,286,863 (102).

49. Helen Waggoner pamphlet, 1924, Redpath Chautauqua Bureau, Special Collections Department, University of Iowa Libraries, Iowa City.

50. Emily Farrow Gregory pamphlet, undated, Redpath Chautauqua Bureau, Special Collections Department, University of Iowa Libraries, Iowa City.

51. Mrs. John McRaven pamphlet, undated, Redpath Chautauqua Bureau, Special Collections Department, University of Iowa Libraries, Iowa City.

52. Cordelia Powell Odenheimer to Janet Randolph, February 11, 1923, Randolph Papers, Box 15, MOC.

53. Odenheimer to Randolph, March 14, 1923, Randolph Papers, Box 15, MOC.

54. Reports of white women's amateur minstrelsy at school functions and club meetings appear frequently in newspaper society pages during this period and date back to at least the 1890s. See, for example, "Lady Minstrels," 3; "News of the Club World," *WP*, April 8, 1917, E2; "Society," *WP*, June 13, 1919, 7; "Winchester Girls in Minstrel Show," *Richmond Times-Dispatch*, January 8, 1923, 9.

55. Cheryl Thurber notes that "having a mammy became a badge of having been 'raised right' as a proper southerner," which became especially important to the UDC after the First World War, as many in the organization worried over its increasingly middle-class membership. Thurber, "The Development of the Mammy Image and Mythology," in Virginia Bernhard, Betty Brandon, Elizabeth Fox-Genovese, and Theda Purdue, eds., *Southern Women: Histories and Identities* (Columbia: University of Missouri Press, 1992), 99.

56. Jessie W. Parkhurst, "The Role of the Black Mammy in the Plantation Household," *Journal of Negro History* (hereafter *JNH*) 23 (1936): 351.

57. James Weldon Johnson, "The 'Black Mammy' Monument," *New York Age*, January 6, 1923, 4.

3. THE LINE BETWEEN MOTHER AND MAMMY

1. Records from Chicago's Cook County court system related to the Delbridge case are no longer available and are believed to have been destroyed. The archive that remains consists of the coverage of this case in newspapers, some of which reproduced court transcripts and police documents in part or in full. This necessarily adds another layer of mediation to the story as it is refracted through individuals, the court, and then the news. My approach to this case and its remaining sources is shaped by two studies of modern legal scandals: Lisa Duggan, *Sapphic Slashers: Sex, Violence, and American Modernity* (Durham: Duke University Press, 2000), and Earl Lewis and Heidi Ardizzone, *Love on Trial: An American Scandal in Black and White* (New York: W. W. Norton, 2001). Within a year of the conclusion of the Delbridge case, James G. Cotter was an assistant in the Illinois attor-

ney general's office and a leading figure among black Republican politicians in the city. He went on to become an assistant U.S. district attorney and ran twice, unsuccessfully, for alderman. "Olson Demands Lundin Join in Party Debate," *CT,* January 28, 1918, 7; "Louis Anderson Lines Up 13 'Foes' in Primary Race," *CT,* January 18, 1923, 10; and "M. V. L. Issues Its Report on First Nineteen Wards," *CT,* February 18, 1929, 5.

2. "Taken from Black Mammy," *New York Times* (hereafter *NYT*), March 3, 1911, 3; "Black Mammy Gives Up Child," *NYT,* March 5, 1911, 4. "Taken from Black Mammy" was reprinted in *WP,* March 4, 1911, 6.

3. James Weldon Johnson, *Along This Way* (New York: Viking Press, 1933), 9–10.

4. "'Yankees Ain't Quality Folks,' Says Mammy," *CT,* December 29, 1916, 7.

5. "Mammy Fights for Her 'Baby,'" *Chicago Daily News* (hereafter *CDN*), December 28, 1916, 3.

6. Ibid.

7. U.S. Bureau of the Census, *Thirteenth Census of the United States, 1910,* Chicago Ward 2, Cook County, Ill., Roll T624–242, 3B. Camilla and James Jackson first appear as a married couple in the 1870 census living in Atlanta. U.S. Bureau of the Census, *Ninth Census of the United States, 1870,* Atlanta Ward 4, Fulton County, Ga., Roll M593–151, 307.

8. "Fight Color Line in Juvenile Court," *CD,* August 19, 1916, 4; "Delbridge Girl Is Found," *CT,* February 14, 1917, 3.

9. Jackson's lawyers produced some of the man's letters as evidence of their client's legal guardianship of Marjorie. One of these was reproduced in "'Yankees Ain't Quality Folks,' Says Mammy," 7.

10. Hortense Spillers contends that notions of *value* are always freighted with race and gender in an "American Grammar" produced by slavery; see her "Mama's Baby, Papa's Maybe: An American Grammar Book," *Diacritics* (Summer 1987): 68.

11. "'Mammy's Girl,'" *CT,* December 28, 1916, 3.

12. "'Yankees Ain't Quality Folks,' Says Mammy," 7.

13. Chicago Commission on Race Relations, *The Negro in Chicago: A Study of Race Relations and a Race Riot in 1919* (1922; reprint, New York: Arno Press, 1968); James N. Gregory, *The Southern Diaspora: How the Great Migrations of Black and White Southerners Transformed America* (Chapel Hill: University of North Carolina Press, 2005);

James R. Grossman, *Land of Hope: Chicago, Black Southerners, and the Great Migration* (Chicago: University of Chicago Press, 1989); Carole Marks, *Farewell—We're Good and Gone: The Great Black Migration* (Bloomington: Indiana University Press, 1989); Joe William Trotter Jr., *The Great Migration in Historical Perspective: New Dimensions of Race, Class, and Gender* (Bloomington: Indiana University Press, 1991). For the fifty thousand figure, see St. Clair Drake and Horace R. Clayton, *Black Metropolis: A Study of Negro Life in a Northern City* (1945; reprint, Chicago: University of Chicago Press, 1993), 58.

14. Gregory, *Southern Diaspora*, 45–49; Grossman, *Land of Hope*, 168–170.

15. Grossman, *Land of Hope*, 168.

16. "'Yankees Ain't Quality Folks,' Says Mammy," 7.

17. Camilla Jackson died in Chicago on February 7, 1934. Illinois Statewide Death Index, death certificate 6003936.

18. "Mammy Fights for Her 'Baby,'" 3.

19. "'Yankees Ain't Quality Folks,' Says Mammy," 7. In the absence of court records it is impossible to know the exact reasoning and case law the judge used to support his ruling that a black woman could not be the legal guardian of a white child. It is unlikely that he found a direct application to the case in Illinois statutory law on guardianship or adoption. Bowles probably relied on the "best interest of the child" standard in custody issues, as it had been elaborated by the Illinois Supreme Court in a 1905 case, *Minnie S. Mahon et al. v. The People ex rel. Margaret Robertson*, 218 Ill. 171.

20. On the court's ruling, see "Negro Mammy Loses One Step for White Girl," *CT*, December 31, 1916, 8. Marjorie Delbridge was sent to the "Mary A. Home" at 4736 Monticello Avenue; see "'Yankees Ain't Quality Folks,' Says Mammy," 7. Concerning her refusal to return, see "Slow to Leave 'Mammy,'" *CDN*, January 8, 1917, 1.

21. The master microfilm of the *Chicago Defender* is missing most pages for January 1917, including the issue in which this article appeared. The *Tribune's* report on the contempt hearing and subsequent reports in the *Defender* provide clues about the charges. "State's Attorney's Aid Asks Protection of Court," *CT*, January 18, 1917, 14; "Marjory [*sic*] Delbridge Case Not Settled," *CD*, January 27, 1917, 1.

22. "Marjory Delbridge Case Not Settled," 1.

23. "Taken from Mammy," *CT*, January 21, 1917, 9.

24. "Marjory Delbridge Case Not Settled," 1.

25. "Take Girl from Her 'Mammy,'" *CDN*, January 20, 1917, 1.

26. "Taken from Mammy," 9.

27. "Take Girl from Her 'Mammy,'" 1.

28. "Taken from Mammy," 9.

29. "Marjory Delbridge Case Not Settled," 1.

30. On supporters, see, for example, "Offers Home and Brother to Marjorie," *CT,* January 24, 1917, 13; "Marjory Delbridge Case Not Settled," 1; "Marjorie Delbridge and 'Mammy' Gone," *CT,* January 27, 1917, 1.

31. "Offers Home and Brother to Marjorie," 13. The home and brother referred to in the headline were not the family with whom Marjorie was sent to live, Mr. and Mrs. Louis Brock, discussed later in this chapter.

32. On the Great Migration and vice reform in Chicago, see Kevin J. Mumford, *Interzones: Black/White Sex Districts in Chicago and New York in the Early Twentieth Century* (New York: Columbia University Press, 1997). On the city's crackdown on Black and Tans in 1917, see Grossman, *Land of Hope,* 170. On the Committee of Fifteen's activities along Thirty-first Street in 1916, see Chicago Commission on Race Relations, *Negro in Chicago,* 342 (map).

33. On the expansion of the Black Belt into Hyde Park, see Chicago Commission on Race Relations, *Negro in Chicago,* 135; and Grossman, *Land of Hope,* 174.

34. Drake and Clayton, *Black Metropolis,* 63–64.

35. "Offers Home and Brother to Marjorie," 13.

36. "It's Brighter for Marjorie," *CDN,* January 24, 1917, 3.

37. "Woman's Club Deadlocks over Marjorie's Fate," *CT,* January 25, 1917, 6.

38. "Marjorie Delbridge in a New Home," *CDN,* January 24, 1917, 3. On the possibility of reading the emotions and body language of photographic subjects that challenge the photographer's authority and intent, see Laura Wexler, "Seeing Sentiment: Photography, Race, and the Innocent Eye," in Elizabeth Abel, Barbara Christian, and Helene Moglen, eds., *Female Subjects in Black and White: Race, Psychoanalysis, Feminism* (Berkeley: University of California Press, 1997), 175–177.

39. "Woman's Club Deadlocks over Marjorie's Fate," 6.

40. See the editorial beginning, "Little Marjory should be taken care of by our citizens," " *CD,* January 27, 1917, editorial page.

41. "Wide Search for Marjorie Unavailing," *CT,* January 28, 1917, 1. Her disappearance was also reported in Washington, D.C.; "14-Year-Old Girl Missing," *WP,* January 28, 1917, 12.

42. "Marjorie Delbridge and 'Mammy' Gone," *CT,* January 27, 1917, 1;

"Marjory Disappears; Police B——," *CD*, February 3, 1917, 1 [page cut off on microfilm, full headline unreadable]. On the rally at Dreamland, see "Plan Contempt Proceedings to Find Marjorie," *CT*, January 30, 1917, 17.

43. "Mammy," *CD*, February 3, 1917, editorial page. The *Chicago Defender* consistently spelled Marjorie's name "Marjory" and argued that white-owned papers were misspelling it; "Marjory Disappears," 1. She was always listed in the census as "Marjorie," however.

44. "Mrs. Brock, Sleepless, Works Hard to Find Missing Marjorie," *CT*, January 28, 1917, 2.

45. Ibid. On Mr. Brock's weight loss, see "Strange Beings Fill Shadows of Delbridge Case," *CT*, January 31, 1917, 17.

46. "Description—How Marjorie Delbridge Looks, Talks, and Was Dressed When She Disappeared from the Brock Home," *CT*, January 28, 1917, 2.

47. On the continuance and the judge's orders, see "Marjorie Mystery Is Bigger as Hours Pass," *CDN*, January 27, 1917, 3. On the contempt charges, see "Plan Contempt Proceedings to Find Marjorie," *CT*, January 30 1917, 17.

48. "Wide Search for Marjorie Unavailing," *CT*, January 28, 1917, 1.

49. "Phipps Woman Denies Knowing of Marjorie," *CDN*, January 29, 1917, 4.

50. Ibid.

51. "Strange Beings Fill Shadows of Delbridge Case," 17.

52. Ibid.

53. Ibid. See also "'Margy's' 'Mammy' Grieves," *CDN*, January 31, 1917, 1.

54. "Wide Search for Marjorie Unavailing," 1.

55. On representations of women and gender in *Intolerance*, see Michael Rogin, "The Great Mother Domesticated: Sexual Difference and Sexual Indifference in D. W. Griffith's *Intolerance*," *Critical Inquiry* 15, no. 3 (Spring 1989): 510–555.

56. On the warrant, see "Strange Beings Fill Shadows of Delbridge Case," 17. "Find Girl Is Not Marjorie," *CDN*, February 1, 1917, 3.

57. "Marjorie May Be Part Negro, Woman Thinks," *CT*, February 1, 1917, 10.

58. Ibid.

59. "That Awful Suspicion," *CD*, February 10, 1917, editorial page.

60. "Delbridge Girl in City, Tapped Wire Discloses," *CT*, February 3, 1917, 13.

61. "'Mammy' Gets One More Day," *CDN*, February 2, 1917, 1; "Delbridge Girl Clew Is Sought by Court Quiz," *CT*, February 2, 1917, 17.

62. "Delbridge Girl in City, Tapped Wire Discloses," 13.

63. "Says 'Mammy' Plays 'Possum,'" *CDN*, February 6, 1917, 1.

64. "Face Contempt Charge Today in Delbridge Case," *CT*, February 6, 1917, 13.

65. "Marjory Is Still M——," *CD*, February 10, 1917, 1 [full headline and article cut off on microfilm].

66. "'Mammy' Jackson on Stand," *CDN*, February 7, 1917, 1. Also on this page, "American Line Cancels Passenger Sailings," "Where to Enlist," and "Hoist Your Flag! Is Plea," *CDN*, February 7, 1917, 1.

67. "'Mammy's' Tale Fails to Move Judge Bowles," *CT*, February 8, 1917, 9.

68. "Marjorie in Custody Again; 5 Face Charges," *CT*, February 15, 1917, 1, 7.

69. "Marjorie, Found, Is Spirited Away Again," *CDN*, February 14, 1917, 1.

70. "Delbridge Girl Is Found," *CT*, February 14, 1917, 1.

71. Ibid., 1, 3.

72. Ibid., 3.

73. Ibid.

74. "Mammy Asks Margy Writ," *CDN*, February 15, 1917, 1.

75. "Marjorie in Custody Again; 5 Face Charges," 1.

76. Ibid., 7.

77. "Delbridge Girl Smuggled Back by Hoyne Aids," *CT*, February 17, 1917, 13.

78. "Marjorie Must Come Back to Court Here," *CDN*, February 16, 1917, 1. On the habeas corpus proceedings in Detroit, see also "'Mammy' Starts Fight in Detroit to Win 'Margie,'" *CT*, February 16, 1917, 13.

79. "Marjorie Says Her Lawyers Kidnaped Her," *CT*, February 20, 1917, 10; on Marjorie's court appearance, see also "Marjorie in Court To-Day," *CDN*, February 19, 1917, 1; "Marjorie Imperils Four," *CDN*, February 20, 1917, 3.

80. "Marjorie Says Her Lawyers Kidnaped Her," 1.

81. "Marjorie Case Ends on Monday," *CT*, February 24, 1917, 13; "Marjory Now Ward of State," *CD*, February 24, 1917, 1. On the last hearing related to the final writ, see "Marjorie Case Settled, Then Opened Again," *CT*, February 27, 1917, 5; "Judge Sabath Orders Marjorie Kept by Court," *CT*, March 1, 1917, 5.

82. "Marjorie Joyous at News of Kin; Sends Her Love," *CT,* May 2, 1917, 1.

83. On Bartelme's position in 1922, see Chicago Commission on Race Relations, *Negro in Chicago,* 334.

84. "Marjorie Joyous at News of Kin," 8.

85. Ibid.

86. Mrs. Louis Brock, "Her Praise—Mrs. Louis Brock Tells Why Marjorie Deserves Love and Care," *CT,* May 25, 1917, 3.

87. "Marjorie Meets Her Grandpa for the First Time," *CT,* May 28, 1917, 17.

88. "Attorneys for Delbridge Girl Face Inquiry," *CT,* October 4, 1917, 10.

89. U.S. Bureau of the Census, *Fourteenth Census of the United States, 1920,* Montgomery, Alabama, Ward 3, Roll T625–36, 3A; U.S. Bureau of the Census, *Fourteenth Census of the United States, 1920,* Chicago Ward 6, Cook County, Ill., Roll T625–309, 5A; U.S. Bureau of the Census, *Fifteenth Census of the United States, 1930,* Chicago Ward 19, Cook County, Ill., Roll 448, 26A.

4. MONUMENTAL POWER

1. This language is taken from the U.S. Senate bill seeking authorization of a federal land grant for the memorial. *Congressional Record,* 67th Cong., 4th sess., February 28, 1923, vol. 64, pt. 5, 4839. Arguably the juxtaposition of the "Great Emancipator" and the faithful slave is far more unsettling from a twenty-first-century perspective than it would have been to those at the unveiling in 1922. Despite black efforts at commemoration, the Lincoln hailed at his monument's unveiling was celebrated as the savior of a reunified white nation, not as an agent of black freedom. On this and the unveiling generally, see Adam Fairclough, "Civil Rights and the Lincoln Memorial: The Censored Speeches of Robert R. Moton (1922) and John Lewis (1963)," *JNH* 82, no. 4 (Autumn 1997): 408–416; and Scott A. Sandage, "A Marble House Divided: The Lincoln Memorial, the Civil Rights Movement, and the Politics of Memory, 1939–1963," *Journal of American History* 80, no. 1 (June 1993): 139–143.

2. On "particular codes of remembrance" through the monuments and memorials of Washington, D.C., see Marita Sturken, *Tangled Memories: The Vietnam War, the AIDS Epidemic, and the Politics of Remembering* (Berkeley: University of California Press, 1997), 47.

3. Mary B. Poppenheim et al., *The History of the United Daughters of the*

Confederacy, vol. 1 (1938; reprint, Richmond: United Daughters of the Confederacy, 1994), 49.

4. Ibid., 92.

5. Gaines M. Foster takes the question of this kind of community memory over the long term as the point of departure for his foundational study *Ghosts of the Confederacy: Defeat, the Lost Cause, and the Emergence of the New South* (New York: Oxford University Press, 1987), 3–8. On UDC monument building in this period, see Karen L. Cox, *Dixie's Daughters: The United Daughters of the Confederacy and the Preservation of Confederate Culture* (Gainesville: University Press of Florida, 2003), 49–72.

6. On the growing southern monument industry, see Foster, *Ghosts of the Confederacy*, 167–168; and Kirk Savage, *Standing Soldiers, Kneeling Slaves: Race, War, and Monument in Nineteenth-Century America* (Princeton: Princeton University Press, 1997), 164, 182.

7. Foster, *Ghosts of the Confederacy*, 128–131; Savage, *Standing Soldiers*, 162.

8. On debates within the UDC, see Joan Marie Johnson, "'Ye Gave Them a Stone': African-American Women's Clubs, the Frederick Douglass Home, and the Black Mammy Monument," *Journal of Women's History* 17, no. 1 (Spring 2005): 70–71; Micki McElya, "Commemorating the Color Line: The National Mammy Monument Controversy of the 1920s," in Cynthia Mills and Pamela H. Simpson, eds., *Monuments to the Lost Cause: Women, Art, and the Landscapes of Southern Memory* (Knoxville: University of Tennessee Press, 2003), 203–218. On calls for faithful slave memorials from outside the organization, see, for example, Johnson, "Ye Gave Them a Stone," 72–73; June O. Patton, "Moonlight and Magnolias in Southern Education: The Black Mammy Memorial Institute," *JNH* 65, no. 2 (Spring 1980): 149–155; Savage, *Standing Soldiers*, 155–161.

9. Mrs. G. Gilliland Aston, "A Monument to the Faithful Old Slaves," *CV* 12, no. 9 (September 1904): 443. On the UCV's campaigns to erect monuments to southern white women, see Foster, *Ghosts of the Confederacy*, 175–178; Cynthia Mills, "Gratitude and Gender Wars: Monuments to the Women of the Sixties," in Mills and Simpson, *Monuments to the Lost Cause*, 183–200.

10. Aston, "A Monument to the Faithful Old Slaves," 443.

11. Mrs. W. Carleton Adams, "Slave Monument Question," *CV* 12, no. 11 (November 1904): 525.

12. Mary M. Solari, "Monument to Faithful Slaves," *CV* 13, no. 3 (March 1905): 123.

13. This time the memorial was to take the form of a stained-glass window for the Confederate Battle Abbey, then still in the planning stages. On the abbey, see Ann Hunter McLean, "Unveiling the Lost Cause: A Study of Monuments to the Civil War Memory in Richmond, Virginia, and Vicinity" (Ph.D. diss., University of Virginia, 1998), 150–157; William M. S. Rasmussen, "Planning a Temple to the Lost Cause: The Confederate 'Battle Abbey,'" in Mills and Simpson, *Monuments to the Lost Cause*, 163–182.

14. Poppenheim et al., *History of the United Daughters of the Confederacy*, 77.

15. On the 1912 call, see "Daughters' Ire Up," *WP*, November 16, 1912, 2. The only non-funereal faithful slave monument including a mammy figure known to have been erected in the United States was unveiled in Fort Mill, South Carolina, in 1898. Savage, *Standing Soldiers*, 155–161. Sporadic calls for monuments to the mammy figure came from the UDC and other organizations but never gained ground and seem to have faded as quickly as they were made. The UDC began its first official faithful slave memorial campaign in 1920 to commemorate Heyward Shepherd, a black railroad employee who was the first person killed in John Brown's raid at Harpers Ferry. He was murdered, according to the UDC, because he refused to join the abolitionist's attack. The monument campaign suffered a number of setbacks, including the discovery that Shepherd had not been a slave and protests from Harpers Ferry elected officials and students at Storer College, a black institution near the monument site. After many changes, the monument (no longer to a "faithful slave") was erected in October 1931. Poppenheim et al., *History of the United Daughters of the Confederacy*, 77–79. See also the reports of the Committee for the Faithful Slave Memorial in the UDC Annual Convention Minutes of 1925, 1926, 1927, and 1931, courtesy of Caroline Meriwether Goodlett Library, UDC National Headquarters, Richmond, Va., which is the source of all convention minutes cited in this chapter; and Mary Johnson, "An 'Ever Present Bone of Contention': The Heyward Shepherd Memorial," *West Virginia History* 56 (1997): 1–26.

16. Census records show that by 1830 the free black population of Washington, D.C., slightly outnumbered the enslaved population by a margin of thirty-three people. This margin expanded considerably over

the next thirty years. In 1860 the free black population numbered 11,131, in contrast to 3,185 enslaved, according to the national census. Constance McLaughlin Green, *The Secret City: A History of Race Relations in the Nation's Capital* (Princeton: Princeton University Press, 1967), 33 (table 1). On Washington, D.C., as a southern city in the early twentieth century, see Sharon Harley, "Black Women in a Southern City: Washington, D.C., 1890–1920," in Joanne V. Hawks and Sheila L. Skemp, eds., *Sex, Race, and the Role of Women in the South* (Jackson: University Press of Mississippi, 1983), 59.

17. Cornelia Reynolds Robinson, "Children of the White House and Cabinet," *WP*, March 16, 1913, M6.

18. "Supreme Court to Present Gift to White House Bride," *WP*, November 14, 1913, 4.

19. "Begin U.C.V. Shaft—Daughters of the Confederacy Hosts to Blue and Gray," *WP*, November 13, 1912, 2.

20. On the opening ceremonies, see *Nineteenth Annual Convention Souvenir Program, November 12–16, 1912*, 5, Folder—"Program: 19th Annual Conv. UDC November 1912, 23rd A. C. Nov. 1916, 24th A. C. Nov. 1917, 25th A. C. Nov. 1919," UDC: National, Box 5, MOC; Hilary A. Herbert, *History of the Arlington Confederate Monument* (United Daughters of the Confederacy, 1914), 17. Taft is quoted in Sarah E. Gardner, *Blood and Irony: Southern White Women's Narratives of the Civil War, 1861–1937* (Chapel Hill: University of North Carolina Press, 2004), 162. For other general descriptions of the evening, see Cox, *Dixie's Daughters*, 147–149, and Cecilia Elizabeth O'Leary, *To Die For: The Paradox of American Patriotism* (Princeton: Princeton University Press, 1999), 81.

21. Moses Jacob Ezekiel, *Memoirs from the Baths of Diocletian*, ed. Joseph Guttman and Stanley F. Chyet (Detroit: Wayne State University Press, 1975), 441.

22. Herbert, *History of the Arlington Confederate Monument*, 77. On the general history of the monument, see Karen L. Cox, "The Confederate Monument at Arlington: A Token of Reconciliation," in Mills and Simpson, *Monuments to the Lost Cause*, 149–162; Cox, *Dixie's Daughters*, 68–72; Kathryn Allamong Jacob, *Testament to Union: Civil War Monuments in Washington, D.C.* (Baltimore: Johns Hopkins University Press, 1999), 164–171.

23. This phrase is drawn from John Berger, *Ways of Seeing* (New York: Penguin Books, 1977).

24. "Gray and Blue Join—Unite in Unveiling Great Confederate Monument," *WP*, June 5, 1914, 3.

25. Agatha D'Aubigne [Agatha Aubrey Woodson], "The Women of the New South," *The South of Today*, vol. 38, Rutherford Scrapbook Collection, 1911–1916, MOC.

26. On Ellen Wilson's role as political wife, see Kurt Piehler, "Wilson, Ellen Axson," in John A. Garraty and Mark C. Carnes, eds., *American National Biography*, vol. 23 (New York: Oxford University Press, 1999), 570. On her influence on domestic policy and segregation, see Green, *Secret City*, 175. Concerning the White House screening of *Birth of a Nation*, see John Hope Franklin, "*The Birth of a Nation*: Propaganda as History," in *Race and History: Selected Essays, 1938–1988* (Baton Rouge: Louisiana State University Press, 1989), 16.

27. For a specific case of very subtle pro-suffrage sentiment on the part of two of the most prominent UDC members in the early twentieth century, sisters Louisa and Mary Poppenheim from South Carolina, see Joan Marie Johnson, "'This Wonderful Dream Nation!' Black and White South Carolina Women and the Creation of the New South, 1898–1930" (Ph.D. diss., University of California, Los Angeles, 1997), 87–97. On the women's suffrage movement in the southern states, see Elna C. Green, *Southern Strategies: Southern Women and the Woman Suffrage Question* (Chapel Hill: University of North Carolina Press, 1997); Marjorie Spruill Wheeler, *New Women in the New South: The Leaders of the Woman Suffrage Movement in the Southern States* (New York: Oxford University Press, 1993).

28. D'Aubigne, "Women of the New South."

29. Mildred Lewis Rutherford, "Address Delivered by Miss Mildred Louis Rutherford, Historian-General, Washington, D.C., Thursday, November 19, 1912," Folder—"Report of the Historian-General, 1909–1912, 1916," UDC: National/General Division, Box 6, MOC.

30. On the founding of the NWP and the D.C. protests, see Sara M. Evans, *Born for Liberty: A History of Women in America* (New York: Free Press, 1997), 164–172.

31. On political changes among black elite Washingtonians, see Jacqueline M. Moore, *Leading the Race: The Transformation of the Black Elite in the Nation's Capital, 1880–1920* (Charlottesville: University Press of Virginia, 1999), 202–205. On Carter G. Woodson's scholarship and his Association for the Study of Negro Life and History, see W. Fitzhugh Brundage, *The Southern Past: A Clash of Race and Memory* (Cambridge: Harvard University Press, 2005), 151–158. On the Na-

tional Association of Colored Women and Mary Church Terrell, see Deborah Gray White, *Too Heavy a Load: Black Women in Defense of Themselves, 1894–1994* (New York: W. W. Norton, 1999). On working-class alienation from elite politics, see, for example, Tera Hunter, *To 'Joy My Freedom: Southern Black Women's Lives and Labors after the Civil War* (Cambridge: Harvard University Press, 1997), chaps. 7 and 8; Robin D. G. Kelley, "'We Are Not What We Seem': The Politics and Pleasures of Community," in *Race Rebels: Culture, Politics, and the Black Working Class* (New York: Free Press, 1994), 35–53; and White, *Too Heavy a Load*, 132–141.

32. On "Red Summer," see William M. Tuttle Jr., *Race Riot: Chicago in the Red Summer of 1919* (New York: Atheneum, 1970).

33. "Detective Sergeant Wilson Victim; Other Officers Hurt; Negro Runs Amuck, Wounding Many in Flight," *WP*, July 22, 1919, 1.

34. "Riots Elsewhere, Forecast by Negro—Colored Men Will Hereafter Protect Themselves, Says J. W. Johnson," *WP*, July 25, 1919, 4.

35. Tuttle, *Race Riot*.

36. Neval H. Thomas, "Washington D.C.—A Paradise of Paradoxes," *The Messenger* 5, no. 10 (October 1923): 838.

37. Hunter, *To 'Joy My Freedom*, 104–105.

38. "For and Against the 'Black Mammy's' Monument," *Literary Digest*, April 28, 1923, 48.

39. The most popular and accessible version of this conception was of course presented in the film *Birth of a Nation* (1915), with its epic contrast of the South before the Civil War and during Reconstruction. Not long after the film's release, U. B. Phillips made a similar argument about the "plantation school." Phillips, *American Negro Slavery* (1918; reprint, Gloucester, Mass.: Peter Smith, 1959).

40. Louisa Poppenheim, "Woman's Work in the South," in *The South in the Building of the Nation*, vol. 10 (1909), quoted in Johnson, "This Wonderful Dream Nation!" 258.

41. Historian Rebecca Montgomery argues that southern women like those in the UDC "were not so much public mothers as public 'mistresses' of a public 'plantation.'" Montgomery, "Lost Cause Mythology in New South Reform: Gender, Class, Race, and the Politics of Patriotic Citizenship in Georgia, 1890–1925," in Janet L. Coryell et al., eds., *Negotiating the Boundaries of Southern Womanhood: Dealing with the Powers That Be* (Columbia: University of Missouri Press, 2000), 181.

42. On the racialization of early-twentieth-century feminism, see Louise

Michelle Newman, *White Women's Rights: The Racial Origins of Feminism in the United States* (New York: Oxford University Press, 1999).

43. In her reading of *Imitation of Life*, Lauren Berlant argues that the white female adult character could achieve abstract public authority and power only by shielding her own gendered body behind the overdetermined racial body of the black domestic, a figure who is clearly coded in the novel and first film version as Aunt Jemima. Berlant, "National Brands/National Bodies: *Imitation of Life*," in Bruce Robbins, ed., *The Phantom Public Sphere* (Minneapolis: University of Minnesota Press, 1993), 173–208.

44. D.C. division membership in 1917 reported in UDC, "District of Columbia Division Report," *Minutes of the Twenty-fourth Annual Convention, Chattanooga, Tennessee, November 14–17, 1917*, 250; in 1922, "District of Columbia Division Report," *Minutes of the Twenty-ninth Annual Convention, Birmingham, Alabama, November 14–18, 1917*, 258. For the monument bill's introduction in the Senate, see *Congressional Record*, 67th Cong., 4th sess., December 8, 1922, vol. 64, pt. 1, 209.

45. *Congressional Record*, 67th Cong., 4th sess., February 28, 1923, vol. 64, pt. 5, 4839.

46. Ibid.

47. *Congressional Record*, 67th Cong., 4th sess., January 9, 1923, vol. 4, pt. 2, 1509.

48. Extant UDC-generated documentation of the memorial campaign, including coverage in the *Confederate Veteran*, is scanty. Johnson, "Ye Gave Them a Stone," 73.

49. The Sixty-seventh Congress closed on March 3, 1923. "Model of Mammy Statue Insults Race," *Washington Tribune*, April 7, 1923, 1.

50. It is possible that many assumed the monument would take the form of an obelisk because that was the design of the Faithful Slave Monument in Fort Mills, South Carolina.

51. "'Mammy' Monument May Not Be Built," *New York Amsterdam News*, August 22, 1923, 7.

52. "Rival's 'Mammy' Statue Arouses Artist's Wrath," *WP*, June 21, 1923, 2.

53. The article briefly describes the campaign as having been started by a state senator in Tennessee in 1907. No mention is made of the UDC, although the report coincided with the conflicts within the organization detailed earlier in this chapter over whether to erect just such a memorial.

54. "Rival's 'Mammy' Statue Arouses Artist's Wrath," 2.

55. Gertrude Richardson Brigham, "Considered Zolnay Alone for Statue," *WP,* June 30, 1923, 6.

56. Freeman Henry Morris Murray, *Emancipation and the Freed in American Sculpture: A Study in Interpretation* (1916; reprint, Freeport, N.Y.: Books for Libraries Press, 1972), xix; reprinted in the *Washington Tribune,* January 6, 1923, 7.

57. *Washington Tribune,* February 10, 1923, 1. In a similar effort to rally protest, the *New York Amsterdam News* ran a front-page headline, "EXTRA! 'Mammy' Statue Bill Passed," above a short summary of the bill's passage, which concluded with the statement, "Practically all colored people are opposed to the move." *New York Amsterdam News,* March 7, 1923, 1.

58. "The 'Mammies' Monument," *Baltimore Afro-American* (hereafter *BAA*), February 9, 1923, 9.

59. "Will Oppose a Monument to Negro Mammies," *Washington Tribune,* February 3, 1923, 1.

60. "Model of Mammy Statue Insults Race," *Washington Tribune,* April 7, 1923, 1.

61. "Want No Black Mammy Monument," *California Eagle,* February 17, 1923, 1. This letter was also printed in part in "Thomas Against Mammy Monument," *Savannah Tribune,* February 23, 1923, 8.

62. Shelby Jeames Davidson to James Weldon Johnson, February 2, 1923, NAACP Papers, pt. 12, Selected Branch Files, 1913–1939, ser. A: The South, D.C. Branch, Jan.–Mar. 1923, Reel 5.

63. James Weldon Johnson to Shelby Jeames Davidson, February 5, 1923, NAACP Papers, pt. 12, Selected Branch Files, 1913–1939, ser. A: The South, D.C. Branch, Jan.–Mar. 1923, Reel 5.

64. "A Disgraceful Statue," *CD,* July 14, 1923, 12.

65. "G.A.R. Women Assail Black Mammy Shrine," *WP,* February 17, 1923, 2. For a general history of the WRC, see O'Leary, *To Die For,* 70–90.

66. *New York World* quoted in "For and Against the Black Mammy's Monument," 48.

67. George E. Cannon, "Monuments to the Negro," *New York World,* February 7, 1923, 10. Cannon was the president of the National Colored Republican Conference and a delegate at a number of national party conventions, as well as the chairman of the National Medical Association, a professional association of black doctors. "For and Against the Black Mammy's Monument," 48.

68. *Norfolk Journal and Guide*, February 10, 1923, 4. On P. B. Young's role as a leader in Norfolk and his commitments to accommodation and gradualism, see Earl Lewis, *In Their Own Interests: Race, Class, and Power in Twentieth-Century Norfolk, Virginia* (Berkeley: University of California Press, 1993), 64–65.

69. "Monument to 'Southern Mammies," *Norfolk Journal and Guide*, February 17, 1923, 4.

70. "Colored Editor Favors Monument," *Washington Tribune*, March 3, 1923, 8.

71. *Norfolk Journal and Guide*, March 10, 1923, 4.

72. *Washington Eagle*, reprinted in "Senate Okeyed Statue Over Protests," *BAA*, March 9, 1923, 1. Reprints also appeared in other papers: see *Richmond Planet*, March 24, 1923, 1; "Proposed Mammy Monument Raises Much Commotion," *Norfolk Journal and Guide*, March 10, 1923, 1.

73. *St. Louis Argus*, reprinted in "For and Against the 'Black Mammy's' Monument," 48.

5. THE VIOLENCE OF AFFECTION

1. "The Fog of Discord," *CD*, May 12, 1923, 12.

2. W. E. B. Du Bois, *The Gift of Black Folk: The Negroes in the Making of America* (1924; reprint, New York: Washington Square Press, 1970), 189.

3. On the modern "spectacle lynching," see Grace Elizabeth Hale, *Making Whiteness: The Culture of Segregation in the South* (New York: Pantheon, 1998), chap. 5.

4. The historical literature on lynching, gender, and citizenship includes Sandra Gunning, *Race, Rape, and Lynching: The Red Record of American Literature, 1890–1912* (New York: Oxford University Press, 1996); Jacqueline Dowd Hall, "'The Mind That Burns in Each Body': Women, Rape, and Racial Violence," in Ann Snitow, Christine Stansell, and Sharon Thompson, eds., *Powers of Desire: The Politics of Sexuality* (New York: Monthly Review Press, 1983), 328–349; Martha Hodes, *White Women, Black Men: Illicit Sex in the Nineteenth-Century South* (New Haven: Yale University Press, 1997); Bryant Simon, "The Appeal of Cole Blease of South Carolina: Race, Class, and Sex in the New South," *Journal of Southern History* (February 1996): 56–86;

Robyn Wiegman, *American Anatomies: Theorizing Race and Gender* (Durham: Duke University Press, 1995).

5. My understanding of the memorial as a form of violence has been shaped by Saidiya Hartman's concept of the violence of the banal. She argues: "By defamiliarizing the familiar, I hope to illuminate the terror of the mundane and quotidian rather than exploit the shocking spectacle. What concerns me here is the diffusion of terror and the violence perpetrated under the rubric of pleasure, paternalism, and property." Hartman, *Scenes of Subjection: Terror, Slavery, and Self-Making in Nineteenth-Century America* (New York: Oxford University Press, 1997), 4.

6. James Weldon Johnson, "The 'Black Mammy' Monument," *New York Age*, January 6, 1923, 4.

7. Henry Louis Gates Jr., "The Trope of a New Negro and the Reconstruction of the Image of the Black," in Philip Fisher, ed., *The New American Studies: Essays from* Representations (Berkeley: University of California Press, 1991), 319–345.

8. J. Martin Favor, *Authentic Blackness: The Folk in the New Negro Renaissance* (Durham: Duke University Press, 1999), 3.

9. The literature on the gendered, as well as class-based, nature of the progress narrative as it relates to the politics of uplift includes Hazel Carby, *Reconstructing Womanhood: The Emergence of the Afro-American Woman Novelist* (New York: Oxford University Press, 1987); Kate Davy, "Outing Whiteness: A Feminist/Lesbian Project," in Mike Hill, ed., *Whiteness: A Critical Reader* (New York: New York University Press, 1997), 204–225; Favor, *Authentic Blackness;* Kevin K. Gaines, *Uplifting the Race: Black Leadership, Politics, and Culture in the Twentieth Century* (Chapel Hill: University of North Carolina Press, 1996); Evelyn Brooks Higgenbotham, *Righteous Discontent: The Women's Movement in the Black Baptist Church, 1880–1920* (Cambridge: Harvard University Press, 1993); and Tera W. Hunter, *To 'Joy My Freedom: Southern Black Women's Lives and Labors after the Civil War* (Cambridge: Harvard University Press, 1997). On the gendering of Western progress narratives in colonial contexts, see Anne McClintock, *Imperial Leather: Race, Gender, and Sexuality in the Colonial Contest* (New York: Routledge, 1995).

10. Walter White to Moorfield Storey, December 11, 1922, quoted in Claudine Ferrell, "Nightmare and Dream: Antilynching in Congress, 1917–1922" (Ph.D. diss., Rice University, 1983), 279.

11. On the East St. Louis riot, see Chicago Commission on Race Relations, *The Negro in Chicago: A Study of Race Relations and a Race Riot* (1922; reprint, New York: Arno Press, 1968), 71–78; Elliott M. Rudwick, *Race Riot at East St. Louis, July 2, 1917* (Carbondale: Southern Illinois University Press, 1964); and Robert Shapiro, *White Violence and Black Response from Reconstruction to Montgomery* (Amherst: University of Massachusetts Press, 1988).

12. Nine white rioters were sent to the state penitentiary, four of them for murder, while twelve black people were imprisoned, eleven of them for the murder of the two officers. Rudwick, *Race Riot*, 97. On the trials in October 1917, see ibid., 111. On indictments and convictions of police and soldiers, see Chicago Commission, *Negro in Chicago*, 72–73, 77–78. The House subcommittee's investigation came after Congress refused to consider Dyer's resolution calling for a full investigation in Washington with public hearings run jointly by the judiciary committees of the House and Senate. Rudwick, *Race Riot*.

13. On the Houston Mutiny generally and responses to it in the black press, see William G. Jordan, *Black Newspapers and America's War for Democracy, 1914–1920* (Chapel Hill: University of North Carolina Press, 2001), 92–98.

14. Simultaneous with Dyer's introduction of his legislation, Representative Merrill Moores of Indiana introduced a similar measure. Lawyers, activists, and politicians would continue to struggle with the issue of a federal anti-lynching bill's constitutionality throughout the interwar period as measure after measure was defeated in Congress. Because none of these bills became law, the issue was never decided by a court, and the civil rights acts of the 1960s made the question moot. From his post in the Military Intelligence Branch of the War Department (MIB), Major Joel E. Spingarn, the white chairman of the NAACP at the time, thought the law constitutionally indefensible and put forth his own anti-lynching bill in the summer of 1918 based on congressional war powers. For a complete recounting of Spingarn's activities at the MIB and the anti-lynching measure in particular, see Mark Ellis, "Joel Spingarn's 'Constructive Programme' and the Wartime Anti-lynching Bill of 1918," *Journal of Policy History* 4, no. 2 (1992): 134–161. On Moorfield Storey's earlier doubts about the constitutionality of Dyer's bill, see William B. Hixon Jr., "Moorfield Storey and the Defense of the Dyer Anti-lynching Bill," *New England Quarterly* (March 1969): 65–81.

15. The 1920 Republican platform quoted in Richard B. Sherman,

The Republican Party and Black America from McKinley to Hoover, 1896–1933 (Charlottesville: University Press of Virginia, 1973), 181. On the Harding campaign and his promises to black voters, see Robert K. Murray, *The Harding Era: Warren G. Harding and His Administration* (Minneapolis: University of Minnesota Press, 1969), 54.

16. For complete histories of the Dyer bill and the NAACP's anti-lynching campaign of which it was a central part, see Ferrell, *Nightmare and Dream;* Sherman, *The Republican Party and Black America*, 178–199; and Robert Zagrando, *The NAACP Crusade against Lynching, 1909–1950* (Philadelphia: Temple University Press, 1980).

17. Murray, *The Harding Era*, 398.

18. *Address of the President of the United States at the Celebration of the Semicentennial of the Founding of the City of Birmingham, Alabama, October 26, 1921* (Washington, D.C.: Government Printing Office, 1921), 7.

19. George C. Rable, "The South and the Politics of Anti-lynching Legislation, 1920–1940," *Journal of Southern History* (May 1985): 204.

20. *Congressional Record*, 67th Cong., 2d sess., December 19, 1922, vol. 62, pt. 1, 549.

21. Ibid., 548.

22. Ibid., 545.

23. Ibid., 549.

24. *Congressional Record*, 67th Cong., 2d sess., January 18, 1922, vol. 62, pt. 2, 1368.

25. NAACP press release quoted in Sherman, *Republican Party and Black America*, 186.

26. On these dramatic changes and the rise of Progressives in Congress, see "Flurry Marks Senate End," *NYT*, March 5, 1923, 1; "Next Congress Seen as Forum of Clashing Blocs," *NYT*, November 4, 1923, 3.

27. *Congressional Record*, 67th Cong., 3d sess., November 28, 1922, vol. 63, pt. 1, 332.

28. "Senate Democrats Start Filibuster, Stop All Business," *NYT*, November 29, 1922, 6; "The Senate's Surrender," *NYT*, December 4, 1922, 16.

29. James Weldon Johnson, *Along This Way* (New York: Viking Press, 1933), 371. On June 13, 2005, the Senate issued an apology for its failure to pass federal anti-lynching legislation despite several opportunities. "A Senate Apology for History on Lynching," *WP*, June 14, 2005, A12.

30. Reprinted in "Expressed by Contemporaries" section, *New York Amsterdam News*, March 21, 1923.

31. "Mockery," *CD*, April 7, 1923, 12.

32. "Use that monument fund. . . ," *Baltimore Afro-American*, March 2, 1923, 9.

33. "Rotten Service," *CD*, March 17, 1923, 12.

34. "Real Democracy," *New York Age*, November 29, 1917, reprinted in Jordan, *Black Newspapers and America's War for Democracy*, 102.

35. "Since Statues Seem to be All the Rage . . . ," *CD*, April 21, 1923, 12.

36. A. L. Jackson, "The Black Mammy Statue," *CD*, April 21, 1923, 12.

37. "This and That and T'Other: A Bit of News, Gossip, Fun and Fiction," *CD*, March 3, 1923, 12.

38. Some other contemporary references to "sheiks" in the black press can be found in the *Baltimore Afro-American*: see "Sheiks," January 19, 1923, 9; "A 'Sheik' Antidote," March 23, 1923; "Modern Sheik Killed in Bed While Asleep," September 7, 1923, 1; also "The Memoirs of an Ex-Sheik," *California Eagle*, April 14, 1923, 10.

39. Siobhan B. Sommerville examines the "sheik" as a queer figure in the 1920s in *Queering the Color Line: Race and the Invention of Homosexuality in American Culture* (Durham: Duke University Press, 2000), 149–156.

40. W. J. Wheaton, "Black Mammy Statue," *California Eagle*, February 24, 1923, editorial page.

41. Reprinted in *New York Amsterdam News*, March 21, 1923, editorial page.

42. The *New York Herald* noted that "representatives of more than two thousand Colored women in Washington adopted resolutions of protest against the erection of the statue," and that they also petitioned the vice president and Congress. Quoted in A. L. Jackson, "The Onlooker," *CD*, April 21, 1923, 12. The board of the Phyllis Wheatly YWCA of Washington, D.C., also staged a formal protest. "Homage to 'Black Mamy' [*sic*]," *New York Age*, April 14, 1923, 4. Joan Marie Johnson, "'Ye Gave Them a Stone': African-American Women's Clubs, the Frederick Douglass Home, and the Black Mammy Monument," *Journal of Women's History* 17, no. 1 (Spring 2005): 77.

43. Reprinted in "For and Against the 'Black Mammy's' Monument," *Literary Digest*, April 28, 1923, 49.

44. Ibid.

45. For Brown's letter, see Johnson, "Ye Gave Them a Stone," 74–76; and Deborah Gray White, *Too Heavy a Load: Black Women in Defense of Themselves, 1894–1994* (New York: W. W. Norton, 1999), 288–289, n. 48.

46. "For and Against the 'Black Mammy's' Monument," 49.

47. Nancy Barkhalter, "Women's Magazines and the Suffrage Movement: Did They Help or Hinder the Cause?" *Journal of American Culture* 19, no. 2 (Summer 1996): 15.

48. "For and Against the 'Black Mammy's' Monument," 51.

49. Gail Bederman explores the ways in which black activists (and others) mobilized the civilization narrative against the white supremacist patriarchy it was intended to support in the context of Ida B. Wells's anti-lynching activism in *Manliness and Civilization: A Cultural History of Gender and Race in the United States, 1880–1917* (Chicago: University of Chicago Press, 1995).

50. Charlotte Hawkins Brown telegram quoted in "Right Kind of Memorial," *New York Age*, February 3, 1923, 4. Another call to fund education as opposed to a statue came from the white director of the Kentucky Interracial Commission, James Bond, shortly after Brown's. "Negro School Favored in Memory of 'Mammies,'" *Louisville Times*, February 6, 1923, 10. Glenda Elizabeth Gilmore examines Brown and her complex political strategies in *Gender and Jim Crow: Women and the Politics of White Supremacy in North Carolina, 1896–1920* (Chapel Hill: University of North Carolina Press, 1996).

51. "Right Kind of Memorial," 4.

52. Carolyn C. Denard, intro. to Charlotte Hawkins Brown, *Mammy: An Appeal to the Heart of the South* (1919; reprint, New York: G. K. Hall & Co., 1995), xx; Gilmore, *Gender and Jim Crow*, 189–190.

53. "Her Living Monument," *BAA*, June 15, 1923, 9.

54. "For and Against the 'Black Mammy's' Monument," 48.

55. Ibid.

56. "Thomas against Mammy Monument," *Savannah Tribune*, February 23, 1923, 8.

57. This is much like Eugene Genovese's later argument in *Roll, Jordan, Roll: The World the Slaves Made* (New York: Vintage Books, 1976).

58. In this context, the authors' authenticity was reinforced by their selection for publication. The role of letters to the editor in shaping news production and "orchestrating public opinion" is explored fully in Stuart Hall et al., *Policing the Crisis: Mugging, the State, and Law and Order* (New York: Holmes & Meier Publishers, 1978), chap. 5. See also C. K. Doreski, *Writing America Black: Race Rhetoric in the Public Sphere* (New York: Cambridge University Press, 1998).

59. Reprint from the *Boston Chronicle* in "For and Against the 'Black Mammy's' Monument," 50.

60. "'Mammy's' Monument vs. Mammy's Son," *Washington Tribune*, March 3, 1923, 8.

61. The *New York Times* noted that in addition to being a lawyer, Walter L. Cohen was president of or had a controlling interest in a number of black-owned businesses in Louisiana, including a statewide insurance company, a chain of drug stores, and an amusement park. "Keeps Negro in Office," *NYT*, February 26, 1924, 6. Cohen's service as a page is mentioned in the acknowledgments to A. E. Perkins, "Some Negro Officers and Legislators in Louisiana," *JNH* 14, no. 14 (October 1929): 527. His earlier federal appointments and party activities are described in "The Horizon," *The Crisis* 25, no. 4 (February 1923): 177. For a brief discussion of Cohen's Republican activism in Louisiana and common post–World War I accusations that he was an "Uncle Tom," see Adam Fairclough, *Race and Democracy: The Civil Rights Struggle in Louisiana, 1915–1972* (Athens: University of Georgia Press, 1995), 10–12.

62. The *New York Age*, for example, reported early that confirmation was practically assured. "Walter Cohen to Be Officer of New Orleans Port," *New York Age*, August 5, 1922, 1. On Parker's trip to Washington, see "Governor Parker, Democrat, La., Has Senatorial Aspirations," *New York Age*, December 9, 1922, 4.

63. "Will Harding Stick to Cohen?" *BAA*, December 1, 1922, 11.

64. With the end of Cohen's recess appointment, Coolidge renominated him in December. This time Cohen was rejected by a vote of 37 to 35. Once again, Republicans had jumped the aisle. In a conference with the chairman of the Republican National Committee, Cohen, and Senate Republicans, Coolidge made it clear that he would not appoint anyone but Cohen to the post, and would continue the pattern of recess appointments if necessary. A resolution calling for the roll-call vote to be made public was introduced in the Senate. Fearing repercussions from black voters and their allies in a presidential election year, some Republican senators preferred to reconsider their vote, and Cohen was finally confirmed. Contemporaries in the press, and some historians later, questioned the constitutional hairsplitting of making recess appointments of individuals who had already failed to gain confirmation for the same post. Senate historian George Haynes, who clearly found the practice appalling, noted its constitutional legality nonetheless. Haynes, *The Senate of the United States: Its History and Practice* (Boston: Houghton Mifflin, 1938), 775–778; Joseph P. Harris,

"The Courtesy of the Senate," *Political Science Quarterly* 63, no. 1 (March 1952): 49–50. See also the following articles from the *New York Times:* "Harding Reappoints Negro Senate Rejected as Controller of Customs at New Orleans," May 17, 1923, 1; "2,000 Nominations Made by Coolidge—Walter L. Cohen, a Negro, Is Again Appointed Collector at New Orleans," December 11, 1923, 6; "Senate Again Rejects Nomination of Negro," February 19, 1924, 2; "Keeps Negro in Office," February 26, 1923, 6. On the initial defeat of Cohen's nomination and the "Traitor Ten," see "Monument to 'Mammy' Wins Senate," *CD*, March 10, 1923, 1. The "Ten" were reportedly Senators William E. Borah (Idaho), H. O. Bursum (New Mexico), Frank R. Gooding (Idaho), Wesley L. Jones (Washington), Robert M. La Follette (Wisconsin), Irvine L. Lenroot (Wisconsin), Charles L. McNary (Oregon), Tasker L. Oddie (Nevada), David A. Reed (Pennsylvania), and Seldon P. Spencer (Missouri). "Party Leaders Deserted Cohen in Senate Fight," *Norfolk Journal and Guide*, March 24, 1923, 1. On other uses of "senatorial courtesy" to defeat black nominees, see Harris, "The Courtesy of the Senate," 36, 49. Nancy Weiss notes that Taft had an explicit policy not to appoint anyone to office who *might be* personally objectionable to congressmen, a practice designed to exclude black nominees from the South. Nancy J. Weiss, *Farewell to the Party of Lincoln: Black Politics in the Age of F.D.R.* (Princeton: Princeton University Press, 1983), 5.

65. See, for example, "Monument to 'Mammy' Wins Senate," *CD*, March 10, 1923, 1; "Maryland Senators Worked for Cohen," *BAA*, March 9, 1923, 1; "Senate Okeyed Statue Over Protests," *BAA*, March 9, 1923, 1; *Richmond Planet*, March 24, 1923, 1; "Proposed Mammy Monument Raises Much Commotion," *Norfolk Journal and Guide*, March 10, 1923, 1.

66. "Monument to 'Mammy' Wins Senate," *CD*, March 10, 1923, 1.

67. Rod Bush, *We Are Not What We Seem: Black Nationalism and Class Struggle in the American Century* (New York: New York University Press, 1999), 83–120; Gates, "The Trope of a New Negro."

68. "Walter H. [*sic*] Cohen," *The Messenger* 5, no. 4 (April 1923): 671.

69. Chandler Owen, "Black Mammies," *The Messenger* 5, no. 4 (April 1923): 670.

70. Ibid.

71. On the history of the National Memorial Association, its response to the mammy memorial, and Dyer's involvement, see "'Mammy Statue'

Opposed with Vet Memorial," *CD*, April 21, 1923, 1. At least one other black soldiers' monument was in the works in 1923. The Illinois state legislature passed a bill for a memorial monument in Chicago to honor members of the 307th Infantry, formerly Chicago's Eighth Regiment of black troops, who were lost in World War I. The governor signed the legislation allotting $15,000 for the statue in June of that year. See "$15,000 Monument," *BAA*, February 9, 1923, 1; "$15,000 for Monument," *BAA*, June 29, 1923, 1. On *The Spirit of Freedom*, see "Civil War Monument Dedication," *WP*, July 16, 1998, D4.

72. Owen, "Black Mammies," 670.

73. Ibid.

74. Elise Johnson McDougald, "The Task of Negro Womanhood," in Alain Locke, ed., *The New Negro* (1925; reprint, New York: Touchstone, 1992), 369–382.

6. CONFRONTING THE MAMMY PROBLEM

1. For a compelling analysis of one black woman's experience negotiating her job as a live-in domestic worker in the mid-twentieth century, see E. Patrick Johnson's discussion of his grandmother's labor history in *Appropriating Blackness: Performance and the Politics of Authenticity* (Durham: Duke University Press, 2003), 104–159.

2. A Negro Nurse, "More Slavery at the South," *The Independent*, January 25, 1912, 196–200, quoted in Gerda Lerner, ed., *Black Women in White America: A Documentary History* (New York: Vintage Books, 1973), 227–228.

3. The phrase "politics of respectability," which has assumed a central place in the analysis of elite and middle-class black women's activism, is drawn from Evelyn Brooks Higginbotham's *Righteous Discontent: The Women's Movement in the Black Baptist Church, 1880–1920* (Cambridge: Harvard University Press, 1993).

4. Two published sources of oral histories, Elizabeth Clark-Lewis's *Living In, Living Out: African American Domestics and the Great Migration* (New York: Kodansha International, 1996) and Susan Tucker's *Telling Memories among Southern Women: Domestic Workers and Their Employers in the Segregated South* (New York: Schocken Books, 1988), are invaluable resources in this endeavor.

5. Alice Childress, *Like One of the Family: Conversations from a Domestic's Life* (1956; reprint, Boston: Beacon Press, 1986). See also Trudier

Harris, *From Mammies to Militants: Domestics in Black American Literature* (Philadelphia: Temple University Press, 1982).

6. Phyllis Palmer, *Domesticity and Dirt: Housewives and Domestic Servants in the United States, 1920–1945* (Philadelphia: Temple University Press, 1989), 12.

7. Evelyn Nakano Glenn, "From Servitude to Service Work: Historical Continuities in the Racial Division of Paid Reproductive Labor," in Ellen Carol DuBois and Vicki L. Ruiz, eds., *Unequal Sisters: A Multicultural Reader in Women's History*, 2d ed. (New York: Routledge, 1994), 405–435.

8. Clark-Lewis, *Living In, Living Out*, 5.

9. Elizabeth Ross Haynes, "Negroes in Domestic Service in the United States: Introduction," *JNH* 8, no. 4 (October 1923): 424–425.

10. Earl Lewis analyzes the organization of domestic workers in Norfolk, Virginia, by the Transportation Workers Association in 1917. Lewis, *In Their Own Interests: Race, Class, and Power in Twentieth-Century Norfolk, Virginia* (Berkeley: University of California Press, 1993), 56–58. Elizabeth Ross Haynes identifies a number of short-lived domestic workers' unions affiliated with hotel and restaurant workers chartered by the American Federation of Labor in 1919 and 1920. Most of these were in southern or western cities: Mobile, Alabama; Fort Worth, Denison, Harrisburg, and Houston, Texas; Lawton and Tulsa, Oklahoma; Brunswick, Georgia; Los Angeles and San Diego, California; New Orleans, Louisiana; Chicago and Glencoe, Illinois; and Beaver Valley, Pennsylvania. By 1923, Haynes argues, the only domestic workers' union still affiliated with the AFL was in Arecibo, Puerto Rico. Haynes, "Negroes in Domestic Service," 435–436. Phyllis Palmer writes extensively of organized workers' attempts to gain inclusion in New Deal legislation in her *Domesticity and Dirt*, 122–133. For a general discussion of domestic organizing after the Civil War, see Donna L. Van Raaphorst, *Union Maids Not Wanted: Organizing Domestic Workers, 1870–1940* (New York: Praeger, 1988).

11. Clark-Lewis, *Living In, Living Out*, 135–140.

12. Jean Collier Brown, *The Negro Woman Worker*, Bulletin of the Women's Bureau no. 165 (Washington, D.C.: United States Department of Labor, 1938), 14.

13. On the National Recovery Act's failure to cover domestic workers and the wide ramifications of this exclusion, see Mary Anderson, "The Plight of Negro Domestic Labor," *Journal of Negro Education* 1 (January 1936): 68–70.

14. Mahnaz Kousha refers to this as the "hidden 'emotional labor'" demanded of black domestic workers in southern households, primarily in the context of their relationships to the white women who employed and managed them. Arguably, this "emotional labor" was not limited to the South and was hardly "hidden." Kousha, "Race, Class, and Intimacy in Southern Households: Relationships between Black Domestic Workers and White Employers," in Barbara Ellen Smith, ed., *Neither Separate Nor Equal: Women, Race, and Class in the South* (Philadelphia: Temple University Press, 1999), 77–90.

15. On migration and southern domestic workers in northern cities, see Jacqueline Jones, *Labor of Love, Labor of Sorrow: Black Women, Work, and the Family, from Slavery to the Present* (New York: Vintage, 1995), 164–165.

16. Elizabeth O'Leary notes this facet of the "servant problem" in her study of domestic work in Richmond, Virginia, in *From Morning to Night: Domestic Service in Maymont House and the Gilded Age South* (Charlottesville: University Press of Virginia, 2003), 55.

17. On the costs and strategic benefits of assuming the "mammy mask," see Darlene Clark Hine, "Rape and the Inner Lives of Black Women in the Middle West: Preliminary Thoughts on the Culture of Dissemblance," in DuBois and Ruiz, *Unequal Sisters*, 342–347; and Johnson, *Appropriating Blackness*, 128–159.

18. Hortense McDonald, "House with No Servant Problem," *NYT Sunday Magazine*, October 19, 1919, 9, 14.

19. "Why Not Import Your Servant?" *NYT*, April 25, 1920, 8.

20. Ibid.

21. On the racialization of domestic service in this period generally, see Glenn, "From Servitude to Service Work." On Japanese women's domestic service, see Evelyn Nakano Glenn, *Issei, Nisei, War Bride: Three Generations of Japanese American Women in Domestic Service* (Philadelphia: Temple University Press, 1986). On Latina domestic service, see Vicki L. Ruiz, "By the Day or the Week: Mexican Domestic Workers in El Paso," in Vicki L. Ruiz and Susan Tiano, eds., *Women on the U.S.-Mexico Border: Responses to Change* (Boston: Allen & Unwin, 1987), 61–76; and George J. Sanchez, "'Go After the Women': Americanization and the Mexican Immigrant Woman, 1915–1929," in DuBois and Ruiz, *Unequal Sisters*, 284–297.

22. June O. Patton, ed., "Moonlight and Magnolias in Southern Education: The Black Mammy Memorial Institute," *JNH* 65, no. 2 (Spring 1980): 150.

23. "The Black Mammy Memorial Institute," fundraising pamphlet, 1910, quoted ibid., 153.

24. Ibid., 153–154.

25. This language mimics the "free labor" rhetoric of the mid-nineteenth century, particularly as it was applied to post-emancipation black southern laborers. Saidiya Hartman refers to free peoples' "burdened individuality of freedom" within capitalism. Hartman, *Scenes of Subjection: Terror, Slavery, and Self-Making in Nineteenth-Century America* (New York: Oxford University Press, 1997), 127. For a discussion of the ways in which emancipation, black codes, and the application of free labor ideology to newly free African Americans transformed notions of contract and obligation around the country, see Amy Dru Stanley, "Beggars Can't Be Choosers: Compulsion and Contract in Postbellum America," *Journal of American History* 78, no. 4 (March 1992): 1265–93.

26. "The Black Mammy Memorial Institute," 154.

27. Samuel F. Harris's history and role in the institute is detailed in Patton, "Moonlight and Magnolias," 150.

28. Ibid., 155, nn. 11, 12, and 14.

29. On the course of training generally, see Haynes, "Negroes in Domestic Service," 399. Average estimates of domestic workers' wages in Baltimore in 1923 were $8.50–$9.50 per week. Ibid., 422.

30. On the desire of clubwomen to professionalize and change black domestic workers, see Deborah Gray White, *Too Heavy a Load: Black Women in Defense of Themselves, 1894–1994* (New York: W. W. Norton, 1999), 132–133.

31. Baltimore Domestic Efficiency Association president quoted in Clark-Lewis, *Living In, Living Out*, 130.

32. On segregation, the southern "servant problem," tuberculosis, and constructions of black women as sources of contagion in Atlanta, see Tera Hunter, *To 'Joy My Freedom: Southern Black Women's Lives and Labors after the Civil War* (Cambridge: Harvard University Press, 1997), chap. 9.

33. William Alexander Percy, *Lanterns on the Levee: Recollections of a Planter's Son* (New York: A. A. Knopf, 1941), 299.

34. Mary Patricia Foley narrative in Tucker, *Telling Memories among Southern Women*, 53.

35. The dates of Delores's employment are not given; this timeline is based on the fact that Mary Patricia Foley was born in 1938.

36. On the impact of *Gone With the Wind* on white expectations for black

domestic workers, see, for example, Childress, *Like One of the Family*, 52; and Palmer, *Domesticity and Dirt*, 73.

37. Judith Rollins has analyzed this facet of the female employer-domestic relationship as one of "maternalism," arguing that this term is more appropriate than "paternalism" because female employers and employees shared the experience of oppression and public exclusion as women and were thus connected through "women's supportive intrafamilial roles of nurturing, loving, and attending to domestic needs." I disagree and argue that this is more a reflection of white women's fantasies about these relationships than their actuality. Rollins, *Between Women: Domestics and Their Employers* (Philadelphia: Temple University Press, 1985), 179.

38. See, for example, Jones, *Labor of Love, Labor of Sorrow*, 182.

39. Marianne Polk narrative in Tucker, *Telling Memories among Southern Women*, 181.

40. Brown, *Negro Woman Worker*, 3.

41. Cartwright quoted in Hunter, *To 'Joy My Freedom*, 106–107.

42. Adams quoted ibid., 107.

43. See, for example, ibid., 60–61, 132–133; and Robin D. G. Kelley, "'We Are Not What We Seem': The Politics and Pleasures of Community," in *Race Rebels: Culture, Politics, and the Black Working Class* (New York: Free Press, 1994), 19–21.

44. Tucker, *Telling Memories among Southern Women*, 147.

45. Elizabeth Clark-Lewis, *Living In, Living Out*, 157.

46. On this post–World War I change in the population of employers of domestic labor, see Glenn, "From Servitude to Service Work," 410–411; Hunter, *To 'Joy My Freedom*, 108–110; and David M. Katzman, *Seven Days a Week: Women and Domestic Service in Industrializing America* (New York: Oxford University Press, 1978), 185. These scholars note that the presence of large numbers of working-class families with hired domestic help was most significant in the South.

47. Some elite black families did hire domestic workers, which in part signified their status. This was quite rare, however. Hunter, *To 'Joy My Freedom*, 110, 229.

48. Melissa Howe narrative, in Tucker, *Telling Memories among Southern Women*, 156.

49. Juliana Lincoln narrative, ibid., 168.

50. Leila Parkerson narrative, ibid., 161–162.

51. Essie Favrot narrative, ibid., 118.

52. Ibid., 118–119.

53. Ibid., 119.

54. Ibid., 94.

55. Quoted ibid.

56. Leigh Campbell narrative, ibid., 48.

57. Corinne Cooke narrative, ibid., 100.

58. Aletha Vaughn narrative, ibid., 209–210.

59. "Domestic and Personal Service" was a U.S. Census and Department of Labor category. In addition to household work and laundering, women's jobs that fell within this category included restaurant and hotel workers, charwomen, elevator operators, hairdressers, and manicurists. Men's service work was also included under this category.

60. "Another Suggestion for the 'Mammy' Monument," *BAA*, March 30, 1923, 9.

61. Ibid.

62. "For and Against the 'Black Mammy's' Monument," *Literary Digest*, April 28, 1923, 48.

63. Carter G. Woodson, "The Negro Washerwoman, a Vanishing Figure," *JNH* 15, no. 3 (July 1930): 269.

64. *Richmond Times-Dispatch*, January 3, 1923, 3.

65. Women's Bureau study of the laundry industry in the South quoted in Anderson, "Plight of Negro Domestic Labor," 69.

66. "A Washer Woman," *Savannah Tribune*, January 18, 1923, 4.

67. Hunter, *To 'Joy My Freedom*, chaps. 7 and 8; Kelley, "We Are Not What We Seem," 35–53.

68. "They Need Your Help," *BAA*, July 20, 1923, 9.

69. Ibid.

70. "Goodbye Mammy, Hello Mom," *Ebony* 2, no. 5 (March 1947): 36.

71. Ibid.

72. On black women's postwar return to domestic service, see Jones, *Labor of Love, Labor of Sorrow*, 257. "Goodbye Mammy, Hello Mom," 36. On the gender conservatism of this cold war civil rights claim and the limitations it placed on black women, see Ruth Feldstein, *Motherhood in Black and White: Race and Sex in American Liberalism, 1930–1965* (Ithaca: Cornell University Press, 2000), 43; and Elaine Tyler May, *Homeward Bound: American Families in the Cold War Era*, rev. ed. (New York: Basic Books, 1999), 18.

73. "Goodbye Mammy, Hello Mom," 36.

74. Freda DeKnight, "Quick Coffee Breads for Sunday Morning," *Ebony*

2, no. 5 (March 1947): 38. Elaine Tyler May notes the prevalence of articles about white celebrities attesting to their mothering and homemaking skills as an example of the post–World War II containment of American women (*Homeward Bound*, 54–58).

75. "Goodbye Mammy, Hello Mom," 36.

76. Montgomery population figures from Stewart Burns, ed., *Daybreak of Freedom: The Montgomery Bus Boycott* (Chapel Hill: University of North Carolina Press, 1997), 2. For statistics on women in domestic service and bus ridership in Montgomery, see Martin Luther King Jr., *Stride toward Freedom: The Montgomery Story* (1958; reprint, San Francisco: Harper and Row, 1986), 27, 71. On the daily experiences of black riders on the buses, see, for example, Jo Ann Gibson Robinson, *The Montgomery Bus Boycott and the Women Who Started It* (Knoxville: University of Tennessee Press, 1987), 26–36. For general information about the boycott, in addition to these sources, see Taylor Branch, *Parting the Waters: America in the King Years, 1954*–1963 (New York: Simon and Schuster, 1988); Mary Fair Burks, "Trailblazers: Women in the Montgomery Bus Boycott," in Vicki L. Crawford, Jacqueline Anne Rouse, and Barbara Woods, ed., *Women in the Civil Rights Movement: Trailblazers and Torchbearers, 1941–1965* (Brooklyn: Carlson Publishing, 1990), 71–83; David J. Garrow, ed., *The Walking City: The Montgomery Bus Boycott, 1955–1956* (Brooklyn, N.Y.: Carlson Publishing, 1989); and Belinda Robnett, *How Long? How Long? African-American Women in the Struggle for Civil Rights* (New York: Oxford University Press, 1997), 53–70.

77. Interview with unknown informant, January 18, 1956, collected in Burns, *Daybreak of Freedom*, 221.

78. Interview with "Beatrice," January 20, 1956, ibid., 222.

79. Interview with unknown informant, January 24, 1956, ibid., 229.

80. King, *Stride toward Freedom*, 54, 77–78.

81. Burns, *Daybreak of Freedom*, 223–224.

82. Ibid., 224.

83. Ibid.

84. Interview with "Irene," February 2, 1956, ibid., 231–232.

85. "Housewife Counter-Boycott," *Montgomery Advertiser*, January 9, 1956, collected ibid., 118–119.

86. King, *Stride toward Freedom*, 79.

87. Ibid., 187.

88. Ibid., 203.

EPILOGUE

1. M. M. Manring, *Slave in a Box: The Strange Career of Aunt Jemima* (Charlottesville: University Press of Virginia, 1998), 163.
2. Ibid.; Arthur F. Marquette, *Brands, Trademarks, and Good Will: The Story of the Quaker Oats Company* (New York: McGraw-Hill, 1967), 157.
3. Daniel Patrick Moynihan, *The Negro Family: The Case for National Action* (Washington, D.C.: Office of Planning and Research, United States Department of Labor, 1965).
4. Ruth Feldstein, *Motherhood in Black and White: Race and Sex in American Liberalism, 1930–1965* (Ithaca: Cornell University Press, 2000), 147–152.
5. Deborah Gray White, *Ar'n't I a Woman? Female Slaves in the Plantation South* (New York: W. W. Norton & Company, 1985), 46.
6. On black feminist responses and the continued impacts of mammy narratives, see Patricia Hill Collins, *Black Feminist Thought: Knowledge, Consciousness, and the Politics of Empowerment*, 10th Anniversary Edition (New York: Routledge, 2000); Patricia Hill Collins, *Black Sexual Politics: African Americans, Gender, and the New Racism* (New York: Routledge, 2004), 140–147; Angela Davis, "Reflections on the Black Woman's Role in the Community of Slaves," *Black Scholar* (1971): 2–15; bell hooks, *Ain't I a Woman: Black Women and Feminism* (Boston: South End Press, 1981); K. Sue Jewell, *From Mammy to Miss America: Cultural Images and the Shaping of U.S. Social Policy* (New York: Routledge, 1993); Kimberly Springer, *Living for the Revolution: Black Feminist Organizations, 1968–1980* (Durham: Duke University Press, 2005), 37–44; Michele Wallace, *Black Macho and the Myth of the Superwoman* (1978; reprint, New York: Verso, 1999).
7. Mary Ann Weathers, "An Argument for Black Women's Liberation As a Revolutionary Force," quoted in Feldstein, *Motherhood in Black and White*, 150.
8. Angela Davis challenged this directly. Davis, "Reflections on the Black Woman's Role in the Community of Slaves."
9. Eldridge Cleaver, *Soul on Ice* (New York: Dell, 1968), 162.
10. Manring, *Slave in a Box*, 168–169.
11. On black visual artists' responses to Aunt Jemima in the 1960s and 1970s, see Michael D. Harris, *Colored Pictures: Race and Visual Representation* (Chapel Hill: University of North Carolina Press, 2003), 83–

124; Marilyn Kern-Foxworth, *Aunt Jemima, Uncle Ben, and Rastus: Blacks in Advertising, Yesterday, Today, and Tomorrow* (Westport, Conn.: Greenwood Press, 1994), 101–104; Doris Witt, *Black Hunger: Food and the Politics of U.S. Identity* (New York: Oxford, 1999), 39–53.

12. Manring, *Slave in a Box*, 172–175.

13. On the 1990s trade in "black collectibles" generally and black collectors of these items in particular, see Lyn Casmier-Paz, "Heritage, Not Hate? Collecting Black Memorabilia," *Southern Cultures* (Spring 2003): 43–61.

ACKNOWLEDGMENTS

IT IS A PLEASURE to have this opportunity to acknowledge the many large and small generosities that have been extended to me while writing this book. I benefited enormously from the knowledge and guidance of archivists and librarians, including those at the Eleanor S. Brockenbrough Library of the Museum of the Confederacy, the Chicago Historical Society, the Caroline Meriwether Goodlett Library at the United Daughters of the Confederacy headquarters, the Library of Congress, the Newberry Library, the New York Public Library Humanities and Social Sciences Library, the Schomburg Center for Research in Black Culture, and the Virginia Historical Society. I thank especially John Coski at the Museum of the Confederacy and Sara Austin, Diane Dillon, and Jim Goodman at the Newberry Library. Kathryn Hensiak Amato at the Pritzker Legal Research Center of the Northwestern University School of Law and Julienne Grant at the Loyola University Law Library were extremely generous with their time in fielding questions about Illinois law via fax and e-mail. Two dear friends provided research help, technical savvy, and moral support in the book's final stages: my unending thanks to Merrily Harris and Jessica Lacher-Feldman at the Hoole Special Collections Library of the University of Alabama. Financial support came from the Department of History and the Graduate School of Arts and

Science at New York University, the College of Arts and Sciences at the University of Alabama, and the Newberry Library in Chicago.

I aspire to emulate some of the extraordinary teachers and scholars I have had the good fortune to know and learn from. Susana Conde-Leverett, Anne Dalke, Madhavi Kale, and Sharon Ullman sparked my curiosity and confidence and taught me the moral urgency of politically engaged scholarship. Adam Green, Robin Kelley, Carl Prince, Jeffrey Sammons, and Daniel Walkowitz each shaped this project and my outlook in powerful ways. I am grateful for the historical artistry, the critical vision, and the advice and friendship I continue to receive from Lisa Duggan, Linda Gordon, and Martha Hodes. Finally, I thank Walter Johnson for his guidance, intellect, and understanding, and his appreciation for the absurd.

Several people read parts of this work and offered keen insights, hard questions, and new avenues for thought. I am especially thankful to Kristin Bayer, Rachel Mattson, Melina Pappademos, the New York University History of Women and Gender group, and my friends and colleagues in the Faculty Interdisciplinary and Interpretive Research Group at the University of Alabama. An earlier version of portions of Chapter 4 benefited from Cynthia Mills's editing. I am indebted to David Blight and Scott Sandage for their careful readings of the entire manuscript, their critical suggestions, and their support. I am also grateful for the work, encouragement, and patience of my editor at Harvard University Press, the incomparable Joyce Seltzer. Many thanks as well to Jennifer Banks, Donna Bouvier, and Lisa Roberts at Harvard and to my copyeditor, Amanda Heller.

For their enduring friendship, scholarship, and inspiration, to Katie Barry, Kristin Bayer, Tanya Erzen, Betsy Esch, Kim Gilmore, Kate Haulman, John Howard, Andrew Lee, Rachel Mattson, Kathleen May, Kevin Murphy, Melina

Pappademos, Liz Renner, Josh Rothman, Micol Siegel, Rebeccah Welch, and Wendy Wisehart—thank you. For their camaraderie and professional support at the University of Alabama, special thanks also to Lynne Adrian, Al Brophy, Jim Hall, Rich Megraw, Stacy Morgan, Jennifer Purvis, Jim Salem, Amilcar Shabazz, Edward Tang, Carmen Taylor, and Veronica Wynn-Pruitt.

This book is dedicated to all the members of my family for their love, support, and faith in me and this project. They have always kept me going and kept me laughing. My parents, Cindy and Mike McElya, are my original models for how to lead an intellectually engaged life. They are fiercely passionate about history, politics, books, and their children. For everything, I thank them. Jim McElya, my brother the adventurer, teaches me every day to approach the world openly, with joy and compassion, and to have fun. He is a wonder and so wonderful. Finally, this book would not have been possible without my partner, Alexis Boylan. She read, edited, gently criticized, and made this work far better. My life would be simply unimaginable without her.

INDEX